Islam
In
Practice

The publication of this book has been partially supported by the Persian Heritage Foundation.

Islam
In
Practice

Religious Beliefs in a
Persian Village

Reinhold Loeffler

State University of New York Press

Published by
State University of New York Press, Albany

©1988   State University of New York

For information, address State University of New York
Press, State University Plaza, Albany, N.Y., 12246

Library of Congress Cataloging-in-Publication Data

Loeffler, Reinhold, 1932–
  Islam in practice.

  Includes index.
  Bibliography: p.
  1. Shī'ah—Iran. 2. Iran—Religion. I. Title
BP192.7.I7L63   1988   297'.82'0955   87-12175
ISBN 0-88706-678-X
ISBN 0-88706-679-8 (pbk.)

10 9 8 7 6 5 4 3 2 1

To Lloyd A. Fallers and Clifford Geertz

CONTENTS

ACKNOWLEDGMENTS

A great many people contributed time, goodwill, expertise or their good office to my research efforts. Although all will be remembered kindly, I would like to thank especially the late Professor Lloyd A. Fallers and Margaret Fallers of the University of Chicago and Professor Nur Yalman, now at Harvard University, for their encouragement; Dr. Helmut Slaby, then Austrian Cultural Attaché in Tehran, for his invaluable help; Professor Werner Dutz, then at the University of Shiraz, for his hospitality and his stimulating interest, and a great number of Iranian friends who, at this state in the Iranian Revolution, I believe best remain unnamed.

The Oriental Institute of the University of Chicago, the Wenner-Gren Foundation for Anthropological Research, the City of Vienna, Austria, the Social Science Research Council and Western Michigan University, my home base, gave financial support at various stages of the research and the writing. Without their help this research could never have been carried out.

Over the years, several departmental secretaries struggled with the manuscript. Of all, Jill Pinkerton and Marilyn Babcock dealt with the lion's share.

Last, but not least, I thank my wife for inspirations and services too numerous to be listed and the people of the village for their hospitality and their untiring willingness to submit themselves to my never-ending and often exasperating questions.

INTRODUCTION

This book documents the individual world views of a score of men in a Shiite Iranian village. As such, it is a study of how Islam is practiced in individual belief systems. It is also a study of what we have rather depreciatingly labeled popular beliefs or folk religion. But most importantly, it is an attempt to pay homage to the personal thoughts and views of common men in the anonymous mass of third-world people and to recognize the dignity and creativity with which these people make sense of their lives.

In the West, we have become used to celebrating individuality. Our mass media thrive on displaying the powerful, the rich, the expert, the beautiful, the violent, and occasionally even the little man who is none of these. Western art and literature since the Renaissance have extolled the portrayal of human individuality in all its realistic concreteness. Historians, always fascinated by the great movers in history, have in recent years become also interested in what the common man as individual has done, thought, and felt in various epochs (LaRoy Ladurie 1978). In philosophy, phenomenology and existentialism insist on the exclusive individuality of each life, probe the nature of human existence, and try to define what it is like to be in the world. In psychology, the new approach of "life studies" inspired by Robert Coles' (1967–1977) monumental work *Children of Crisis* emphasizes the irreducible personal dignity of every individual. In fact, some fear that in recent years we may even have over-cultivated our fascination with the individual self into a culture of narcissism (Lasch 1978).

But this mainly concerns Western man. Outside our sphere, people

A Note on the Transliteration: The transliteration rules of the Library of Congress for Farsi were followed for Persian and Luri words, except for diacritical dots below letters, which were omitted, and some words and names that are anglicized entries in Webster's Dictionary.

tend to be perceived as mass. There, individuals live their lives in neglected oblivion, as mere fragments of villages, tribes, and states.

Anthropology is an attempt to lift this oblivion. Although over its career it has produced its chimeras (Pandian 1985), denied coevalness to its subjects (Fabian 1983), and served as instrument of imperialist powers, it has nevertheless done more than any other science to include people in an authentic human discourse.

The primary form this enterprise takes is to discover the ways of life and thought of a whole people, the group patterns, the shared culture. In this, however, anthropologists have never lost sight of the individual. From the early biographies of American Indians and the admirable monographs of Cargo cult leaders to the case studies of the Manchester School and the analyses of the psychological tradition (e.g., Obeyesekere 1981) single individuals have been thrown into relief. They have been portrayed as role models (Casagrande 1960), as interpreters of culture (Lewis 1969, Shostak 1981), as metaphors (Geertz 1968), as political exponents (Friedrich 1965; Kracke 1978), as cultural wizards (Castaneda 1968), or, in film making, as central figures (Gardiner 1963; Fernea 1978). But it was probably Paul Radin (1959) and Erik Erikson (1980) who have most eloquently argued for a recognition of the independent creativity of individuals, regardless of time and cultural setting.

As for portraits of single individuals in the Middle East, a whole spate of works has appeared in the last decade (Antoun 1987; Atiya 1982; Crapanzano 1980; Critchfield 1978; Eickelman 1985; Mottahadeh 1985; Munson 1984; Taheri 1985). The present study is part of this tradition, contributing, however, a number of novelties: it is concentrated more than others on a systematic exploration of the specifically religious aspect of the world views of individuals; it is the first presentation of such world views—in fact, of any comprehensive study of religion—in regard to village Iran; and it features not a single individual or a few, but a relatively large sample covering all major socio-economic and educational backgrounds of senior men, thus exhibiting, although preserving individual particularity, the cultural system at large, demonstrating the enormous range of individual forms the system can take, and allowing the single individual to be situated within it.

This mode of ethnographic presentation arose out of a dilemma. Having not really worked with informants, but having lived and talked with many men over a long period of time, I had become acutely aware of the vast differences in their religious beliefs and knowledge. How could I do justice to this diversity in a conventional ethnographic format? But keeping all individuals separate had, as far as I knew, never been done before. When I discussed this problem with the late Lloyd Fallers, who just had had to deal with it himself in what tragically became his last publication (Fallers 1974), he emphatically encouraged me to maintain separation.

Certainly, this format will find its critics, mainly those who want to see the general patterns worked out. But it does have a number of distinct advantages: it preserves the unique flavor of an individual's creation and so conveys not only what it feels like to be a peasant in South Iran, but what a particular person of particular circumstances feels like in this setting; it preserves the particular structure of a world view, the special context in which beliefs are situated and the special way in which beliefs are held; it shows the various strategies with which symbols are put to use to mediate the particular circumstances of a person's existence; it preserves the wide range of religious knowledge, religious systems, and forms of religiosity in a single community and so offers a more factual picture of the practice of Islam than a summary account could give; and it preserves primary source material for later analysis by other scholars.

With all the emphasis on individual particularity inherent in this format I am, of course, not arguing against the validity and necessity of making generalizations and finding common patterns. Taking diversity seriously may imply, however, that making such generalizations and finding patterns is a more complex and intricate enterprise than has so far been acknowledged.

Evidently, then, this is a study of human practice, and so a contribution to the developing theory of practice (Bourdieu 1977). This means that I am concerned with religion not solely as a set of doctrines, norms, and legal precepts to be enacted by individuals, but as the way in which individuals interact with these patterns and use them to interact with their environment. More explicitly, I am concerned with the ways in which, under the constraints of social, cultural, existential, and psychological forces, individuals make sense of, come to terms with, and create religious concepts, thereby shaping their world views and concomitantly—because these world views in any of their expressive and thereby objectivated forms constitute part of culture—their culture. As well, I am concerned with the ways individuals use their world views to conceive, make sense of, and justify self and others, good and evil, fortune and misfortune, life and afterlife, status and power, interests and actions, and create a feeling of prevailing order and justice as well as a sense of personal authenticity, identity, and worth.

This exploration of what individuals make of their religion and what religion makes of them is obviously quite different from the elegant pictures presented by orthodox scholars (Tabātabā'ī 1975). It is, however, essentially the same approach that underlies recent works on religion in Iran (Akhavi 1980; Fischer 1980; Mottahadeh 1985) though it takes a different form in each case. As these three works deal with the Shiite religion on the level of the clerical establishment, the present volume on Shiite beliefs as practiced on the village level may serve as a fitting, even necessary, complement.

In my presentation I have decided to let the single individuals speak for themselves. Not only does this better acknowledge their individuality and autonomy, but it also keeps their views more effectively clear of the unintended meanings, suggestions, implications, and cultural overtones of the ethnographic interlocutor. For the same reasons, the translations have been kept as literal as possible. Language is not a clean instrument of symbolizing like mathematics or abstract logic. Beyond the overt message, it communicates a flood of cues about the speaker's cultural background, social status, regional origin, occupation, education, and so forth. This principle is of course made use of by gifted authors when they impart different dialects or speech styles to the characters of their novels, plays, and films. Therefore, letting the individuals talk in idiomatic American would necessarily create the impression that they are essentially Americans who happen to hold these views, a suggestion I wanted to avoid. Whoever has once heard on Iranian television John Wayne talk in the smooth intonation of Tehrani Farsi in a western saloon will realize how absurdly cultural cues can become mixed up by linguistic alterations.

Even so, however, the medium of the written word curtails some of the original information. Much of what is conveyed by the immediate impact of the individual's personality is lost. Lost also are the cues and messages transmitted by facial expressions, gestures, enunciations, and intonations which function as a running commentary to the spoken words. Particularities of speech patterns (e.g., eloquence or the laconic) and idea formulation (spontaneous or reflective; assured or struggling) which provide additional clues do not show up clearly in the written word. And conventions of style and translation suppress subtleties of meaning as the diction of some persons needs more editing than that of others to render meanings intelligible. Exact English equivalents of terms and idioms often are lacking. An individual's choice of words (literate, technical, old-fashioned, and so forth) is, in many cases, only imperfectly replicable. Finally, grammatical particularities, like the use of the first person plural for oneself, which is especially frequent among the less-educated, cannot always be retained for reasons of clarity. These conditions also make styles of presentation appear more similar than they actually are.

All pre-revolutionary case studies were collected in the course of three years of anthropological field research in a large tribal village in South Iran in 1970–1971 and 1976. The material grew out of informal conversations held in private, with only occasionally the man's wife or a young child present. From the beginning, I considered such privacy essential for a free expression of views although it turned out to be rather difficult to achieve. Contrary to a general stereotype, Iranian peasants do not just sit around idly, not even in winter. They keep very busy. And when they are at home for a short lunch break or after dark, other people are around—family, neighbors, friends, guests. Thus, besides talking with the men when they were alone at home, I also used such opportunities as working with them in their fields or accompanying them on their way around. During the winter months when men were alone in herding outposts, I lived with one or another at a time. We prepared our food, did some work in the fields, fed the animals before they left with the shepherd in the morning and again when they came back in the evening and were visited by other men in the evenings. The intimacy developed in the course of such extended isolation set the tone for our conversations and became for both of us a lasting experience. Religious things were just one of the many topics we talked about. Given the time we had I could afford to let religious themes develop spontaneously out of concrete contexts. In this way, I came to know in 1971 and 1976 the world views of some seventy-five individuals. From among these I selected twenty-one for this presentation. The distribution by status groups is as follows:

	Land-lord	Mullah	Peasant	Trader	Teacher	Crafts-man	Worker	Youth	Woman	Total
Total	4	1	38	5	6	6	2	7	6	75
Selected	1	1	14	2	2	1	—	—	—	21

Editing the original statements consisted of several complex steps. First, of my own questions, only a lead question was reproduced. Second, with a few exceptions, ideas were arranged in a general, loose sequence starting with aspects of each person's existential situation, proceeding to morality, reward, punishment and eschatology, and ending with ritual and popular beliefs. And third, ideas pertaining to the same topic but expressed at different occasions were collated and arranged into a coherent form, meticulously preserving, however, the original wording and the original linkages between ideas. In this process, repetitions were omitted; statements that were more explicit and elaborate were chosen over those that were less so; lengthy and winding stories, like case histories of illnesses, were sometimes condensed; and insertions were made in rare instances where they were considered absolutely necessary to maintain authentic meanings or to substitute for information conveyed by tone or gesture. In all this, I painstakingly avoided additions, deletions, and changes in the wording, context, and linkage of ideas which might suggest something different from what was intended. This process of integration without change as well as the search for English equivalents that best preserved the range of connotations implicit in the vernacular original proved to be the most exacting part of the work. Much of the trouble could have been spared by using an extensive apparatus of notes. However, I wanted the text to stand on its own and to make its reading not more cumbersome than necessary.

The selection of individuals excluded the workers, educated youths, and women. By workers I mean men who, at the time of the research, gained their livelihood from manual wage labor in a city and who in their attitudes identified themselves with the growing industrial working class rather than the peasantry, although they still maintained households in the village. As to the educated youth (high school diploma and above), world views were from 1976 on highly politicized and because some of these views may not conform with the political powers of the day, I cannot responsibly make them public.

With the women, finally, I could never build up the kind of intimate relationship I had with men, although I could talk with them freely on an occasional basis. My wife and field companion did, however, enjoy the access and rapport necessary to gain in-depth insights into women's world views, and her studies have already resulted in a number of publications (Friedl, 1980; 1983; 1987).

THE SETTING

The village lies some 7000 feet high on a small, basin-like plateau in the inner ranges of the Zagros mountains in southwestern Iran. It is by far the largest village in a wide area. Back in 1971, when this study was begun, it had a population of 2200 people living in some 400 adobe brick houses which formed a tight cluster intersected only by a few narrow, dusty lanes. Each house typically consisted of a single 12x15 foot room and a verandah of about the same size sitting on top of the stables in the lower story, and sheltered one nuclear family of two to seven persons.

Surrounding the village on all sides lies its irrigated land, a mere 500 hectares of rocky soil. Most of it is made up of small fields on which a wheat crop in one year is rotated with summer crops such as legumes, clover, potatoes, onions and, in the 1970's, sugar beets in the next. The remainder, about 15%, carries vineyards and orchards of apple, apricot, almond, and walnut trees. Beyond this irrigated area extends austere, stark, oak-covered mountain-scape of which the village claims on either of its sides a stretch nearly seven miles long and 2.5 miles wide. This region, although also used for some dry cultivation of wheat, serves predominantly as the pastureland for the villagers' flocks of sheep and goats.

The village was founded some 100 years ago when an innovative, progress-minded chief persuaded his small, heterogeneous tribe to discontinue their nomadic life style and permanently settle in what had been their summer pasture area. There, aided by energetic elders, the chief pushed for more improvements. Thus, although embroiled in the tribal wars which ravaged the region at the time (Loeffler 1978), the village grew and flourished in quite unprecedented ways. It could boast of an extensive irrigation system, vineyards, orchards, a bathhouse, a mosque, and a resident mullah decades before such things appeared in other communities. Urban traders and craftsmen attracted by a growing market, moved to the village and so contributed to its development as a rural center. As the population grew, daughter villages were founded in the surrounding area and new land was colonized. Finally, when Reza Shah established political order in the region in 1930, the chief, by now in his sixties, moved to realize yet another of his innovative ideas. He travelled to Tehran and pleaded at high government levels for the appointment of a teacher to the village. Eventually, and after great persistence on his part, his request was granted. Soon the first man on the job, a gifted educator who also transmitted some of the liberal ideas of the time, could count some sixty boys as his pupils. In many families it became customary to send one of the sons to school. Thus, in this village a significant number of commoners started to receive a secular education a full generation earlier than in the rest of the region, a fact which greatly influenced future developments. By 1938, the first villager of peasant extraction had been appointed as teacher of the village, but after three years, political suppression forced him to suspend instruction. He resumed teaching in 1949, to be joined by more local teachers in the decades ahead.

The chief also created new socio-economic conditions. As the irrigation system was built and the land was made arable, he claimed that as tribal chief who had initiated and directed these innovations he was the owner of it all and therefore entitled to a share of the crop. Commanding a group of armed retainers, supported by neighboring chiefs, and at least implicitly acknowledged by the central government, he was able to put his claim into effect and force the peasants to comply with his demands. It was, however, generally acknowledged that though an autocrat and de facto landowner, the chief never wantonly abused his power, but ruled with justice and a basic concern for his people. This order came to an end when, after his death, one of his grandsons, the Landlord of this book, a rather ruffian character who shared nothing of his elder's enlightenment, seized power, and after the collapse of central control in 1941 erected the reign of ruthless oppression referred to by many individuals presented here. It was in this context of oppression that the Representative felt impelled to take up the cause of the peasants (Loeffler 1971). From around 1950 onward he lodged complaints about the conditions at government offices, deftly bypassing the local officials who were notoriously bribed by the Landlord. Although the latter attempted with mounting intensity to neutralize him—on one occasion he even succeeded to get him jailed for six months under trumped-up charges—the Representative's strategy of appealing to ever higher levels in the government proved increasingly effective in curbing the excessive extortions and wanton use of power by the Landlord. But for the Representative this was not enough. He asserted that the Landlord was not entitled to any dues at all because his position was based on force, not legitimate right. Rather, it was the peasants themselves who by right of having taken the land in possession and having made it arable with their own hands were the rightful owners of the land. This ideology also brought the Representative into conflict with the land reform officials who took the legitimacy of past relationships for granted. The Representative, however, advanced his claim with such unrelenting vigor and adroit persistence that the officials finally conceded he might have a point. In 1971 a special commission arrived in the village to hear the arguments of both sides and examine title deeds to the land. After that, although an official decision to the effect was never issued, the peasants were no longer pressured to make payments on their landholdings and the Landlord received no compensation. For the Representative and the peasants this meant that the government had not only established order and security, but eventually justice, and they credited the Shah with the entire process of their liberation from the Landlord's oppression.

Once landlord power had been curbed and the peasants knew they would no longer be willfully stripped of the proceeds of their labor, they industriously began to expand the cropland but soon reached the last niches of possible cultivation. They also allowed their herds to grow, and an increasing number of households engaged in the local transhumance cycle.

In winter the sheep were stable-fed in the village, but the more hardy goats, which could feed on leaves and supple twigs, were grazed from herding outposts in the mountains to save on animal feed. The group of men associated in a herding unit took turns in staffing these outposts. In early spring, the sheep were also moved to the outposts, and the women took over the management there while the men, busy with their agricultural work around the village, only periodically visited the outposts to meet arising needs. At the beginning of summer, camps were set up in higher locations. Then, in late summer, they were drawn closer to the village to make use of the forage offered by the harvested fields. In fall, the units moved back to the outposts from where in early December the household and the sheep returned to the village. In 1970, a third of all households practiced this pattern. The rest, usually the ones with herds of less than 20 animals, grazed these year round from the village itself. This intensive use of all available pasture grounds by a growing animal population soon led to severe overgrazing and deterioration of resources. Around 1970, the income potential from both agriculture and animal husbandry reached its practical limits while the human population kept growing at an annual rate of over 3%, and the people's needs and expectations were steadily rising. At this critical point in the local economic history, two decisive things happened: the investment in education began to pay off and the labor market opened

up. These two developments came to provide the basis for further progress
(Loeffler 1976).

The introduction of schooling in the 1930's had swiftly generated a
cultural climate which placed a high value on educational achievement.
Early on it also came to provide the community with excellent and dedicated teachers able to cope with the problems of mass education in a rural
environment. By 1965, elementary school attendance among males had
reached 78%, which was more than twice as high as in the wider region
where schooling was just getting started. Even more significant, high school
attendance of males topped 40% in 1970 when the boys, under great economic hardships, still had to be sent to schools in cities, and it reached
60% on the eve of the revolution, by which time the educational system in
the village extended from kindergarten through senior high school and employed a staff of seventy teachers and administrators. As a result of this
educational explosion a steadily growing proportion of the younger generation qualified for salaried positions which until the revolution were readily
available to them. For example, the number of villagers with salaries as
teachers increased from thirteen in 1965 to sixty-seven at the time of the
revolution.

The other major source of outside income became seasonal migrant
labor in the cities. By 1974, wages paid for unskilled labor in Iran had
reached a level which allowed peasants working for three to five months in
a city to save amounts of money they considered very much worth the
effort. Consequently, peasants of the village took up this kind of work in
such numbers that by the time of the revolution over one-quarter of the
male population over fifteen years were engaged in it. Besides, wage labor
became available in a nearby small town and in the village itself. Finally,
there was a smaller but longer established group of men who went to the
more lucrative but less convenient labor market of Kuwait. This massive
turn toward wage labor did not affect—at least not on the village level—
agricultural production. Animal husbandry, however, declined: by 1979 the
proportion of households engaged in the transhumance cycle, which of
necessity required year-round local residency, had withered to a mere 7%.

Thus, within a decade the income and occupational structure of the
village had been transformed. By the time of the revolution, 25% of the
household heads either earned a salary or had a regular income from one of
the businesses, crafts or enterprises which had developed concomitantly to
the growth of capital in the village. The remainder still pursued their peasant work, but in addition over half of them earned wages from migrant
work and many more engaged in wage labor available locally, usually on
construction sites. Furthermore, in many cases a wife, unmarried son or

daughter contributed a salary or wage to the household budget. Overall, there was hardly a household without at least one salary or temporary wage earner.

There was virtually no emigration from the village, though. People maintained their households in the village even when their post was somewhere else, which was usually not very far away. The resulting cash flow into the community drastically changed living conditions and the physical appearance of the village. People used their new wealth mainly for the creation of better housing. Spreading into orchards and farmland, they built new, spacious, multi-room stone houses, furnished with modern plumbing, gas ranges, electricity and, in many cases, refrigerators and other conveniences. Characteristically, the new homes, which often were shared by two or three closely-related nuclear families, were all enclosed by a stone wall, urban style. Apparently, what people had found most wanting in the traditional pattern besides space and facilities was privacy. Building activity was so intensive that by 1980 some 225 new units covering two to three times the area of the original village had been completed or were under construction; nearly 75% of the households (now numbering 500) had moved into new quarters, discarding their former adobe houses, which soon started to fall into ruin.

With the revolution and, later, the war, this economic upsurge came to a halt. Salaries remained frozen at pre-revolutionary levels. High-school graduates frequently found no employment. Migrant labor opportunities in the cities became rare. Wage levels and the prices peasants got for their cash crops (mainly butterfat, meat, grapes) did rise but not in pace with the tremendous inflation. Construction materials, automobiles, and other machinery for investment became prohibitively expensive. As a consequence, the people's potential for economic development was considerably lowered. The resulting frustration on the part of most villagers forms an important ingredient in their view of the new regime. More about this, however, in the last chapter.

Sociologically, the village is composed of some twenty major, rather shallow, patrilineal descent groups of heterogeneous derivation. These structures, however, do not function as corporate units defining social action. Rather, each individual family maintains a social network based on bilateral, affinal, and spatial relationships, and it is through the activation of relationships within sets of such networks that social groups crystallize over specific issues and for specific purposes such as the formation of agricultural partnerships, herding units, factions in disputes, or the crowd participating in life-cycle rituals. Of special importance in these networks is the relationship of a man to his wife's father and brother. This relationship carries obligations of assistance and allegiance of such strength that it may even take precedence over the son-father relationship.

Cutting across such groupings is the hierarchy of economic rank. To the casual observer the traditional system appeared rather homogeneous. All villagers were peasants; all worked hard from dawn to dusk, summer and winter; all lived in adobe houses bare of modern amenities; and all ate the same kind of food. In fact, however, there existed pronounced economic differences. In terms of landholding, the upper third in the hierarchy owned some 60% of the land, whereas the lower third, including the landless, held barely 10%. These inequalities were compounded by the disparities in livestock possessions. As it was, some of the larger landowners also possessed the largest herds in the village, whereas many of the smallholders owned only a few animals. Because it was the flocks—and not the generally small landholdings—which yielded most of the cash products and so constituted the real source of wealth, this distribution vastly enlarged the economic distance deriving from the disparity of landholdings.

Thus, on top of the village's class system were a few individuals like the Wealthy who owned some four to six hectares of land and sixty to one-hundred animals, possibly also making some money from a bit of sideline trading. The bulk of the population ranged from the more well-to-do—like the Fundamentalist and the Mashhadi—owning some two to four hectares of land and some thirty-five to sixty animals—to the poorer households with around one hectare of land and, at best, twenty animals, like the Lower Peasants. Then there were still the poor, some 15–20% of the population, who had very little land and a few animals, like the Poor, or no productive resources at all. Among the latter were the descendents of immigrant traders and craftsmen who were never given ownership rights to village land and therefore were entirely dependent on share-cropping contracts with "natives." Finally, there were a few households of blind, crippled, and disabled whose subsistence mainly derived from alms given by other villagers.

Standards of living varied with these differences in property and income. The more prosperous, though never flaunting their position, could afford a livelihood somewhat cushioned from dire exigency. The floors in their houses tended to be covered with rugs; their clothes, bedding, and household utensils were good and proper; their food regularly included rice and a fair supply of protein; and their sons could be sent to high school in towns or even cities. By contrast, in the poorer households the floor was covered only partially and with some cheap material; clothing and bedding were threadbare and often inadequate; food at times consisted merely of bread, with little on the side; and generally the feeling of teetering on the brink of sheer survival was pervasive.

The economic upsurge in the 70's changed this stratificational system. The salaried individuals who derived mainly, although not exclusively, from the traditionally better-situated households, came to form the new financial elite of the village. Their regular cash incomes provided them with an affluence unprecedented by village standards. In the other classes, economic mobility set in under the impact of wages and earnings from trade and craft enterprises. As a result, all classes, including the poor, improved their position in absolute terms, but concomitantly overall economic distances widened and the inequality in income distribution increased markedly.

Until very recently, formal village institutions were strikingly absent. There existed no constituted council of kingroup representatives, no circle of elders, no strong man, and no mosque organization which could have exercised regulation of social life. Instead, such regulation came essentially from the force of public opinion as activated by and channeled through network pressures, ad-hoc mediation processes, and symbols of etiquette, honor, reputation, and religion. Not that there were no tensions to speak of. On the contrary, the unusually large size of the village, the crowded housing conditions, and the scarcity of resources constantly generated conflicts which often remained unresolved. Innumerable conflicts and mutually opposed claims permeated the social fabric and new disputes arose daily over the most diverse issues. Yet the informal mechanisms proved effective enough to contain, if not to settle, these conflicts, and to enforce the norms regulating economic and social processes such as the use of land, water, and pastures, or the maintenance of the village poor. In fact, under the circumstances they fulfilled these functions with amazing smoothness and effectiveness. Violence occurred very rarely, and, when it occurred, did not go beyond an exchange of blows: at least over the past 30 years, it has never led to killings or serious injuries. Nor did the local gendarmerie play any other roles than representing the ultimate guarantor of law and order and transmitting major cases of conflict to urban courts.

As to their religious persuasion, the people of this village are Shiites of the generally Iranian Twelver form. At the time the individuals presented grew up, most villagers received their religious education in unstructured and informal contexts, that is, at home, with peers, in conversational exchanges, and at occasional sermons. Few persons attended the traditional school (*maktab*) which up to around 1950 was taught intermittently by local literate men (*mullahs*). This variegated and rather individualistic form of education may partially account for the great diversity of world views reflected in the cases presented. Anyway, despite the lack of formal learning, people are, as these cases show, neither uneducated nor unsophisticated in religious matters, a finding which refutes urban and western stereotypes of rural people.

The village had a resident mullah, which before the revolution was rather unique in the region. The son of an immigrant trader, he had studied in Qom in the late 1930's and then returned to the village to practice his profession. His income derived from portions of the religious alms some of the villagers paid, from the official fees he collected for recording marriage contracts, from the honorariums he received in this village and other places for performing religious ceremonies, and from his diverse business investments. He gave no formal religious instruction except in sermons and personal advice, and he made no performance or even appearance in the mosque except at the rather rare communal rituals—occasions when he usually expected some payment for his services.

There were no religious associations in the village. Nor did people commonly gather in the mosque although by 1950 they had built it by communal effort. Only about four or five men, the Mullah not among them, used to regularly go to the mosque and say daily prayers there. Quite generally in the village, for two major reasons formal religious ritual was not much in evidence. For one thing, core-orthodox Islam, as such, offers only relatively few and little elaborated communal rituals. In its austere and absolute spirit it places almost exclusive emphasis on the dyadic relationship between God and the individual, grossly neglecting such rituals as seasonal or crisis rites, which play important communal roles in other religions. Shiite additions, mainly mourning celebrations for the Imām Husayn and his family, compensate somewhat for this paucity of ritual in the orthodox core. Thus, in this village, communal ritual was limited to the services on some evenings in Ramadan, a communal prayer at the end of Ramadan, the funerals, and the specifically Shiite celebrations in the months of Muharram and Safar. Only in the latter context, on 'Ashūrā and on 28 Safar, the anniversaries of the martyrdom of the Imāms Husayn and Hasan, respectively, did communal rituals take the form of great, solemn, elaborate celebrations engaging virtually the entire community in ritual drama and self-representation.

For another thing, the Islamic core rituals, commonly known as the Five Pillars of Islam, appear little adapted to peasant existential situations. Peasants, at least those of this village, obviously have no means to make the pilgrimage to Mecca. They feel unable to pay the obligatory religious alms. They find it physically impossible to sustain the month-long fasting, especially when it coincides with their heavy summer activities. And as to reciting the daily prayers, many, especially the lower peasants, say that beneficial as this may be, they cannot get to it: the continuous demand of tasks and chores keeps them too busy, and, besides, in their soiled clothes out in the fields or with the animals, they cannot meet the requisite of ritual purity.

These are not cheap rationalizations. The peasants' existence is back-breaking hard work from dawn to dusk, day after day. On occasions, as when working the fields under a scorching summer sun for twelve straight hours a day, or in winter when taking fodder to the outposts over high passes in knee-deep snow, their chores turn into feats of incredible endurance. In all, they work swiftly and incessantly, with only short breaks for lunch or an occasional glass of tea, obviously under pressure to get everything done. Under the circumstances, the constraint of taking time out to somehow achieve ritual purity and say the prayers only would add to the stress, given the hectic tune they step to.

But neglect of the orthodox ritual does not make them an irreligious people, as had been suggested for a similar group of southern Iran (Barth 1961:135; Douglas 1973:37). In such an assumption there is a failure to recognize the particular nature of peasant religiosity. For the people of this village, true Islam does not consist in the fulfillment of formal ritual obligations. Instead, it centers around the belief that a great compassionate God bestows mercy on them in this world and the next, and that, in turn, as in a mirror, man has to have compassion on all creatures and do them no harm. Being a true Muslim does not come from saying the prayers but from having compassion: to give to the poor is better than to make the pilgrimage to Mecca. Thus, while the religion's normative structure as well as the thrust of the clergy's presentations projects the strict observance of prayers and fasting as criteria for a good Muslim, in the peasants' view a good Muslim is one who does good to others. With this shift in emphasis from ritual criteria, which they cannot meet, onto a basic social morality, which they believe they fulfill better than others, peasants adapt the religion to their particular existential situation and afford themselves the image of being good Muslims in spite of their failure to meet critical obligations.

The ideas which appear to lie at the core of the villagers' structure of their world view provide also the basic formula for seeking supernatural assistance, i.e., to give to people to please God and so obtain favors many times greater in value than what was given away. This formula underlies all the innumerable offerings, sacrifices, dedications, contributions, alms, vows, *sufrahs,* invitations, and gifts made to obtain favors, ensure well-being, secure protection, avert evil, help the dead, give thanks, or simply show compassion. Such offerings form the heart of peasant ritual life as attested by their diversity and continual practice. They are called for in a multitude of contexts defined by cyclic patterns (weekly, monthly, on Thursday night, *Naw-rūz,* on *'īd qurbān,* on *sūri safar,* on holidays, in the months of *Sha'bān,* Ramadan and Muharram) or crisis situations (illness, danger, after an ill-boding dream, before a journey, at a passage in the life cycle) or special occasions (a good harvest, prospering herds, escape from danger, building a house, returning from a successful hunt, receiving dairy products from the outpost, or even when transporting a load of grapes through the village). In performing these rituals, villagers generate a constant stream of symbolic acts confirming their common understanding of what I have described as the core structure of their world views.

I will present more abstractions of religious patterns in the analytical frameworks of the two concluding chapters. For the moment, the foregoing may suffice as characterization of the religious background in the village. The general background for the cases which follow is, of course, provided by the Shia religion, summaries of which the reader may find in Nasr (1969), Shehabi (1958), and Tabātabā'ī (1975).

THE WORLD VIEWS

1

The Mullah: Uncommitted Formalism

The Mullah, a middle-aged man, represents religious learnedness and authority in the village. He completed four years of formal studies in theology and sacred law in Qom, the religious center of the Shia in Iran, and is supposed to use this knowledge for the spiritual benefit and ritual guidance of the people and to present a model of Islamic morality. In the eyes of the villagers, however, he has not lived up to these expectations during the twenty-five years of his residency in the village. For this reason, and also because of the general disrepute in which the clergy is held, ranging from biting anticlericalism to general distrust, he is not well accepted by the villagers.

People have become especially alienated by the Mullah's habit of leaving the village for a town outside the tribal area during Ramadan and Muharram, the two most significant religious months of the year, to earn more money. When, in 1970, the villagers asked him to stay, he demanded an honorarium of five *toman* per household. For this fee he held two *rawzah* services each night with impressive pathos, complete with religious instruction, sermon, recitation of the passions of Husayn and his family, prayer, and invocations. Inevitably, these performances earned him the caustic comment that for five toman he cut off the head of the Imām Husayn several times a day. But there is no doubt that the huge participation in the rituals on Tāsū'ā and 'Ashūrā was due to his performance.

During Ramadan and Muharram the following year, however, the Mullah left the village again, this time to serve the administrative center's new mosque, which enjoys the patronage of well-salaried government employees and officials. The peasants were upset about it, but the Mullah defended himself, saying that unlike the city people, the villagers were ignorant, impious peasants who were unwilling to honor his right to proper

17

remuneration. In the eyes of the villagers his excuse was invalid, because his substantial income from various enterprises such as ownership of a store, shares in flour mills, partnerships in a transport business and herds, together with a small salary and fees for services, provided him a living standard surpassing anybody else's in the village.

His shift from a peasant community to a congregation of government officials indeed reflected more than just a consideration of earnings and audience receptivity. It meant definite upward status mobility. In the preceding fall he had attended the congress of clergymen held annually under the auspices of the government and designed to form a Religion Corps analogous to the Literacy and Development Corps. The mullahs were lectured by government officials on themes like the role of religion and the clergy in modern Iran and the correct reading of the scriptures in regard to modernization. They were also admonished to stop criticizing the regime in their sermons by way of allegorical symbolism and refined allusions. This week long training in the new language of the national culture enabled him to address successfully an audience of government officials. Given the prospect of social advancement, he did not miss the opportunity to use these means.

Besides failing to attend properly to rituals, he also seemed to fail in presenting a good moral example. In the eyes of most villagers, he is not committed to safeguarding village morality, and there have been rumors of improper advances to married women in the past. He is never seen at the mosque for prayers, and only officiates at marriages and burials for renowned persons. (Common peasants turn to certain fellow villagers for services like saying the prayers over the dead). He does not act as mediator in quarrels either. Soon after his arrival from Qom he became involved in personal and political disputes which discredited him considerably amongst the peasants. In the political arena he took the side of the landlords who then, twenty-five years ago, enjoyed almost absolute power over the peasants. His political stance was sealed by his marriage to one of the landlords' daughters and has not changed since. In the past he even condoned the oppression of the landlords by performing rituals on their behalf.

All this compounds to discredit him hopelessly in the eyes of most villagers and to compromise his religious credibility. People believe that what he says about religious issues he says only to earn a living, not out of deep conviction. Also, the air of honesty, dignity, and religious solemnity which surrounds his manners and speech is seen rather as something he owes his job than something that reflects substance. Thus, the negative image people have of the clergy is both confirmed and actively shaped by the Mullah's behavior.

It is difficult to determine how influential his presence and his activities actually have been on the religious life of the community. Judging from overt evidence, his impact has been very limited.

In the past, he was unable to prevent what to the peasants were the gravest sins: the abuses of power by the landlords. Neither could he stop the raiding expeditions of both landlords and villagers.

At present, participation in the traditional rituals at certain core festivals, such as Tāsū'ā or 'Ashūrā, is strikingly higher whenever the Mullah performs them, but he does not have the authority to introduce any religious innovations.

There are indications that certain expressions of piety, such as saying the prayers and fasting, have increased over the past decades. But this has happened more as part of the general Islamization process which occurred in the wake of the opening up of the tribal area than as result of the Mullah's specific activity. The observable increase in mosque contributions and pilgrimages is also related to this and, of course, to the general rise in living standards. Religious taxes (*zakāt* and *khums*) were never paid and the Mullah has not been able to change this.

Nor has the Mullah much influence on the fulfillment of the prescriptions. The villagers send their daughters to school if and when it is economically feasible, whether he approves of it or not. About one-third of the village women use contraceptive pills, but only one or two actually know the Mullah's opinion about it. As to dancing at weddings, there are only two women (one of them his wife) who explicitly refrain from it because the Mullah says it is sinful. The others dance whenever the social situation calls for it, confidently waiving the Mullah's scruples. The observance of ablutions and ritual bathing may be stimulated by his sermons, but people are not willing to accept his orthodox standards. Once, in the mosque, he gave orders to wash more carefully than usual the glass I had used, only to be severely criticized by a villager who told him that a Christian was not more polluting than a Muslim.

In fact, the Mullah himself implicitly admits his limited impact on the people when he considers them impious peasants, not very much different from the way they were when he came to the village from Qom twenty-five years ago. This means that by his own standards he has failed to induce the change in religious attitudes he declared his avowed goal as a young mullah. Surely, however, his personal shortcomings are only one factor in his failure, probably even a minor one, beside traditional attitudes, cultural norms, general evolutionary trends, secular education, and the collapse of the power structure he was connected to. (1971).

What are man's duties?

Man's duties are to recognize God and to live by the rules of the religion. There are five different types of behavior: obligatory (*vājib*), forbidden (*harām*), desirable (*mustahabb*), disapproved (*makrūh*), and neutral (*mubāh*). Failing to do the obligatory acts and doing the forbidden ones is sinful, whereas doing the desirable acts and abstaining from the disapproved ones earns merits.

What is obligatory behavior and for what reason is it obligatory?

The daily prayers and the preceding ablutions are obligatory to satisfy and please God, to worship Him, and to ask for help. Fasting is obligatory to give rest to the body. Giving alms, *khums* to poor Sayyids, and *zakāt* to poor non-Sayyids and for public works is obligatory because it collects wealth for the strength of Islam. Bathing (*ghusl*) after intercourse, childbirth, and menstruation is obligatory because there is sweat and filth on the body, and bathing after touching a corpse because one may contract a disease. In general, washing is obligatory if the things touched were polluting (*najis*), like blood, semen, or excrements. If things are just plain dirty (*kasīf*), washing is only desirable, except when the body is so covered with filth that at ablutions before prayer water cannot reach the skin. In this case washing becomes obligatory too. For a woman it is obligatory to cover, not necessarily with a veil, all her body except face and hands because a fight might start if a beautiful woman is seen: the eyes that see her will cause the heart to want her. For a male, circumcision is obligatory: otherwise he is filthy.

What are forbidden acts?

Stealing, lying, murder, false accusations, abuse, and beating a person without reason are *harām*. Slander is *harām* because the victim is annoyed by it; wine-drinking because, if drunk, a man cannot recognize his mother, daughter, or other forbidden relative and might sleep with her; the habit of opium smoking because a person stops working; eating pork because pigs feed on dirt and have a worm; eating the meat of animals whose throat has not been cut because when the blood stays in the body, the meat gets rotten; and adultery because it is a violation of other people's property.

Taking interest is forbidden because it distresses people. But the prohibition stipulates only that no interest be taken of the same kind: that is, it is unlawful to take back twelve kilogram of honey if you gave only ten kilogram, or take twelve toman cash for a loan of ten toman cash. It is lawful, however, to give ten toman worth of sugar and take back twelve toman worth of butterfat if it was first stated that the sugar given was worth twelve toman; or to give a hundred toman plus some sugar and take back 150 toman; or to give seven or eight toman cash if stating that, in fact, the loan was in the amount of ten toman, and in return taking some produce worth ten toman.

Hearing music is forbidden because it tends to become a habit and keeps people from working. But some authorities dispute this prohibition. Some say growing a beard is forbidden, but others say that it is obligatory, although the beard need not be long. The regulations regarding these two issues are based on consensus, not on the Qur'ān. In any case, their violation is a small sin as compared, for example, to murder.

What are desirable acts?

These are acts whose practice is better than their non-practice. If done they earn merit, but if not done, there is no sin. There is a very large number of such acts, such as,

—Helping people by giving money, food, and assistance, by remitting debts, and so on. Reason tells us that this is good. It makes people happy.

—Cultivating the land, raising animals, tending gardens, digging irrigation channels, trading, and doing business. This has merit because it increases possessions. It safeguards a man from becoming poor and becoming a thief. Also, a poor man cannot give good food to his children.

—Having social relations with one's relatives, loving one's neighbor, visiting the sick, accompanying a funeral procession, respecting father and mother, respecting one's husband, and loving one's wife, because this makes people cheerful and happy.

—Putting perfume on one's clothes, so people won't be offended by bad odors. Also it is based on the tradition that Muhammad valued three things in this world: good smell, women, and prayer.

—Giving parties of any kind. This communicates love to people, and, possibly, among the guests is a poor man who will be helped, and even animals profit from the bones and other waste.

—Studying and teaching, because they enlighten and make good use of one's faculties.

—Learning how to ride, swim, shoot, and such, because these are skills that serve the protection of the country, and, also, because learning is better than not learning, and knowing is better than not knowing.

—Watering and feeding the animals because they have souls.

—Frequenting the mosque and saying the prayers there. About the Friday-noon prayer there is, however, a dispute: Some say it is obligatory to say it in the mosque, but others say it is only desirable.

—Taking a wife and giving a daughter in marriage, because these serve the social life, sexual satisfaction, and the procreation of children. To take a wife becomes obligatory, however, as soon as one starts doing forbidden things, such as adultery.

—Washing filth off one's body, brushing one's teeth, stopping to eat before one is fully satisfied, removing pubic hair because it is dirty, dressing in white clothes on which filth shows easily: all this is meritorious because it prevents disease. Muhammad for sure knew about bacteria and therefore he gave us all these regulations about purity, bathing, washing, and ablutions. But in his time he couldn't talk in these terms. People would never have believed in him and his message. How wonderful his knowledge was becomes evident only today.

—Economic progress, according to some authorities, is neutral, according to others, desirable. It is considered desirable because it is good for the society. A few people may become destitute in its course, but without development everyone would become destitute.

What are disapproved and what are neutral acts?

Disapproved acts are those whose non-practice is better than their practice. If you don't do them, it earns merit, but if you do them, it is not sinful. About that last point, however, opinions are split: some say that doing these acts is sinful, although, to be sure, much less so than doing forbidden acts. Such acts are, for example: defecating and urinating on a road or into water; saying the prayers in the bathhouse, where one's attention is distracted, or in the dry river bed of summer torrents, where there is danger; going without work, as one has to care for a family; soiling one's body; dressing in black clothes; cutting down green trees; selling expensively and bargaining excessively; doing butchery work, which makes one uncompassionate; smoking cigarettes, which is unhealthy for the body; sending daughters to school, where something may happen to them, but educating them at home is not disapproved of.

Neutral or indifferent acts are, for example, eating, sleeping, walking, joking, and such. But again, joking may earn merit if done to make other people happy.

What is the order for family relationships?

The father has the "right of order" over a son till the son is fifteen and over a daughter till she is nine years old; that is, till the ages at which their reason matures. Up to these ages obedience is obligatory for them; after that, only desirable. The right of order is also held by the viceregent (vakīl) who is elected by the people, like the Shah, and by a master over his apprentice, but not by a husband over his wife. The husband does have, however, a "veto right" vis-à-vis her; that is, he may not allow her to do certain things.

A man ought to work and care for his family and be ready to fight in the defense of the country and in a holy war (*jihād*). A woman ought to be ready for her husband, make herself beautiful for him, care for the children, and do the household chores; she must not go out without permission of her husband. A son ought to carry out the orders of his father and must not do anything without his permission. A daughter ought to do what her father tells her; she ought to have modesty and restraint and must not sit and eat with men who are not closely related to her.

How can one explain the fact that some people observe all these rules and regulations and others don't?

There are four forces in man: rage (*ghazah*), as when one person hits or abuses another; desire (*shahvat*), as a man's desire for food, women, status; fear (*sahm*) and reason (*'aql*). Evil behavior results whenever the first three of these forces are in any state of excess. It is the excess which is bad, not their presence, as such. If they were totally absent, it would not be good either. Someone who follows only these three forces is worse than an animal. But a person following reason and controlling the other three forces is noble. Such a person, like Jesus and Muhammad, is higher than the angels because angels don't have the option to do evil. Essentially, every man is capable of following reason and achieving moral excellence, but only some do it—in the same way as the stones of dates are all alike, but some grow into a tree and others don't.

To what degree then is man responsible?

This relates to the distinction between matters which are given by creation (*takvīn*) and matters of duty (*taklīf*). Man can exert no influence upon matters of creation, like the shape of the nose, but in all matters of duty man is responsible. An idiot is not liable, of course, but any person who is able to discern between good and evil is responsible for his moral behavior, irrespective of whether he has seen a good example from his father or has grown up in the house of a thief and learned bad habits. He possesses reason and must follow reason to become good. If it becomes hard to do this, he must force himself and use restraint. In this effort it helps if he stays away from temptation, associates with good friends, and reads good books.

God's punishment for disobeying the rules is hell in the next world and in this world it is whatever the Qur'ānic laws prescribe: cutting off a finger for stealing a small amount, the hand for more, death for murder.

Also, earthquakes, droughts, and so on, may come as God's punishment for evil behavior, as happened in the case of the city of Lut.

Is poverty God's punishment too?

That's possible, but not all who did something evil are necessarily punished that way: there are evil-doers who are rich. For in this world God is merciful (*rahman*), that is, evil-doers also may profit from God's kindness; but on the Day of Judgment God will be merciful and just (*rahīm*). Quite evidently, poverty is the result of a person's behavior. After all, God has given to every man the energy to work. So, if he becomes poor, it is his own fault: he just did not use his reason and energy right. To a degree, his poverty might be also the fault of the social group he lives in.

The same is true for a man who gets sick: it is his own fault. He was careless in his food habits, ate something dirty, ingested some bacteria. In cases where this cannot account for the disease, it may be something that God has sent for a man's benefit and he simply does not understand it. It's as in the story of the man into whose mouth crept a snake while he was sleeping and who was forced by his companion, who had seen this, to eat all kinds of bad-tasting leaves. It was not until the snake escaped and the friend explained his behavior, that the man understood the reason for the trouble he had been caused. A disease may serve the same purpose: if God had not sent it, the person might have done some evil, or something even worse might have happened to him.

By the same token, if God gives blessings—if, for example, a field yields fifteen times the amount of the seed instead of the normal ten—he gives it either as a matter of creation, upon which man has no influence, or as a reward for virtue and hard work. But at the same time, the high yield is also due to the man's hard work in plowing, irrigating, tending, and improving his field.

What happens after death?

In the first night after the burial, the soul of a deceased, which has been around somewhere, re-enters the body in the grave and the two angels Nakīr and Munkar descend to question the person about past faith and deeds. At this interrogation it becomes manifest whether the person is destined for heaven or for hell. In the first case, the soul is carried to a pleasant place near Najaf where, through an open gate, it is allowed to look into paradise. In the other case, the soul is carried to a place of torment where a gate to hell is open. The souls stay in these places until the Day of Judgment. It is not known when the Day of Judgment will come, not even the Prophet and the Imāms knew it: only God knows. On that day all bodies of the dead will come to life again and God will sit in judgment over all men as their sins and merits are weighed on the scales. Then a person will be taken either to hell or to heaven. Hell is like a hard and arduous prison of torment and fire where people stay—similar to sentences in this world—for one year, two years, or longer, or even eternally. In paradise there are ranks according to merits: those of higher standing live, for example, in better quarters—such as houses of sultans—than others.

Isn't remission of sins possible?

Certain sins, like the belief in no God, or two gods, are not forgivable at all. Other sins, but only those against the "right of God," can be redeemed by merit. For example, if one does not say a prayer, it is a sin that can be made up for by giving alms; but there are no norms as to how much merit is needed to compensate for certain sins. Also, repentance may be made for committing such sins, and God may forgive them on this basis. But sins against the "right of man" are up to people. Such sins cannot be effaced by merit. Rather, whatever has been taken from the other person has to be restituted. And such a restitution implicitly constitutes a repentance. Very hard, however, are crimes such as murder, adultery, and oppression because what has been taken cannot be restored. If a restitution is not made in this life, one will have to pay compensation on the Day of Judgment by giving one's own merits to the offended party. If one does not possess sufficient merits, God may possibly give one what one needs. Otherwise one will be tormented for one's crimes. It is also possible that one will be forced to assume, in proportion to one's offences against the other person, some of the sins committed by that other person and that one will be tormented for them.

And the Imām Husayn's intercession?

The learned men affirm the existence of the Miniature World ('ālam-i zarr), in which all men issued from the body of Adam like small ants. But they don't support the belief that the Five Persons—Muhammad, Fatima, Ali, Hasan, and Husayn—existed already at that time: their existence should be taken merely allegorically. By the same token, they reject the belief that in the Miniature World the Imām Husayn drank the Cup of Good Deeds which, in consequence, entailed his suffering and passion. Rather, the Imām Husayn simply saw that the people of his time had deserted the religion and he sacrificed himself for the propagation of the true faith. As to his intercession, if he wants to intercede, God will certainly listen to his plea. But, in any case, this would concern only sins against God, not sins against people.

The same is true for the Prophet. The general opinion is that he will intercede, but again, only in cases of sins against God and only if a person's sins are few. If a person has committed many sins, Muhammad himself will take offence and won't intercede.

Doesn't the religion place too much emphasis on rituals and prescriptions, such as prayer, rather than on moral behavior, like honesty?

No, on the contrary: the emphasis is on moral behavior. If rituals and prescriptions are, in fact, carried out better than the moral rules, then this is for several reasons.

First, certain regulations, as the prohibition of pork, are observed because of habit: people would vomit if they ate pork. Others, as the prohibition of adultery, would cause fighting and killing if they were violated. So the observance of certain regulations is supported by custom, but moral rules, such as not stealing and not lying, are not.

Second, praying and fasting doesn't harm people, so they do it. But to agree on projects that would benefit the community as a whole would mean possible harm for one or the other, so they don't do it. They can't overcome their private concerns. They don't have the moral zeal to do so.

Third, the religion has the method, as laid down in the *shari'at,* to enforce the moral rules, but the state doesn't accept it. In Saudi Arabia, where the *shari'at* is the accepted law, there is very little stealing and lying. So it is the fault of the state, not of the religion if these things are done. The learned men disagree very much with the state on this point but they don't have any power.

Isn't the observance of rituals like praying, fasting, and veiling declining in the cities partly because it has become inconvenient?

No, it's not because it is inconvenient. Bank robberies aren't done either because their prohibition is inconvenient. If women don't cover their heads—as many do not do now—this is just personal misdemeanor, in the same way as a bank robbery. People have free will. If they choose to do evil it is personal misdemeanor and has nothing to do with the religion.

Aren't certain teachings of the religion in conflict with generally accepted modern views and behaviors?

No, they aren't. There were misinterpretations, though. For example, the passages in the Qur'ān about the creation of man are not to be taken literally. They just mean that man somehow was created by God. There is no conflict with what scientists say about the evolution of man.

Or the belief in spirits, *jinn.* In the Qur'ān one passage speaks about the creation of *ins* and *jinn* [sura 51/56]. It was thought that these mean "men" and "spirits," and that thus the belief in spirits was validated by the Qur'ān. In fact, however, *ins* refers to city dwellers and *jinn* refers to people living outside cities, like tribesmen and villagers. *Jinn* does not mean spirit

in this context. The way people conceive of this passage is plain superstition.

Or the evil eye. There is a passage in the Qur'ān in which Muhammad is warned that some were casting the evil eye against him. But that
doesn't mean it is right to believe in the evil eye.

Or the veil. The Qur'ān only says that a woman must cover her head
in a way that all hair is concealed. This can be done by a scarf or kerchief:
it mustn't be a full veil, which hinders work.

Or modern hygiene. True, it is said that water which has flowed at a
certain speed over a certain distance is pure. Of course, such water is not
necessarily clean in a hygienic sense. But this rule was made for the whole
world. If one had said to the Arabs that muddy water was impure, they
would have perished because they couldn't have used any. And as to the
present time, there is a passage in the Qur'ān which says that it is forbidden
to kill oneself. This means that once it is known that certain water contains
bacteria and causes diseases, it is forbidden to drink it. Today, muddy
water, even if flowing, isn't to be considered pure: it is unhygienic and is
forbidden.

Or birthcontrol pills. There is nothing said in the Qur'ān to forbid
them. Some ignorant people say that taking the pill interferes with the will
of God. If this were true, one would also have to say that taking medicines
interferes with the will of God—which is evidently wrong because God has
charged us to take care of our health.

What about the prayer-invocations (du'ā')?

Don't you believe that there is a power which can heal diseases? Prayers are supplications to God. One says, "It is up to You, oh God; I can't do
anything." So God's grace is one effect of the prayer. The other is the psychic effect: it is a reinforcement in the same way as when one says to
somebody on the road, "The village is quite near; you will get there soon,"
when, in fact, he will have a long way to go.

But the prayers written on a piece of paper. . . .

. . . and hung around the neck of a child, and so on? That's superstition. It's superstition just as killing an animal when a twist forms in a
wheat field: this is meant to ward off a misfortune; but such a misfortune
would be either due to a psychic effect—people talk about the rich field, the
person becomes haughty and conceited, and so is likely to make a
blunder—or to the effect of the evil eye in consequence of the people's
envious talk. And in the same way it is superstition to believe that a *damband* can check a wolf, or that pausing after a sneeze prevents mishap, or
that giving eggs to a neighbor at night brings bad luck, or that studying the

stars can reveal the future, or that certain days of the week and dates of the month are inauspicious.

But the mullahs have tolerated the superstition, such as prayer-writing, quite generally.

There are even some who don't ride in a car because they consider it forbidden, and others who say that inoculations and Western medicine are forbidden. But only illiterate, foolish characters say that. And besides, one has to understand the position of the mullahs. If a man comes to a mullah and the man isn't at all interested in the prayers, or the law, or the wisdom of the religion, but instead asks, "Is it good to go to a certain place today or not?"—what shall the mullah say? He is forced to give some answer to this question even if he considers it all nonsense; otherwise the man will regard him as an illiterate and ignorant person.

Thus the religion has not been an obstacle to development?

Maybe some religious men have been, but not the religion. The religion says that science should be encouraged even if it were to be found only in the stars. The religion indeed demands the pursuit of science—though not by every individual. It is a group obligation, that means, only one or the other of a group of people has to engage in it. Also, it is said, "Educate your sons in the true spirit of the time," which means that it is requisite to adjust to the changes time brings about, such as no longer fighting with arrows and swords but with rifles and jets. No, if we are backward, it's not the fault of the religion.

Rather, we are backward because of inner fragmentation: different states, different provinces within the state, and so on. If a village like this cannot achieve unity for the purpose of building a road, a bathhouse, or a clinic—how can a state? The three forces I mentioned earlier hinder man from subordinating himself to someone else. But the religion doesn't say they shouldn't. On the contrary, the religion suggests that they should do so for the benefit and strength of Islam. But people don't do it—just as they don't say the truth either.

It is also said that Islam must be backward because most of the modern inventions were actually made in the West. But inventions are ideas, and ideas have nothing to do with religion as such. Also, it is by no means established that this claim is true. In fact, in Iran there were men such as Ibn Sīnā and Omar Khayyam, the great mathematician. And Saʿdī said:

"In the heart of every particle you split,
behold the sun in its midst."

This means he understood already then, 700 years ago, what only today we know as atomic theory. What an enlightened mind!

Above all, the wisdom is written down in the Qur'ān. For example, formerly people thought that the earth was stable and the sun revolved: this was a general opinion, but it's not written in the Qur'ān. The Qur'ān, in fact, says:

> "And you think the mountains you see don't move.
> Yet they move like the clouds." [27/88]

It is only now that this passage is understood correctly. And even if it had been understood earlier, it still would have been impossible to say it because people would not have believed it. This shows also how knowledgeable and enlightened the Prophet must have been to say this 1400 years ago. We ourselves have ignored all this knowledge. But the foreigners learned the whole science from the Qur'ān.

The wisdom of the Qur'ān shows you that Islam is the most perfect religion. Reason tells you that. For it stands to reason that a religion which says, for example, that a certain mountain is God or that the cow should be worshipped is wrong. And likewise, it stands to reason that a religion which says that Jesus is the son of God, and that divorce is forbidden, and that birthcontrol pills are forbidden cannot be perfect. Reason tells you that.

2

The Former Landlord: Religion of Power

The Former Landlord's grandfather was a tribal leader who became a landlord in the course of the settlement of this village and its environs. The
Former Landlord himself was one of the most powerful landlords in the
region, controlling resources and exerting influence in an area far beyond
the village itself and wielding a despotic rule over the peasants. Countless
anecdotes of daring, cruelty, generosity, and political acumen sketch him as
a ruthless and successful leader who moved by his own laws, enjoying what
life had to offer a man of his forceful character and respected position.
Since the early 60's his powers had been declining steadily with increasing
government control over the area, and his claims to the land were successfully challenged by the peasants. Therefore, during the land reform, he lost
without compensation practically all his income from the land. In his mid-
sixties now, he lives in poor economic circumstances and has lost all his
former social status. Of his eight sons only two stayed with him and his
former supporters have gone their own ways. (1976).

*People say you are impoverished because you oppressed them in the past
and have to pay for it now . . .*

Taking the landlord's share they call oppression! But the land was our
property! It was ours by right of our ownership! All the irrigation channels
were built by my grandfather. He brought stone cutters from Isfahan; he cut
through the rocks; he spent money; he dug the channels. He founded this
place. He built the houses; he built the fortifications; he built the bath-

house; he built the mosque. Then he built the other irrigation channels, and one-sixth of each new habitable place he declared as religious endowment. For example, Husaynābād means that the Imām Husayn has made this place habitable and that one-sixth of its income belonged to him; this was then spent to serve food to the people in the month of Muharram, or for some other charitable purpose. These people weren't natives of this place; my grandfather brought them here. He gave them a place to stay, he gave them houses, he gave them fields. So, to take the landlord's share is our right. It's the share of our property for which we paid taxes to the government. Since 100 years we have been paying taxes. The government recognized us as the landlords, the Treasury demanded the taxes from us, and we paid them.

These people were a wretched tribe. They were unable to improve their conditions, they were unwilling to do so. My grandfather had to beat them to build the houses in which they now live. He had to beat them to build the irrigation channels which now water their fields. Otherwise they never would have done it. Now they say, "We did it!"

In fact they came and implored us to rent land to them. We rented it for 100 *man* of wheat per section, or we went to the threshing ground and divided the crop into three parts, two for the peasants, one for us. Now, when the land-reform office will be collecting the land payments from them, it will become evident whether this was oppression or not. I was taking 100 man per year; 100 times 15 rial is 150 toman—be it 200 toman; it wasn't more than that. Now, according to the list of payments that the village council itself submitted to the land-reform office, they have to pay 2,000 toman per year for each section. That's ten times as much as I took. Just wait till the money will be collected from them; then it will be known if I oppressed them!

But didn't one of their elders file complaints with the government against these payments?

Shit he ate, filing complaints. The land-dispute commission wrote in its latest report that while he only claims that the peasants themselves were the owners of the land and that the landlord's share was taken from them by force, the former landlords do have titles to the land while the peasants don't, and that they have been paying the landlord's share in the past. Therefore, the commission wrote, his claim is unwarranted and is being dismissed. What he says is nonsense. These people begged to rent land from us. With his own hand he wrote the rental contracts. I still have them. He came to me and said he would go to the peasants and make the contracts for me. He wrote the contracts, he got the people, they put their fingerprints on, the gendarmerie signed, the military signed, the 'ulamā' signed, and he brought them to me and I gave him fifteen man of wheat as alms.

This man didn't have a thing. He was a servant in my house. I gave him land, I gave him a lamp, I gave him bedding, I gave him food. Some years ago the land reform office asked me to whom I would entrust the safekeeping of the landlord's share till the government would decide the issue. I named this person since he had been elected head of the village council. So they gave him the landlord's share in trust. He stole everything. Then he said the mice ate it. They put him in jail for that, though I waived the claim to my share. Such a person! Such a crime! If he had had my possessions and power, he would have destroyed the world with it.

So, you didn't oppress them?

No, God knows that I didn't oppress them. God knows, I have well taken care of them. Every pauper, every cripple I provided for. There is this blind man in the village. Ask him who cared for him when he was a child, and blind. All those years I was helping the poor and destitute. If one needed fodder, I gave it to him; if one needed barley, I gave it to him; if one needed bread, I gave it to him. There was that rascal who taught the Qur'ānic school; kerosene lamps had not yet come to this area at all when I brought one from Tehran for him. The quilted bedding which is now used I brought here at a time when nobody even knew what it was. The men in the village who were my agents got everything from me; all my possessions were in their hands and they took what they could. Now they act as if I had done them harm. Wretched people, all of them.

The village down the road I built myself. The families living there now had been raided in their old place and I brought them here. Not a sigh they had. One cow they had between them and one donkey, and the donkey had a broken leg. First I gave them 180 sheep and goats, which they divided among themselves. For ten years I gave them seeds and oxen and fodder; I built houses, built stables, and settled them. Once one of their elders became ill. I took him to Isfahan myself. I spent 10,000 toman to have his belly cut open to make him well, and then I brought him back. On the way back we met the khan of a neighboring tribe who asked me whether the man was of my family. I said no, a peasant of mine. He said, "Never take any trouble for a miserable peasant." His words are still in my mind. By God, when that peasant sees me now, he acts as if I had done him an injustice. They were beggars, I provided for them.

This tribe was a wretched and trustless people. I bought rifles for them and hired men from other tribes to protect them from the khans and tribes around us. The tribes up and down were all our enemies. When the government ordered disarmament, I had ninety-six rifles to hand over. These had been for the protection of the tribe, the protection of the people's herds, of their possessions. I did not let them be raided and plundered. They were a miserable tribe, and I took care of them. I fought with the khan, or made peace with him, or did whatever politics were needed: all the time I took care of them.

How come then that they all say you oppressed them?

The "oppression" was that they were robbers and I took them and handed them over to the government. In 1941 they captured rifles from the military posts. I took them away from them and gave them back to the government. This made them angry. At that time the rifles were worth 10,000 toman each, but I handed them over. No matter what the khans said, no matter how much the people kept saying, "Who is the Shah? What have you got to do with him? Let's go and plunder!" I said, "I have been loyal to the Shah and the government from the beginning and I will continue to do so till the end of my life."

But the people say you were the greatest robber?

Never; it's they who went, up and down the country, raiding caravans, travelers, herdsmen, and bringing back the loot. All the time they went. My half-brother didn't stay home a single night; he was constantly out robbing. In his youth he even made the pilgrimage to Karbala. The war minister once wrote a letter to his father complaining about his robberies and other misdeeds. I have kept this letter. I want to show it to him sometimes and say, "Look, these were your deeds."

No, here in the village they couldn't steal, or cheat me. At that time there was order. I had agents, agents from among themselves, who had to oversee them. When one did something wrong I punished him. There was no such thing, as today, when a thief can bribe the gendarmerie and go stealing again. Anyone who stole was punished. During the time of Reza Shah, from '31 to '41, I myself was the government executive charged with the maintenance of law and order in the whole area, the confiscation of rifles, the seizing of black tents, the founding of settlements, the control of robbery. We also brought a teacher here and built a school house where the children were taught till the end of Reza Shah's period.

But then, people say, you stopped education and razed the school building to the ground.

That's nonsense. We built it ourselves. Why should we destroy it again? After the time of Reza Shah the caretaker of the school left—he was employed by the governor's office—and snow and rain ruined the building.

It wasn't built with cement or plaster as buildings are today. It was built of sun-dried bricks, and when nobody took care of it, it fell into ruins. A house that is not taken care of in winter goes to ruin. We also built a clinic here, and it fell to ruins. Should we have destroyed that too?

Did you also provide for religious celebrations?

Already in my youth I built a Husaynīyah here. Every year I spent 5000 toman for *rawzah khvānī* and mourning celebrations. I made the vow to dedicate all the income from the water mill to this. I gave sheep, rice, wheat. Also, there were the proceeds from the religious endowments of the villages which I spent in this way. On the first ten days of Muharram, in the month of Ramadan, and at the other festivals I invited the people. They all came.

Why did you do all this?

To give in the way of the martyred Imām, in the way of God; to give a lunch or dinner to the people, the poor and destitute. The rules of Islam have to be followed: to build a Husaynīyah, to build a mosque, to hold mourning celebrations, to say the prayers, to read the Qur'ān, to recite the prayer-invocations, to hold rawzah khvānīs, that's the order of Islam. A Muslim has to practice these things. I have learned this from my grandfather: he built the mosque, he held rawzah khvānīs. My father was the same way. He was constantly devoted to worship and prayer. He never failed to worship, and to give in the way of God, to practice generosity. For the sake of such acts the Lord will pardon on the Last Day.

What would you say is the essential thing in the religion?

The religion of Islam has to be practiced truthfully and sincerely, not in some phoney way. The rules of the religion, the worshipping, all have to be carried out truly and sincerely. This means, always to say the prayers, not to put them off, not to miss them, to be always ritually pure, to see that one's clothes are not soiled and unlawful. There are some who will say the prayers for seven or eight days, but then go without prayers for two or three months. That's not right. But with me it's a habit, like my opium smoking. From childhood on I have had the habit of saying the prayers and prayer-invocations. It's absolutely impossible that I ever miss the prayers. Friday nights I am sitting up till morning, as long as I am able to, and recite the prayer-invocations. Most of the important prayer-invocations I know by heart.

Our former governor was also a great believer in these prayers. Once I wrote one down for him, one that is good for one's well-being and health, for safe travel, for approaching the great and returning with esteem—you couldn't find it with the wisest dervish nor would the 'ulamā' know it. The governor told me several times that he had tried it out and that it had been very efficacious for him. He was a very pious man.

True, he was drinking, but that's no big thing. Doing repentance for it will be taken into account favorably. I was drinking a lot too. Nobody could drink as much as I could: good wines, best liquors, liquors specially made by a friend in the city. But in 1961 I made the pilgrimage to the Imām Rezā and did repentance. From then on I have never drunk again. Sure it has been forbidden by the Prophet, but it's not serious. Whenever one does repentance for it, one's repentance will find approval. To oppress and to seize other men's property, that is serious, or committing adultery: for that the Lord will never approve of one's repentance; He will never accept it.

Why did you then repent your adulteries?

The Lord is very forgiving, He is most merciful. He forgives great sins, even the greatest sins. But, of course, adultery is not good.

But it is said that you even killed some of your peasants?

That's a lie. God is my witness, it's a lie. They made it up that I killed that man. By this God, He knows it's a lie. I have done no such thing. What happened was that the man was ill and died, and my half-brother and his people incited his family to say I killed him so as to get some land from me. They did this and went to court filing a charge against me. A commission came and a doctor investigated the body and found that the man had died of his illness. It was a lie. By Hazrat-i 'Abbās, it was a lie, a lie.

So, in your opinion, what are the reasons for your loss of power and wealth?

If it were God's punishment, why didn't then my former agents also become impoverished? No, it's not that. It's because I spent my wealth for the government and the people. I maintained the garrison that was stationed here, provided them with food, built houses for them, built a military station. I took care of the people of this tribe, bought rifles, ammunition and horses for them, supported a corps of riflemen to maintain order in the area. All of this involved large expenses. Then, of course, we handed our rifles over to the government, the horses were no longer needed, and our land was sold by the land-reform office to the peasants without us having as yet received any compensation payments. Also, for over ten years we have not been receiving our landlord's share; the peasants are bribing the gendarmerie not to collect it, and we, of course, are not allowed to collect it ourselves—otherwise we'd get it in a flash.

That's the way destiny is. Fortune, the world, is this way. But what difference does it make? Formerly when we were wealthy, we gave our wealth to the people. Now that's no longer needed, and I don't want it anymore. God is providing us with what we need for a livelihood, and if it's not more, may it be so. We had debts at the bank, but the Shah ordered to annul them. A marshal N. in the army communicated to him that I was a person who had been loyally serving the government; who during the time of Reza Shah had established law and order here, seized the robbers, confiscated the rifles, and maintained the garrison; who handed his rifles over by himself when disarmament was ordered, and so on. So the Shah adjusted this. And the power I had was given to me by the government, and it's for the government that I have put it to use. Several times I went to war against insubordinate tribes, captured the rebels, and handed them to the government. Now I no longer have these hardships and troubles. It's better so. Now I am at ease.

3

The Old Trader: Virtuoso Devotionalism

The Old Trader gives his age as seventy-four. Ten years less may come closer to the chronological facts, but the figure he gives expresses more distinctly what he considers to be his stage in life: that of an old man who is prepared to leave the world. Six of his children are married, and in his household, which is still loosely joined with two of his married sons and their mother, remain only his younger wife and his youngest son, twelve.

The Old Trader has been a trader all his life. The son of an immigrant from a village outside the tribal area who owns no agricultural land, he started out as an itinerant peddler. After having made some money, he joined four well-to-do peasants in the partnership of a local store, which since then he is running for the group. This he does with the diligence, patience, skill, and the meticulous correctness of the traditional bazaar merchant. Due to this and also to the generally rising standard of living in the village, the store has been thriving in the past years. In spite of this prosperity, his style of living—again in genuine bazaar fashion—has remained extremely austere, not better—maybe even poorer—than that of most peasants.

Renowned as pious, truthful, and impeccably honest, he serves the community as a model of the true orthodox believer. He performs the prayers and other rituals with the matter-of-course ease of long established routine and has made the pilgrimage to Mashhad not only once but several times. His profound knowledge of religious doctrine, learning and regulations, of special prayers, magic practices, and communal rituals makes him the authority, guide, and organizer par excellence for these matters. If the district governor calls for a celebration of a national holiday in the mosque, the Old Trader will take care of the religious part, chanting the Qur'ān and reciting special prayers. He usually says the prayer over the dead at a burial.

In the Muharram celebrations he acts as a tireless organizer and especially as the entrusted caretaker of all contributions. In 1966 he still arranged and played a leading role in *ta'ziyah*-like performances during the Muharram procession, but, sensing a lack of community interest, has given up on this since then.

All this behavior, religious and secular, he clearly strives to pervade with the ideal Islamic attitudes of deep faithfulness, humbleness, unfailing thankfulness, and remembrance of God. The created image is perfectly convincing and is only slightly tarnished by the fact that his first, older wife complains—supported by the village women—that her husband neglects her and does not care for her adequately. (1971).

How many prophets are there?

From the creation of Adam till the time of the Prophet there were 124,000. Some were prophets of a tribe, others of a city, and others of a family only. Of these 124,000 prophets, twenty-five became *ulū'l-'azm* (endued with constancy and patience), like Joseph, Jonah, Job, and Jacob. Five of them became *mursal* (those to whom is sent). This means, the Lord, blessed and exalted, sent them a special message: a book of heaven was revealed to them. One was Hazrat-i Ibrāhīm, who was given the Books of Abraham (*suhuf*). One was Hazrat-i Dāwud, the father of Hazrat-i Sulaymān who was given the Psalms (*zabūr*). One was Hazrat-i Mūsā, "the one who talked to God," who was given the Pentateuch (*tawrāt*). One was Hazrat-i 'Isā—peace be upon him—who was given the Gospel (*anjīl*). The last one was Muhammad—God's blessings and peace be upon him and his family—who was given the Qur'ān. These five became mursal, they were higher than the others.

God also declared that after Muhammad, the son of 'Abdullah, there would be no other prophet till the Day of Judgment. The other four prophets to whom books were sent were told by God to herald Muhammad's coming. This is written in their books. Of course, you have read all this, too. It is in your Gospel, although Muhammad's name is of course different in your language.

Hazrat-i 'Isā is called the Spirit of God, that is, he has no father, he came into existence from the spirit of God. He didn't die, either. He was taken to heaven. Their high priest ordered him killed, but only the outer appearance of Hazrat-i 'Isā was crucified; 'Isā himself was carried to heaven. He was a good prophet.

The Prophet Muhammad was not taken to heaven. He died. When he lay dying, 'Izrā'il came to fetch his soul. The Prophet said, "Oh sister, brother, 'Izrā'il, it is all right with me. But what will you do to my people?" 'Izrā'il went to heaven and came back with the sura *"alam nashrah"* [sura 94], in which God says to the Prophet, "For your sake I will pardon so many on the Day of Judgment that you will be satisfied." The Prophet understood and said, "Now, take my life, but whatever pain you want to give my people, give to me, instead." And he wept. So kind is our Prophet! Oh, how kind he is!

Hazrat-i Muhammad had no son, just one daughter, the mother of the Imām Husayn. They married her to Hazrat-i Ali, the Amīr al-Mu'minīn, who was the Prophet's cousin, his son-in-law, and later his vice-regent (*vazīr*). The Shia say that the Amīr al-Mu'minīn is the viceregent and successor of the Prophet. The Sunni say that the successors to the Prophet are Abū Bakr, Umar, and 'Uthmān. They consider Ali the fourth caliph of the Prophet, which is not true. They were a powerful and oppressive lineage, but not successors to the Prophet. In their prayers they don't say that Ali, the Amīr al-Mu'minīn, the Commander of the Faithful, is the governor and executor (*vali*) of Allah either.

Is it known when God created man?

When the Lord, blessed and exalted, created Adam, the Father of Mankind, he gave him 50,000 years. That is, from the creation of Hazrat-i Adam till the Day of Judgment it's 50,000 years. Of these, 11,380 and some years have passed. We all are the Creation of Adam—all the peoples are the offspring of just this one man. But before Adam there was another kind of man, and before that there was yet another one, and so on. There was always man. The world was never empty. And again, after us—after the Day of Judgment—another kind of man will exist. We will disappear, this sky will be rolled up, this land will turn into sea. Then God, blessed and exalted, will make another creation. The world will not remain empty.

When Adam was created, that was the First World, which is called the Miniature World ('ālam-i zarr). After Hazrat-i Adam had been created, many tiny ants came from his body. Some of these ants were white, some were black. They asked the Almighty, "Why are some ants black and some white?" God said, "All are the descendants of Adam. White they come to the world, but when they die, those whose deeds are bad turn black, and black they return. Those whose deeds are good return white." That's how it was in the Miniature World. Now is another world, the Middle World, and the Day of Judgment is still another world, the Last World. That makes three worlds.

For what reason did God create Adam?

The Lord, blessed and exalted, created Adam so that from him the Five Persons could issue: the Prophet, the Amīr al-Mu'minīn, Hazrat-i Fatima, the Imām Hasan, and the Imām Husayn. He created him so that He may forgive the sins of the people for the sake of the Five Persons.

When Adam was in paradise, there were several palaces there. Every day Gabriel opened them, and Hazrat-i Adam and Eve, his wife, walked around in them. Only one small palace he did not open. Finally, one day, Hazrat-i Adam said, "Oh, Gabriel, brother, open this one, too." The angel got permission from the Lord and opened the door. Inside, they saw a throne and a girl sitting on it with a necklace around her neck, a crown on her head, and two earrings in her ears, one yellow, one red. Gabriel said, "This is the daughter of Muhammad, son of 'Abdullah—God's blessings and peace be upon him—and her name is Fatima. The crown on her head is the sign of her father, the Prophet of the Last Age, the last of 124,000 prophets in your lineage. Her necklace is the sign of her husband, the Amīr al-Mu'minīn. The two earrings represent her two sons, Hasan and Husayn. The yellow one stands for the older son: his body will turn yellow. And the red one is the sign of her younger son: he will be martyred, his blood will be shed."

At this point Hazrat-i Adam mourned for the Imām Husayn. He, the ancestor of all of us, was the first one to mourn for the Imām Husayn. Thus, the mourning for the Imām Husayn began in paradise and it will last till the Day of Judgment. All prophets, whoever they were, all shed tears over the Imām Husayn.

For example, at the end of their prayers Hazrat-i 'Isā and Mūsā wept for Hazrat-i Imām Husayn. They knew. God informed them. It is written in their Pentateuch, it is written in their Gospel. When Hazrat-i Mūsā was told the meaning of the word 'Āshūrā, namely, that it is the day on which the Prophet's grandson would be killed, he said, "Almighty, accept me, too, among the people of this prophet." Hazrat-i 'Isā made the same request.

How did Imām Husayn's martyrdom come about?

In the Miniature World there was a Cup of Good Deeds and a Cup of Evil Deeds. The unbelievers like Umar and 'Uthman and Yazīd and Mu'āwīyah and Abū Sufyān drank from the Cup of Evil Deeds. The others chose the Cup of Good Deeds. Abraham only moistened his lip: his family had troubles later. Jacob drank a little: he was burdened with separation from his kin. Job drank a little: his whole body was stricken with worms. The Prophet drank a tiny bit: for this he later was hurt in the wars with Abū Jahl. When it was Imām Husayn's turn, he was ready to empty the cup. But Gabriel held his hand and said, "It has its conditions. You will have to give your head. Your wife will be led into captivity. Your young people will be killed. Your small child will be martyred. You will lose all your property, and even your bones will be crushed under the hoofs of horses." "I agree to it all," said Imām Husayn, "But what will be the return for all this?" Gabriel, speaking in the name of God, said, "In return for your martyrdom I will forgive the sins of the people of your grandfather and of the *shī'ah* of your father. For the sake of the captivity of your wife and the others' wives I will pardon the women. For the sake of Ali Akbar and Qāsim and the other youths I will pardon the young men of the Prophet's people. For the sake of your child I will pardon the children of your people."

Then he drank the Cup of Good Deeds, and they wrote a contract, and the Prophet and Moses and Jesus and Abraham—all the twenty-five great prophets and the five prophets who were sent a book—put their seal on it, and it was kept until the day of 'Ashūrā.

What then happened on the day of 'Ashūrā?

On that day, in the plain of Karbala, Gabriel descended and presented the contract to the Imām. Many things happened. For example, the night before, a certain dervish heard the crying of the children who were burning with thirst. He filled a water bag and took it to Hazrat-i Husayn for them. But the Imām Husayn said, "Oh, Dervish, we have no need for water. But I want to prove my identity to the people now so that later in the presence of the Prophet, they won't have any excuse." And he thrust his lance into the ground and water came up. When the dervish saw the miracle, he asked for permission to join the battle, and he was martyred, too.—Oh, poor dervish!

Also, it is written that Safar, the sultan of the jinn, was just making love to a boy when one of his men interrupted him. "Ashes on your head! The son of the Amīr al-Mu'minīn is fighting now in the plain of Karbala and you are busy making love!" The sultan set out with his army and asked the Imām for permission to fight for him. The Imām Husayn said, "You are invisible, but they are men. That's unfair." Safar said, "We will take on the shape of human beings." But the Imām Husayn said, "No, after the death of my son life is worthless for me anyway." So Safar went back. But his mother took her breasts in her hands and said to him, "If you don't sacrifice yourself for Husayn, I won't make the milk of these breasts lawful for you." So the sultan of the jinn returned and was martyred.

The Imām Husayn fought with invincible bravery. He remembered his oath to kill so many that even the stirrup of his horse would be dipped in blood. He and his brother Abul Fazl killed a great many men. Finally, when the others had all been martyred, Gabriel descended, handed him the contract and said, "The Lord, blessed and exalted, says, "If you want the fame of bravery, kill as many as you like. But if you want the privilege of intercession for your people, stop!" The Imām Husayn took the writing, kissed it, and said, "For the peace of the world I will stop fighting. I have not submitted to bondage. I have not yielded to injustice. I have fought violence and oppression. I have done no offence." He alighted from his horse and so he surrendered, otherwise they would have never been able to overpower him. Then they fell over him and with swords and rocks and clubs they hit him till, all spent, he broke down. His body was covered all over with wounds—1950 wounds!

Nobody dared to cut off the Imām's head, which had to be brought to Yazīd, because everyone knew that the Imām was the son of the Prophet's daughter. So they brought a Christian—Nasrānī Ibn Sa'd was his name—and told him to do it, promising rich reward. This man, in a dream the previous night, had been told by Hazrat-i 'Isā, "You must not do any evil that would make me ashamed before Muhammad, son of 'Abdullah, the Prophet of the Last Age. Tomorrow they will tell you to sever the head of a man. Don't do it!" Then Jesus had shown him paradise. Now as he came before Hazrat-i Imām Husayn to cut off his head, he saw a radiance and a light in his face and he wondered. Hazrat-i Imām Husayn told him who he was, and reminded him of his dream and of what Hazrat-i Isā had said, and then he, too, showed him paradise. At this, the Christian requested to become a Muslim, joined in the battle, and was martyred too.

Finally Shimr, whose name means "merciless"—his actual name was 'Abdullah—came with nine other men to cut off the head of the Imām Husayn. But whatever he tried he could not do it. The back of the Imām's neck had been touched by the lips of the Prophet and Hazrat-i Fatima and the Hazrat-i Amīr al-Mu'minīn. Shimr could not cut through there. He had to strike from the front.

For the sake of this innocently shed blood they will be pardoned on the Day of Judgment: this people of the shī'ah of the Amīr al-Mu'minīn, the people of the Prophet—all of them.

Also the thieves and haughty ones?

The Prophet will forgive. He will also forgive for the sake of the good deeds people have done: at some time they may have made a dedication, given some alms, or said, "Oh Husayn, come to my help!" God, the Prophet, the Imām Husayn, their mercy is very great.

What difference then does a good life make?

Well, from now on till the Last Day evil-doers are caught in hell! Only on the Last Day He will forgive! Until now only 11,000 years have passed.

For the rest, until the Day of Judgment they are caught in their sins. There are another 40,000 years. That's hard!

Will Shimr be forgiven too?

What do I know? Their mercy is very great. For example, when those of Husayn's party who had been taken to Damascus as prisoners were released, Yazīd came to Zayn al-'ābidīn, Husayn's son, and said, "Oh, son of the Prophet of God, I left the right path; I was deceived by the devil; I did evil in order to dominate the world. Show me a way to salvation." Zayn al-'ābidīn said, "Between the sunset prayer and the night prayer recite twice the prayer *ghufaylah*. Then God will forgive you." And he told him the prayer.

When his aunt, Zaynab Khatūn, learned about this, she said, "Oh, son of the Prophet of God, after all this violence, the killing of your father and brothers and uncles and all the others, why did you teach him this prayer so that God will forgive him?" He said, "Aunt, we are a benevolent family. Nobody who comes to our house ought to leave in despair. I told him the prayer, but he won't be able to say it at the prescribed time."

And indeed, every time Yazīd wanted to say the prayer he was attacked by such abdominal pains that he could not do it. He just could not say it. The order of God! Miracle of the Imām! He sent for doctors from everywhere, but they could not do anything. Finally a doctor from England, a Christian, came. He asked for a thread, a needle, and some tiny pieces of meat. He strung the meat on the thread, forced it down into Yazīd's stomach, waited a few minutes, and pulled it up again. With each piece of meat two or three scorpions came up. The doctor beat his head in horror. "What did you do?" he cried. "You either killed the Prophet or a successor to the Prophet. You cannot be cured."

So Yazīd kept being seized by pains, and, thanks be to God, could not say this prayer. One day he set out hunting. As he was pursuing a gazelle, a coffin of fire carried him off, and he was gone.

But the prayer that Zayn al-'ābidīn told him exists and is said by many people. Everyone who says it at the prescribed time earns great merits. The Lord remits his sins, and he won't see hell.

Would God forgive even stealing and murder by this prayer?

No, not now. On the Last Day perhaps he will forgive. These sins are very serious, the sins against people. The Lord forgives sins against His own rights, like prayer, fasting, merits. But sins against people weigh heavily on a person's back. God cannot remit them. Only on the Day of Judgment He will forgive. Then He is bound to.

Going back to Adam: don't people say now that man descends from animals?

No, no, man is of earth. The body of Adam was formed out of earth. When the Lord, blessed and exalted, after the vanishing of the previous man, wished to create Adam, who is called the Father of Mankind, Gabriel went to get earth from paradise for his body. As he was gathering it in his long Arab shirt, by the order of God, the earth started to speak, "God wants to create Adam. Take your hands off me, I want no part in the fire of hell." So Gabriel did not take it. Michael came, was addressed in the same way, and did not take it either. Nor did Isrāfīl. As the fourth, 'Izrā'il, came—the one who takes the soul now—whatever the earth said, it was to no avail. He took some and carried it to heaven. The Lord, blessed and exalted, ordered the body of Adam formed from it, and He breathed the soul into this mould. So the material of man is earth. The people lie, who say that man is derived from animals.

After Adam had been created, all the angels of heaven came and bowed in reverence before him. Only one angel, Iblīs, the devil, did not do it. Haughtily he refused, saying, "I am created out of fire, this one is of earth. I won't bow." So God ordered him driven off His court. Iblīs said, "I have a petition to the throne of God: Tell me the "Greatest Name" of God!" The "Greatest Name" is an important prayer-invocation. He said this in a tone as if he would then give reverence to Adam, but when they told him, he exclaimed, "With the power of this invocation I will hinder the salvation of your servants so much that all people will go to hell." The Lord, blessed and exalted, said, "The prayer shall vanish from your memory." And he forgot it, thanks be to God. Now he can't, he can't!—Ah, this God, how gracious He is, how kind!

But still, the devil retained his power, and God won't take it from him till the Day of Judgment. He leaves him alone for the purpose of testing the offspring of Adam, to let them prove that they won't be seduced, to see who is worthy. God said, "Man travels as in a caravan. There is a thief along the road, be careful that he won't get you." The thief is who? It's the devil.

In paradise Hazrat-i Adam was given paradisic fruits to eat. These fruits became sweat and evaporated without defecation. But then the devil seduced him, saying, "Eat from this wheat! It's a good fruit, better than all others." And Adam ate the wheat. He didn't know that the wheat has the effect of bowel movement. No one who has eaten it is allowed to stay in paradise any longer. So Adam was expelled from paradise. As he passed through the gate with Gabriel he said, "In the name of God, the merciful, the compassionate!" Gabriel said to him, "You have said a great word, a word for which God will show mercy to all your offspring until the Day of Judgment."

About this, Hajji Hafiz said: "My father sold the garden of paradise for two grains of wheat. I wouldn't be a worthy son of my father if I wouldn't buy it back with one grain of barley."[1] That means, Hazrat-i Adam was deceived into selling paradise for two grains of wheat, but his offspring can buy paradise back even with barley, that is, with worldly possessions—by giving help to the poor and destitute and miserable, by giving bread, by giving a shirt to one who goes naked.

Anyone who is good, who is near God, does well. God puts things all right for him here as well as there. How great, how great! A good man is always alive. When he dies here, he will be taken to paradise. After the questioning in the grave by the two angels Nakīr and Munkar the good-doers are taken to paradise; the evil-doers, the sinners, are taken to hell.

Anyone who is evil, who says, "I am somebody," who goes the road of the devil, will have nothing either in this world or in the next: a man in misery. God makes him destitute in this world—for sure he does: God can't be fooled—and punishes him in the next as well. He is tortured in the fire of hell. Oh, God, come to our help!

On the Day of Judgment God will remit hell finally—if God wills. We hope that our Prophet will supplicate on our behalf: he is very close to God, very near. Sure, there will be a hell after the Day of Judgment, but this will be for another creation, for another mankind.

How are sins recorded?

Two angels are always with man: one on his right side, the other on his left. One records his good deeds, the other his evil deeds. When you have formed the intention to do a good deed, like, for example, a dedication, or alms to the poor it already will be written down before you even have done it. But the intention of an evil deed isn't written down. Even if you do the evil deed, the angel won't write it down for three days because God says, maybe you will repent. Only if you do not repent for three days, the angel will write it down. So they have these two books.

Then they have a pair of scales. The merits and the sins are thrown onto the scales to determine which one is heavier. Then if a person has been harassed, a certain amount of his own punishment is given to the offender. Of course, he may also pardon him.

And as to his merits?

For merits many sins will be forgiven, but only light ones, such as having spoken ill of a person, or having troubled someone lightly—such offences are remitted for alms or dedication or some other merit. Violations of people's property are not forgiven, unless the creditor himself forgives it. As to the prayer, that must be said. A person will be held responsible for it.

Depending on the extent of the neglect, he will be punished either by greater torment (*'azāb*) or lesser torment (*'aqāb*).

So how will a person be judged?

For the merits of a person proportional amounts of his sins will be taken away. If all his sins are removed in this way and only merits are left, he will be carried to paradise. But if there are still more sins left, that's hard. Then he will be punished in proportion to them by greater or lesser torment. But it can also be that a person is first tormented for his sins and then carried to paradise for his merits.

What must a person do to be good?

Men and jinn were created to worship God. Every day a person should allow eight hours for sleep and rest, eight hours for work, and eight hours for worship. Of course, everybody has his ability, but if he can fulfill these eight hours of worship—two of them during the night—then it's good, very good.

Someone who is content in illness, who reconciles himself to suffering, who thanks God in distress, who shows himself worthy is good before God. Someone who doesn't show himself worthy, who says, "Why did You do this to me?" is evil before God. Suffering is a test: its purpose is to reveal whether a person is worthy or not.

If one has done evil, the devil has it easy to seduce him further. He must do repentance, right away, and he must restitute all stolen unlawful goods, because offences against people's property aren't remitted by God.

We have the Right of People and the Right of God. God will forgive offences against the Right of God, that is, if a man was negligent in his prayers or fasting or worship. But offences against the Right of People, like stealing money, He won't forgive. Only the rightful owner may remit these. If I know the owner, I have to return things to him. If he is not known or the owner has died, I have to give to the poor the exact amount of what is on my neck. That's the rule of Islam. In any case there is no excuse whatsoever such as ignorance. After all, God has told us through the prophets.

The nature of man must be right. People here weren't right from the beginning, and they aren't now either. They were stealing, went raiding, robbing. The food they ate was unlawful. Thus, from the very beginning their nature was impure. If a man goes begging here, his brother won't give him a thing, his father won't feel bad about it, neither will his son. That's because of ignorance and lack of spirit and zeal. A person must have zeal and a sense of honor.

How many times a day should a person pray?

The obligatory prayers are said three times a day: the morning prayer, two prostrations; the noon and afternoon prayers, which are said together, each four prostrations; the sunset prayer and night prayer, also said together, three and four prostrations. So, each day there are seventeen prostrations. These are obligatory. If a person doesn't say them, it's as if his religion was not right.

But voluntary prayers are many. For example, after midnight eleven prostrations are said, which is called the "night prayer"; or, between the noon and afternoon prayers, the so-called "voluntary prayer" (*namāz nāfilah*), seven to ten prostrations, is said; between the sunset prayer and the regular night prayer the "prayer for forgiveness" (*namāz ghufaylah*), two prostrations, is said. These are voluntary: if you say them, it earns merit; if you don't say them, you won't be held responsible for them.

There is another kind of prayer, invocations (du'ā'), which are also voluntary. Such prayers exist for everything. One, *du'ā' mashlūl,* Hazrat-i Amīr al-Mu'minīn taught to a person who was lame. Prayers are said so that a person's muslimhood be proven. The body and face of a person who recites the prayers and says invocations appears to radiate a special light.

Prayer-invocations (du'ā') for sickness and pain are of a different type. These are looked up in a book (*jam' d'avat*), and figured out on the basis of a person's name, month of birth, the kind of disease, and so on. Such prayers exist for all diseases and pains. For example, for a toothache, which comes from a worm shaking the tooth, it's part of a sura of the Qur'ān.

Another du'ā' is the "worm-binding" (*sīmband*). Sometimes a sort of worm (*sīm*) appears in a field and eats the growing wheat. When they write this prayer—the Sayyids of a nearby village have it—this worm will leave by the order of God. There is also the "binding of the jaws" (damband). It's taken from the Qur'ān and protects sheep and goats against a wolf. Another such du'ā', the "binding of the lock" (*quflband*), is made to prevent a miscarriage when a pregnant woman starts having untimely labor-like pains. Four short chapters of the Qur'ān are spoken over a padlock which is then snapped shut. When a woman has a hard delivery, a du'ā' is written on a small saucer, and the woman washes it off with a little water which she then rubs on the inside of her thighs. For everything there are such du'ā'. These prayers have efficacy. They are very good.

What about vows and alms (sadaqah)?

Vows are made to an Imām, or to a mosque. You promise to give a certain amount if your wish is granted, or you make a dedication and ask for a favor, such as that a sick child may get well again. Alms (sadaqah) are given to the poor. In this case one takes some money or some wheat, puts it on the head of the sick child, and then gives it to a poor person. For this, God will have mercy and dispense the evil. Sure, to sacrifice an animal when a twist (*kākul*) forms in a wheat field belongs to the religion too. One says that such a twist eats the head of the field's owner. For the sake of the blood of a sacrifice God will dispense this evil. How great, how great! A wonderful God we have!

Are the calendars which foretell the future accepted by the religion?

Of course the religion approves of them. Some make mistakes, but especially the one by Habīb'ullah Nujūmī is correct in whatever it says. If it says it will rain, it will rain. If it foretells a backache for today, I will have a pain in the middle of my back. It tells the truth. It's marvellous. These men take great pains to learn this science. They read, have books, travel a lot, climb mountains in snow and ice, fast. It is said that they live on an almond a day. Of course they eat more than that, that's a symbol. The aim of eating little is that their mind would not be distracted by a full stomach.

Why don't you sell whistles and toys in your store?

Doing business with them is unlawful. The whistles are useless; besides, blowing them is sinful. These whistles, these plastic toys, these toy cars, these sun glasses, these useless watches the children wear . . . doing business with anything that is neither food nor clothing is unlawful. A Muslim mustn't sell them. The wares in our store are either food, or lamps, or pots, or detergents, or other necessary things. Money made from them is lawful.

How much profit is it lawful to take?

One half, or one, or two of ten is lawful. A bit more is still lawful if it is gained by bargaining. But if it is out of proportion, or the other is not bargaining, like yourself, then it is unjust. This detergent here cost me five rial. If I said ten rial, you would pay it, but it would be unjust. I would have done violence to God. Adding half a rial would be enough. If God gives his blessings—that's good. But if I did injustice, there would be no blessing—it would vanish, everything would vanish. Be satisfied with little so that God may give you rightly. But if you act with injustice, and greed, and deception all you have will vanish completely.

What religious rules has a woman to observe?

In general, the same as a man. A woman must have modesty and chastity. She must not talk or sit with people who are not intimately related to her, and she must pass modestly and swiftly through lanes and public places. A man not, he is free. He may go wherever he likes.

Until she is nine years old, a girl has no formal religious duties. But if she wears a veil even as a small girl, it's all right. Wearing the veil is very good for the modesty and chastity of a woman. After the age of nine she must say her prayers and observe her fasting till her first menstruation. Then, for these periods, she must not do the prayers and the fasting, and after these periods a ritual washing of the whole body is obligatory (*ghusl hīz*). A ritual bathing is also obligatory on the tenth day after parturition (*ghusl nīz*). After the child has been born, and cleansed, and dressed, she will purify her hands up to over the wrists for purposes of eating but she can't say the prayers till after this ritual bath. Thus, for a woman there are two ritual washings in addition to the three which are also obligatory for a man.

For forty days after childbirth a woman has to be very careful. Another woman wearing one of those stone beads which affect a child, or a person coming tired from a long journey may enter the room—those things are dangerous for the child. Also, if she is visited by a woman who has not yet completed her forty days either, her child is in danger and she herself may not become pregnant again. There is a proven du'ā', called *chihil-i bur,* for protection against this; a white and a black thread are twisted to a string, seven knots are tied into it, and over each knot a special prayer (du'ā') is spoken. For the mother a long string is made, for the child a shorter one, and both wear it on their bodies.

What about the education of girls?

They must go to school at the age of seven like the boys. Knowledge is very good. "From cradle to grave seek knowledge," says a poem. Science has no end that man could see, but whatever level a person reaches is good.

Didn't the religion disapprove of it?

Yes, the religion says that they shouldn't go. My heart would want that things would be according to the rules of the law (sharī'at) which says that a woman shouldn't leave the house at all, that only those intimately related to her should see her, that a girl mustn't go among people, and if somebody wants to have her educated, she must be taught in the house of her father or brother or husband.

But now, well, things have come to be this way. Now different times have come. These earlier times are no longer possible now. Now girls and boys see each other in school. They ask each other for marriage. They themselves go to their fathers and mothers and ask to be married. Now it has come to be this way.

Are the people's morals getting better or worse?

They were much better in the past. Even thirty years ago the religion of the people was much better. Today compassion and justice have become rare. People don't say the prayers. And they drink liquor, too.

In fact, the poets and learned men of the past have told us that it will get worse and worse, that the religion will become darker. In the old days boys and girls did not go to school together. Now they do. The women didn't ride on horseback. Now they do. Now they go by car, they go by airplane. We were told these things would happen. And they will get worse until the Imām of All Time, the Twelfth Imām, will appear.

These will be arduous times. For some years there will be drought and dearth. People will leave the faith and the religion. The Deceiver (*dajjāl*) will come, riding a donkey; he will give dates to the people and they will follow him. Then, after forty days, the Imām will appear. Anyone who will follow him is a Muslim, anyone who won't is an unbeliever—a very grave misdeed. Then he will redeem the people. Their hearts will be enlightened and they will become good.

The Christians will become Muslims sooner than the others. They will say, "We knew how to make cars and build airplanes; but the sons of the Prophet had the gift of covering instantly the entire distance of the earth." The son of the Imām Rezā, for example, left Medina and in the blinking of an eye reached Khorasan. The Imām Husayn fought in Karbala on the day of 'Ashūrā, and on the same day rescued Sultan Qais of India from the teeth of a lion. The Prophet split the moon in two, a miracle which is called *shaqq al-qamar*. Because they had these gifts, it is evident that they were in the right, and, therefore, the Christians will approve of the Imām of All Time and will do so even earlier than the Muslims.

But right now it is rather bad. Indeed, I don't know what is happening now. Maybe the Imām of All Time is about to come. Yet, I don't think this will happen in my lifetime. But how great would it be to see the Imām, how great!

4

The Young Trader: Literal Zealotry

The Young Trader comes from a family of fairly well-to-do, respected peasants. His grandfather reputedly even died a heroic death in courageous defense of peasant rights against a former landlord. By occupation, however, and by his general outlook, he is not a peasant, but a trader. While working as a migrant laborer in a city he suffered an injury which he claims disabled him from doing farmwork. He used his insurance payments as business capital and took up trading. Now in his late twenties, he owns and runs jointly with a partner one of the more successful small stores in the village. He also has acquired some literacy and learned the traditional bazaar methods of bookkeeping. Quite frequently he travels to Shiraz and other towns on business to re-stock his store. In the towns he associates mainly with the traders of the traditional bazaar sector, thereby learning to identify with their opinions.

His family of two children is still relatively small and is still joined in one household with his older brother, his wife and four children, and his mother. While he contributes clothes, tea, sugar, and other trade items, his brother cultivates their undivided land and produces most of their agricultural and dairy necessities.

He appears to be a very conscientious observer of prescribed rituals like prayers and fasting, and has made the pilgrimage to Mashhad already several times. During the Muharram celebrations he regularly joins the flagellators, untiringly swinging an especially heavy chain. This is the more significant as most of the flagellators in this village are not married men but boys. The thorough practice of rituals is complemented by an intellectual interest in his faith, which prompts him to read religious literature.

He expresses himself freely and easily, appearing as an outgoing, so-

ciable and happy character. But he stands for his convictions: Rumor has it
that he beat up his wife when she tried to use the contraceptive pill. (1971).

Why do you consider Hazrat-i Ali to be so great?

Hazrat-i Ali—peace be upon him—existed from the beginning. It is
impossible to say whose son he was. He guided all the prophets. Once,
when Hazrat-i Adam haughtily said that there was nobody higher than
himself, he was taken to the seventh heaven and shown Hazrat-i Fatima
wearing a crown, which was Hazrat-i Ali, and two earrings, which were her
two sons, the Imām Hasan and the Imām Husayn. Thus, these four existed
already before Adam.

But God arranged it so that Hazrat-i Ali was born as the cousin of the
Prophet. Once, when he was only a child, Gabriel bowed before him, and
Muhammad asked the angel why he had done so. Gabriel told him that it
was in respect to Ali's greatness.

How great the Hazrat was you can see from this: When the Prophet
set out for his ascent to heaven (*mi'rāj*), Hazrat-i Ali wanted to be taken
along, but Muhammad refused. The Prophet left, but on his journey he was
stopped by a lion who requested his ring for letting him pass. And when he
was dining near the throne of God, a hand appeared from behind a parti-
tion and joined him in the meal. And while Muhammad was eating half an
apple, the hand took the other half. The next morning Hazrat-i Ali asked
the Prophet what had happened. The Prophet told him and showed him the
half apple from heaven. Hazrat-i Ali took the other half from his pocket
and Muhammad saw that it was the matching piece. Then Hazrat-i Ali gave
him back the ring which the lion had taken. That is, Hazrat-i Ali had been
the lion and was near the throne at the same time as the Prophet. There-
upon the Prophet said, "I don't know Ali as God, but neither do I know
him to be separate from God."

Still, one cannot say that Hazrat-i Ali is higher than the Prophet. The
Prophet himself said, "It is like Ali being my head and the rest of my body
being myself."

Hazrat-i Ali had divine knowledge, but the Prophet didn't have it
before Gabriel delivered it to him. Also, Hazrat-i Ali had divine power: if he
had wanted to, he could have destroyed the world with the whisk of a
finger. When he was an infant of three months, the dragon which used to
haunt Mecca came again and the people fled the city. Hazrat-i Ali seized
the dragon, which was thirty meters long, with his hands, from which the
bands fell off which were holding him in the crib, and tore it apart.

Yes, Hazrat-i Ali—peace be upon him—had great power. Did you hear the story of Marhab Khaybari? This was a king, an idolworshipper, who had built an impregnable castle in which maybe more than two million people lived. The Lord sent Gabriel to the Prophet, ordering him to conquer the castle, and the Prophet moved the army against it. Abū Bakr attacked first and was defeated. So were Umar and 'Uthmān. Then Hazrat-i Ali, who was somewhat sick at that time, arrived from Medina. Alone by himself he rode into the battle. Marhab Khaybari wasn't a joke: he was a hero like those in the story of Rustām. When Hazrat-i Ali reached the moat, he alighted and went onto the water which, by the order of God, became solid as stone under his feet. On the other side he was countered by some heroes of the castle and he killed them. Marhab Khaybari himself came. He struck his sword against Hazrat-i Ali, but to no effect. Then Hazrat-i Ali struck him in the middle of the head, and all the way down he was split into two parts.

Thus, Hazrat-i Ali spread the faith of Islam with his power, his sword, his miracles, and his word. Once he entered a church, and the priest in the pulpit became dumb. Hazrat-i Ali came forth and started to preach and converted the whole congregation.

It is because of this power that we say, "Oh, Ali!" in any danger and that this is very efficacious. Once a car with Jews swerved off the road on the Pīr-i Zan Pass between Shiraz and Bushire. At this moment they cried out, "Oh Ali!" and converted. The car plunged down and was smashed to a thousand pieces, but they themselves were completely unharmed.

All this shows that the religion of Islam is superior to all others. The religion itself is perfect. It is we ourselves who are rotten. Islam is the pure religion because it comes from God. Hazrat-i 'Isā himself has said, "Another prophet will come, listen to him!" So the Prophet of the Last Age is the best prophet. We approve of all prophets, but none is better than the prophet Muhammad, the Last Prophet. These prophets were sent to guide man onto the right path. God sent them.

What about the Imām Husayn?

Hazrat-i Husayn was very brave. After the Prophet had died, Hazrat-i Ali had been killed, and the Imām Hasan had been poisoned, their task fell to the Imām Husayn. He waged a sort of holy war against injustice. Against Abū Bakr and Umar and 'Uthmān he proclaimed: "People are equal!" He didn't tolerate it that they were haughty, that they plundered people's property, that they took away their wives. He told them to stop, to work honestly instead. He fought them. And this is everybody's duty: to defend his property, to fight for it. Surrender is sinful. We in this village didn't surrender to the landlords.

Finally, they martyred him. In commemoration of that day we make a celebration every year. We make it for him because he is our Imām and because we love him. We make a contribution to the mosque because we love him. Those who feel very great sorrow even flagellate themselves.

Do you feel the same about the other Imāms?

Yes, when we make a pilgrimage to Mashhad, we do it because Hazrat-i Rezā is our Imām; and because of compassion, for he was a stranger in this land and was killed here; and to pay respect to him, in the same way as one greets his father in the morning.

What a sight it is, the shrine of Hazrat-i Rezā! Maybe a hundred, two hundred, three hundred large rooms, who knows how many. . . . Once you are inside, you don't know through which door you entered. And there are at least a million people inside the sanctuary. It's like a swarm of locusts—you can't count them. They are there day and night. I went at midnight, thinking it would be more quiet then, but in fact it was more crowded than at noon; and the same at four o'clock in the morning. People stand so tightly packed, you can't move. Only if one is very strong can he elbow his way through to the shrine of Hazrat-i Rezā itself. And the new rooms they have built! Magnificently they built them! It's a view . . . what shall I say? The shrine of Shāh Charāgh in Shiraz is only like a corner of a single room of Hazrat-i Rezā's shrine. And then the golden dome—this dome is built of golden bricks. No king in this world has so much gold as this dome.

Do these Imāms have great power too?

Certainly. This is the family of the Imāms. God loves them. Whatever they wish from God, He does for them. In Mashhad, the people who are sick or make a great request of Hazrat-i Rezā fasten a chain around their neck. Its lock springs open when their wish is granted. Every day many people are healed there. Hazrat-i Rezā is very miraculous. You have seen with your own eyes how ill the wife of one of your neighbors was before she was taken there—no doctor could cure her. Now she is all right: at the shrine of Hazrat-i Rezā she got well. Yes, the Imāms have great influence with God.

Down the valley there is a small shrine of a sister of Hazrat-i Rezā. During summer, the families living around this Imāmzādah deposit some of their belongings there while they move higher up. Nobody has the power to take even a box of matches away from there because the Imāmzādah will strike any thief. One night, a man of a nearby village became stupid, a fool, the devil seduced him. He stole some of the people's things there. But as he made off with them his eyes became blind and he couldn't see anymore. He started to implore God and to repent and pledged to become a caretaker of the Imāmzādah. At that, he got well again. He could see again. He returned, put the things of the people back in place, and later married the daughter of the woman who takes care of the shrine.

There is also a shrine on the other side of the mountain, the Imāmzādah of Sayyid Mahamad, an offspring of a brother of Hazrat-i Rezā. Some years back a man of one of the tribes took to the mountains and became a highwayman, robbing and killing people. One day, a group of women had come into the mountains to gather greens and wild vegetables when that man attacked them and wanted to do an infamy. At that moment a horseman appeared on the other side of the huge rock where they were—a rock about five times as large as this room—and shot his rifle. The bullet pierced the rock and killed that man. Then the horseman disappeared. A group of men happened to pass by, but he vanished before their eyes—it was the Sayyid Mahamad. The rock lies beside the road and you can see the hole. Not a thousand M-1 rifles, not even a cannon can make that hole.

Another Imām, Imām Ja'far Sādiq, wrote the remedies for all diseases down in a book. At a time when there were no doctors, he wrote down the divine knowledge that the Lord had given him. He was the first doctor. He wrote, for example, that this herb is good for a certain illness, how it must be prepared to make a certain medicine, what medicine there is for a toothache, a headache, and so on. This Imām also wrote down prayer-invocations (du'ā'). God has 1001 names and these are used to ask Him favors. The prayer writers know how to do this. The du'ā' too have much proven curing power.

Once a person with a disease of the nose came to one of the hospitals in Shiraz. A smear was made, and medicines applied, and their effects studied under the microscope, but no Western medicine killed the bacteria. Then, by accident, some cold water got on it and immediately killed them. At that, a Muslim doctor showed the American doctor a passage in the book of Imām Ja'far Sādiq, where it says that before the prayers ablutions should be made—rinsing water down the arms, and up the nose, and so on—and that this kills the bacteria. The American doctor was so struck by the superiority of Islamic science that he became a Muslim.

For a Muslim, what is right behavior?

To carry out what the religion says. The father of my partner was a very pious man, better than the Mullah. Whatever the Mullah said the religion requests, he carried out. He was so pious that when he cast a curse over an evil-doer, it really took effect.

Our religion tells us especially to share with our neighbor today and that God will take care of tomorrow. What one gives to a needy person one possesses in That World, it earns merit: like giving help to one who is alone, giving money to one who is sick, giving bread to an orphan, ransoming a prisoner, and so on. For that reason, attending the Friday prayers in the mosque earns special merit. Gathering in the mosque affords an opportunity to see who is poor, to collect money for him, and to give it to him. In our village this isn't done though. The Mullah doesn't come, he is negligent. Of course, the contributions to the mosque in Muharram earn merit too; one who participates actively in the ceremonies earns even more.

On the other side, causing harm to other people and violating their property is sinful. In this store, for example, I couldn't steal from my partner. If I embezzled only one rial, I would be held responsible for it on the Day of Judgment. Also, it is forbidden to take interest. A debt of one-hundred toman is a debt of one-hundred toman and I wouldn't increase it, no matter how long the payment is delayed. Well, yes, an item I bought for, let's say, ten toman, I might sell for only eleven toman when I see that the customer will pay in cash, but for twelve toman when he buys it on credit—but making a profit of two toman on ten toman is within lawful limits.

As to ritual obligations, if a person fails to perform them, he is hurting himself. If he doesn't say the prayers or observe the fasting, he fails to carry out an order of God, and so commits a sin, and so is doing violence to himself in the same way as if he hit his head with a rock. My brother who is farming isn't observing the fasting. He says, "The work is too hard, my body can't do it." But hard work alone doesn't produce the daily bread: God gives it. God has arranged it that one shall work for eight hours, sleep and rest for eight hours, and worship for eight hours. Sometimes a person works for twenty-four hours and doesn't have a thing—he has no blessings. If one shares one's possessions with others, then God gives blessings. Many people don't pay the obligatory alms (khums) because they want to keep everything for themselves. But, in fact, paying the khums doesn't diminish one's own possessions at all. One can test this. Let's say a person harvested 200 man of wheat. If he will take off the khums—which should be a fifth of the produce—and then weigh his wheat again, it will weigh the same 200 man again. God makes it this way. My brother isn't paying the khums. There are many others who do pay it, though. I don't pay it either. I don't have to because I don't make any profits in the store.

With all evil behavior it's like this: The devil says, "Go ahead! Do it!" while reason keeps saying, "No, don't do it!" Most people don't deliberate though. They don't think of the Last Things and just do the evil. One must keep the Last Things in mind. For in this world we are travellers. Our real place is there.

What are these Last Things?

When a person dies, his soul goes off to some other place—just as when one is dreaming. If this man in the past has committed unforgivable sins like adultery, blasphemy, theft, usurpation—like seizing land from orphans who cannot defend themselves—then, in the hour of his death will come Isrāfīl, a very ugly and frightening angel, and seize his soul to take it to the fire of hell. He will be told, "Why did you run after others' wives? Didn't you have a sister to see that it is evil to look at others' wives? Why did you . . ."; and so on. But to a person who believes in the Imāms and the Prophet and didn't do evil, to him comes Hazrat-i Ali himself in the most critical minute after death, when he is put into his grave, and then his soul will be carried to paradise.

Then, on the Day of Judgment, all men will come to life again. The special attendant of every person who has written down all the person's deeds will present this book now, and on the basis of this book judgment will be passed. A good person will go to the Prophet, a bad one to hell, which is like a prison, eternal for some, shorter for others.

We used to say that at this judgment good and evil deeds are weighed against each other. But I don't believe—as others do—that then the amount of deeds on the heavier side will be reduced by the amount of deeds on the lighter side. In this way a person could pay off his sins—which cannot be true, at least not in regard to sins against people. Rather, a person will be rewarded in proportion to his good deeds and punished in proportion to his evil deeds. For an evil deed a person has to suffer. He cannot redeem it by paying it off with merits. Neither is it redeemable through a pardon by the offended person. That's not possible. A murderer must go to hell for a time in proportion to his sin.

So a remission of sins is not possible?

The attendant which I have mentioned writes down instantly and twice all good deeds. Evil deeds, however, are not recorded until after three days. If, in this period, a person repents them, they will be forgiven, except if he violated other men's property—even if he stole only a few grams of something—and made no restitution: this sin will not be forgiven.

What happens in cases of adultery?

This same thing surely will happen to himself. Once a man did such an indecency to the wife of another. When he left, he noticed a small boy looking at him in a very strange way. Years later, this same man happened to catch a young man with his own daughter, and he saw that it was the same boy. Now he understood. He renounced to retaliate and let him go. But whether or not God will forgive this man—for he has seen the same evil that he did to others—or forgive that young man—for the offended man himself waived his claim—is impossible to say.

Likewise, the relations of a killed man may renounce their claim after having received, let's say, a daughter of the killer's party as compensation payment. It is possible that then God will forgive, too.

Is illness God's punishment?

Inevitably it is. Or rather, it may be so. That is, if a person did something evil he will be without doubt punished for it in this life in one way or the other. But whether a particular disease is a punishment for sins, we don't know.

In the same way, poverty may be God's punishment. We see it with our Former Landlord. In former times he may have roasted twenty or thirty chickens—stolen from the people—for dinner; today he frequently hasn't any dinner at all. But it may also be simply that one is poor one day and rich on another.

Why then are evil and misery in the world?

If evil did not exist, good would not be recognizable. And also, if there wasn't any evil—for example, no earthquakes—nobody would even think of saying, "Oh, God!" If I had all amenities, all the best, never became sick, had no trouble, had a car, had money, had the best apartment, had piped water in the yard: what good would that do me? But if a poor person nevertheless constantly praises God and has God in mind, it is very good.

Couldn't one also be pious in good circumstances?

There are some who can't, like Fir'aun, the king of Egypt at the time of Moses, or Shaddād. Shaddād was an orphan. It's a long story which I don't know in detail, but eventually Shaddād attained kingship, and the Lord gave him so much wealth that he claimed to be God and built a paradise, a paradisical garden. Just as he wanted to enter it, and stood with one foot outside and one foot inside the garden, Gabriel descended and took his life as punishment for his haughtiness.

But not everybody is like this. For example, Imām Reza with all his possessions and lands and money and gold and wealth still gave the khums and zakāt and alms to the poor.

Thus, to some God keeps giving riches to see how well they prove themselves. There are some whose attention is turned toward God hour for hour, day for day, no matter how rich they get. For example, in Tehran, Isfahan, and Shiraz are rich people who build a big mosque, which costs millions, or a bathhouse, or a bridge. They say, God gave us wealth, we have to give, too.

But others are evil. Once they have become wealthy, they say, "We have acquired this wealth ourselves. It's not God who gave it to us." They forget God. The Lord tolerates them, though, to see how far they will go.

Do you feel people are generally turning this way?

No. As I have said, in the big cities there are people who spend millions in the way of God. And this Development-Corps man from Shiraz in the village—he says the prayers most perfectly. Those people in the cities who are not saying the prayers and those women not wearing the veil—which is absolutely obligatory—those are Bahais. This group has become big in the cities; actually, most urbans are Bahais nowadays. That's a rotten religion. They say every period has its own prophet. They make no marriage contract, only ask the boy and the girl, and there are witnesses, and that's it—no prayer or anything. Those schoolbooks which talk about evolution and such nonsense, they are written by Bahais, Armenians, and Jews.

True, many students don't fast. But their mind isn't sound at all, otherwise they wouldn't make demonstrations against the Shah twice a year. Has there ever been a better Shah? The whole world is in his brain. He is very near to God!

But he favors birth control.

About that the religion hasn't said anything. It's impossible to say whether the religion approves or disapproves of it. But I don't approve of my wife taking these pills. If God wishes to give four or five or however many children, then this is good so. It is in His hands how many children He gives.

What is the purpose of sacrificing an animal, for example, when a new house is built?

This is done because there are some, for instance, . . . well, we say, they have the evil eye. If such a person passes by a new house, and looks at it, and says, "What a nice house this is," it is possible that the house gets destroyed. The shedding of the blood checks that . . . bad eye.

It's now known who these people are. They are people who are envious, devil-like. They don't want others to have more, or better things, or to be equal to them: they want us to be their servants. This kind of people we call "Mu'āwīyah-like" because their behavior is like that of Mu'āwīyah, the father of Yazīd, who was envious, who didn't want people to gain anything, but desired to have everything in the world for himself.

Among the people there is also the belief that gossip is bad. When a person gets talked about, and ten people say, "Look, he got to be well off," or something like this, then he will suffer a loss. Or when the wheat turns out well, it forms a twist in the field. Then people say, "The Lord gave him abundant blessings this year." And soon you see him suffering a loss—his child dies, or his cow, or one of his sheep. To prevent this, the blood of an animal is sacrificed. I don't know how this works and I myself don't believe much in these things.

5

The Old Teacher: Idealistic Humanism

Now in his fifties, he is the oldest teacher in the village. His life story is the story of the beginnings of education and the end of the tribal chiefs' oppression. A peasant's son himself, he obtained a four-grade elementary school education in the 1930's from the first secular teacher in the village, an urbanite sent by Reza Shah's government. In 1938 he himself was appointed as one of the first native teachers of the whole tribal area. But after three years his activity was cut short. With the collapse of Iran's governmental power in 1941, the supreme tribal chief, the Khan, returned from his exile in Tehran and re-established his reign in the region. He forced the Old Teacher to stop teaching because he did not want people to become educated and because he suspected the teacher of instigating the people against him. Two years later the Khan even imprisoned him, kept him chained for ten days, and forced him to sign a declaration that he would not accept any government appointment without the Khan's consent.

For the next five years the Old Teacher could not do much more than tend his fields, but in 1948 a military garrison was established in the area and in 1949 he was allowed to resume teaching in his native village. There he had to master an educational onrush: up to ninety-five students, spread over four grades, crowded his classroom. After urgent pleas for help, the school administration eventually appointed a second teacher, also from a local family. In the same year, 1953, fifth-grade instruction was introduced.

But the Khan still wielded considerable influence even if his physical exercise of power had become restricted. He intrigued against the unwelcome teacher by depicting him as a communist who agitated against the Landlord and the paying of tributes until the Old Teacher was recalled from his post and sent to the village of a staunch henchman of the Khan. Warned that the Khan planned an attempt on his life, the Old Teacher wrote to the

school administration, saying that he was aware of the danger awaiting him
at his new post, but that he would accept it if the administration insisted,
and that a copy of his letter was being sent to Tehran. The letter produced
the desired effect and the assignment was changed to another village. After
a year, with the help of a doctor's certificate and a month's salary worth of
bribe, he succeeded in persuading the superintendent to re-assign him to his
home village.

From then onward, without further disturbance, he could attend to
his great endeavor, the general enlightenment of the people. Not even the
Khan's insurrection of 1963, which shook the region for half a year, interrupted his teaching activity. In 1958 sixth-grade instruction was introduced, and in the same year the Teacher Training Institute in Shiraz
admitted the first two students from the village, who returned as teachers
the following year. More new local teachers were appointed during the next
ten years, and classes were split along grade and gender lines. By 1970,
fifteen teachers, including five women, were employed in the village and its
landlord suburb.

Now the Old Teacher is a veteran who expects to retire soon. But his
educational zeal and fervor, which so markedly structure his attitude and
personality, are as strong as ever. One afternoon I met him in one of his
gardens studying a text on higher mathematics "in order to keep up with it,"
as he said.

Even stronger is his concern for the education of children. One late-
fall evening, walking back to the village from work in a garden, we came
across a boy feeding goats with branches he had cut off a tree. Tenderly
putting his hand on the boy's shoulder, the Old Teacher asked him why he
had stopped coming to school. The boy lowered his head shyly. Only after
some affectionate insistence by the Teacher he revealed that his father had
hired him out as a shepherd. The Old Teacher was upset. As he walked
away, he asked desperately, "How can a father, for the sake of a few toman,
deprive a child of such a thing as education?"

The Old Teacher is considered to be one of the richest villagers. Not
only has he earned a salary over a longer period than anybody else, but he
also owns more land than many peasants who have to subsist on it. Most of
this land he has transformed into some of the finest vineyards and orchards
of the area in years of relentless effort and intensive care. "Zarathustra has
taught us to hold trees in high esteem, and this spirit is in our family too.
My grandfather considered it a sin to cut down a tree," he says. In the
afternoons, after school, he invariably can be seen busy in one of his gardens. Only recently he planted new fruit trees provided by the Development
Corps.

This untiring industry is matched by a frugal life style. Only two old carpets cover the floor of his living room. In winter he moves into a smaller room to save on the expenses for firewood. He even keeps some sheep and goats to be as self-sufficient as possible, like any peasant. The family's store of raisins, walnuts, and almonds is treated like a treasure, consumed sparingly and with a sense of preciousness. It should last well into the next year in case of a crop failure. By the same token, tea-drinking is rare in his house. This is quite unique in view of the general addiction to tea among this people. It stems from the rational insight that tea and sugar account for at least 1000 toman, that is about half the total annual cash budget of a family. This thrift is taken by many as exaggerated and earns him the reputation of a somewhat tightfisted miser.

His only legitimate reason for spending money freely appears to be education, and nothing seems to be too costly when it comes to that. Last year he transferred his oldest son from a high school in the small town where most of the village boys are sent—if they are sent at all—to one in the much more expensive city of Shiraz because he believes that education is better there. He sends food to the boy with villagers who travel to Shiraz. This reflects his permanent concern for his children's well-being as well as his attempts to reduce costs.

His second son passed the final elementary examinations as best student of the village and subsequently made it also through the highly competitive entrance examination into the prestigious tribal secondary school in Shiraz. The Old Teacher definitely expects him to go on to university and has similar expectations for his other five sons. He regrets being barred by moral tradition from sending his two daughters, who completed six years of elementary school, on to secondary school in the city. For some time he even considered moving there himself to better care for his children and to give his daughters a chance to attend high school, too, but he feels he cannot afford this. (1971).

How did you come to think the way you do about the chiefs and the people?

When the chiefs were still in power, the people were downtrodden, intimidated, exploited, tortured, mutilated, killed. I felt desperate, until by chance a professor from the University of Shiraz came up here: a very noble and learned man. He inspired hope and confidence in me. He told me he

was sure that the oppression would end soon, that the chiefs would lose
their power, that the peasants would be freed, and no longer subjugated to
injustice, violence, and extortion. He wanted to find a way to prevent the
exploitation of the people by the money-lenders of the towns. Although he
came from a princely family himself, he behaved entirely differently from
our chiefs. He never gave commands, he was polite, considerate. His visit
was like a revelation for me. I saw the light. Later, he sent me a book,
Crime and Punishment, by Dostoevski. When I read it, I understood that he
wanted to show me that people like us existed elsewhere, too, and that
there is hope for change. In a way I felt like Raskolnikov, the hero of the
book, myself.

While the chiefs stood for raiding and oppression, I stood for security,
peace, respect for life, the Shah, development, the ending of oppression. To
the children in school I talked this way, too. I told them what the state, the
nation, and the law is and that the chiefs had no right to do what they did.
Of course, people informed the chiefs about it and they tried to silence me.
One of them sent his men and had me carried off to his village. Hands and
feet in chains—like in the Khan's castle some years earlier—I was kept in a
room for nine days, until several influential men persuaded the chief to set
me free.

How do you see life in the village now?

Now it is much better. There is education, security, agriculture, a
water pipeline has been built. People work much harder now that they feel
safe. Formerly, I didn't work as much as I do now. You never were sure
what the chiefs would do to your garden, to your crop. Still, the dispute
between the people and the landlords has not yet been settled. But there is
no doubt that the right is with the people. They cleared the fields, they
planted the crops. The landlords came afterwards and claimed the land by
sheer force. Also, the people are still exploited by the money-lenders and
traders of the towns. The tribes have been ruined by the urban traders. A
loan corporation would be needed to end that. Maybe four or five years
from now one will be established.

Also, many of the government officials here still don't do their job
properly. Suggestions from us villagers are consistently ignored. For example, small factories should be established locally for meat freezing, hide
processing, dairy products, carpet weaving, fruit canning, and brick manu-
facture. But enormous sums are spent instead on some project or the other
we don't see the need for, and after some time it turns out that it has been a
mistake.

Ever since our water pipeline and the public faucets were built almost
two years ago, I wanted to pipe water into my house. I am ready to bring a

professional plumber from the town and pay for everything, and, as you see, I have already done most of the digging. But the Development-Corps man and his agency still haven't approved it. They say that first twenty or thirty people must be ready to pay fifty percent of the costs of their private lines, then the government would contribute the other fifty percent, and then the pipes would be installed. It's all words. It's a game. They play with their power. Like I, myself, dismissed my class recently because I was busy with the wedding at my neighbor's. I had a pretext for a play with power, so I used it, and the students liked it, too. Similarly, a lot of politics is involved in the employment of teachers. Recently, a teacher for adult education was appointed who is illiterate!

At the anniversary celebrations of the White Revolution (6 Bahman) you announced that you would donate ten suits to poor children. Do you give them away in the way of God or in the way of the Shah?

The Shah is the means of God. God works through the Shah, as He works through any shah. Without a shah there would be nothing in Iran. Sure, other countries have different forms of government and it is all right for them, but in Iran there probably would be anarchy without a shah. In the same way as God gives us this Shah, and in the same way as the Shah gives to us as he sees our needs, so I wanted to give a very tiny bit.

I bought ten boy-scout uniforms and sent them to boys of poor families, but in such a way that they did not know the suits were coming from me. Good deeds are better if the recipient does not know the donor. Otherwise, a relationship of gratitude and dependence may be created, or the donor may derive a reputation from something that was not meant to serve that purpose.

Isn't it a great burden for the peasants to send their children to school?

Very much so. Many of them haven't even gotten their daily bread and yet pay for a boy in high school. Some are sending one boy to school while employing another as a shepherd. That's unjust. A father must give the same chance to every child and he ought not look at his own interest. If he can at all afford it and the son has the ability, he must pay for his education. Otherwise the boy becomes his enemy later on. The father of the boy we met commits a grave sin by hiring his son out as a shepherd for a piece of bread and so destroying the future of the child.

I eat only simple food, and the trouble I take in tending the gardens and keeping the animals I take only for the children. They are the goal. To pay for their education is the weight on my chest. For my son in the tribal secondary school I was ready to pay a fee of 2200 toman—or anything—if only he got accepted. But money did not decide, only performance. After he had passed the exam, they told me I need only pay 1100 toman. I offered to pay 1000 toman more so that they could admit a student whose family does not have the money. They declined, but I heard them talking about it in the hall, and one of them asked me where I was from. When I told him, he was greatly amazed since, he said, about the tribes he had known only that they were thieves, mean, and disregarded education.

Will your son return here after his studies?

If he won't it will be a mistake and my education was a failure. He ought to make his skills available to the people here. If there won't be a position for him to use his abilities, he must create one. After all, I did the same when I became a teacher. And he must work with the people—not like these officials who never leave the administrative center. They could equally well sit in Tehran. The veterinarian, for example, ought to travel around and inspect our animals regularly. By the time we see that they are sick and call him in and he eventually arrives, it is too late.

You talk about evolution in class. Isn't it in conflict with what the religion says?

To me it appears more likely to be true. What is said in the Hadith—or wherever it is—namely, that they gathered a handful of earth from all over the world and built a human body out of it, and so on, and this and that—it does not make sense. Now that we know better, we must say that this was said only on the basis of a certain wisdom. The writer had some insight—not that he knew as we know, though—but he could not bring forth the evidence for it the way it is possible now. He said it in this form so that people would believe. For example, in the Hadith is the rule of the Prophet that defecating into water is sinful. He knew that there is some thing, some active force in dirty water which causes people to get sick. But he did not have the means—like the microscope, for example—to make this evident.

What does this mean for the mullahs?

Well, the descendants of those mullahs of the past must turn around now. Their beliefs must change. For example, my father, whom I did not know because he died when I was two or three years old, he may have held certain beliefs which I—with a different attitude—possibly count as superstitions. If, let's assume, the mullahs in his time said that the world rests on the horn of a bull, he believed it. But I can not agree with this. I rather see it as a superstition. There is clear evidence. Books are written about it. Astronomy, geography, mathematics tell us how it is. I have more faith in these books than in the accounts of the mullahs.

The children who go to school learn a better religion now. The religion is better now—at least in certain regards—than in former times because it is purer: the superstition has been taken out of it. In the past, for example, the mullahs said that it was forbidden (harām) to build foreign factories in Iran. This would remove the people from the religion, they said, yet they declared it permissible to buy finished goods from abroad. Another superstition is the belief that one can remove one's sins with a special prayer, or that God will forgive if one says, "Repentance!" But what one has done, he has done. The only thing that counts is his behavior from now onwards. There were also—and still are—people who had their corpse taken to Karbala because they believed that in this way their sins would be forgiven.

It is also a superstition if one, for example, falls from the roof and believes that this was the decree of God, that it has been written on his forehead. After all, one has eyes, and one should think.

Some of these superstitions—like the one regarding the factories—have been spread by mullahs who were brainwashed in England, Iraq, America, to spread them here so that the foreign countries could sell their expensive goods to us and Iran would not start producing them. It was a strategy of foreign countries to make Iran weak.

Superstition is everything that damages or impairs the economy of the country. The veiling of women, for example, is a detriment because if a woman has her hands full gathering her veil, she cannot work. Also, superstition is everything that weakens the faith in the Shah. Like all the spokes of an umbrella converge onto the "pillar" in the center, and without a pillar there would be no umbrella, so Iran could not exist without a shah.

How, do you think, did evolution work?

I think that the radiation of the sun was involved. The light which emanates from the sun in the form of rays consists of particles which are life-creating. These particles of sunlight fused with the decaying preceding existences to create higher forms of existence. In this way life developed in the sea, moved onto the land, forests emerged and decayed, and so on, until finally an animal called Man emerged. I don't know how this happened in detail, but because we know that we need the light of the sun to live, it is evident that some portion of these particles of sunlight become part of my body, and this plant, and that animal. What again will come after us out of the vanishing of this man—this I do not know.

Will you know it after death?

I don't know. Certainly I believe in hell and heaven: "Heaven" stands for a world of peace and pleasure; "hell" for a world of misery—here or there, what difference does it make? A number of people say that paradise is where there is well-being. Life after death, this is just a word. My belief is that, for instance, the soul . . . the soul . . . so to speak—that's the way we say it, I don't know—the soul . . . exists. It is something that urges you to do something. Now, how this is, and where it is, and where it goes, and where it comes from—this we don't know. What happens after death, we just don't know. But in hell and heaven I do believe. Be that now for keeping order in the world, for the management of the world, or for whatever, I believe in it.

We have a game here, a trick we play on a road companion. When we pass a big rock, we say to him, "This rock is muffling all sound. However loudly I shout you won't hear me behind it." If the other is simple-minded, he will believe it. He will go behind the rock and while I walk away, he will think that I am yelling and yelling and that the rock stops him from hearing it. And when he finally comes around, he sees nobody. This is the way our minds are tied up. We don't know what really is there.

They say paradise is a pleasant place with flowers and gardens and houris—that's laughable—a place of pleasure. Pleasure! Whatever pleasure we find right here—that is paradise. Whatever trouble and distress we experience here, that is the World of Hell for us. Yes, it is right here in this world: we don't sell cash for credit. If it is good here, it is heaven. If it is bad for us, it is our hell.

And then?

By God, I don't know. Man is weak, he can't know. Neither can the mullahs. We cannot see into these things. I think about them, but I am not getting anywhere. So I say with everybody else, "paradise." However it may be, the notion of hell invokes fear. Since most people act morally out of fear, it disciplines them. But if a wronged person forgives his offender, just as a judge is satisfied, I think, God, too, would have no business anymore.

All these ideas are my own. I don't want to interfere with the beliefs of others, but there are many things I just can't see, such as that the breast-beating and weeping in Muharram should be of any use. I think this way: If I greet you, it has a meaning. From a philosophical point of view it means, "Be assured that in everything—words, thoughts, and deeds—I am safe for you!" If then I did something evil to you nevertheless, it would be inconsistent. Thus, to exclaim "Ali" ought to mean that you should be like Ali, that you should acquire Ali's qualities. To love Ali and Husayn means to be brave and valorous like them—but not to weep. This is of no use.

Do you think that God punishes in this world?

Yes, I believe that punishment comes in this world. But for us it is a problem why my child should be miserable because I did some evil. I think it is like this: the evil deeds of a person accumulate like water poured into a glass. As water overflows a full glass, so the misdeeds of a person spill over into the next generation. Also, it has to do with inheritance. My son is innocent, but just as he is the heir of my possessions and of my debts, so he is necessarily the heir of my deeds, too. There are many such cases in the village. That's the way I think—not that I have proof for it, though.

What is the meaning of religion?

Religion means to do good. It means what Zarathustra said: "Think good, speak good, do good." Faith is the very belief in good actions, such as not to harm anybody. All religions of the world say this. But beyond that, our knowledge, our information is deficient. We can't see why it is so, why it is good. It is as if we had a veil in front of our eyes. We don't know.

The regulations of the religion mean the same. Isn't the meaning of the prayers that we ought to do good, that we should obtain our bread by our own work and not by violating the rights of others? There are some who make the ablutions, say the prayers, and so on—all very pedantically—but who deceive, lie, steal. Their prayers are worthless. What matters are the deeds.

How do you explain such behavior?

Above all, our early education is rotten. If I am not good, for sure my child won't be either. Moreover, we don't understand the prayers because we say them in a language we don't understand. We say only the external form, so to speak. Yet we are told we must say the prayers. The Mullah even said on the pulpit that even the thief must say them. He did not say, for example, that the meaning of the prayers is that one shouldn't steal. He even said that if you kill seventy people, and say a certain prayer seventy times, then all your own sins and those of seven generations back on your father's side and of seven generations back on your mother's side will be forgiven. All this is instilled in childhood, from then onwards it exists. Certainly they say you shall not steal, but when you think about it, you realize that they mean: "Don't steal it so that I can steal it myself."

The grapes for these raisins were not quite ripe, but since there is no discipline in the village, you have to harvest when all others harvest around you. Otherwise your crop will be destroyed, for example, by animals grazing unguarded. For some time in summer my oldest son has to sleep out in the orchard to watch it. The only way to remedy this lack of discipline is to see that a child, as he grows up, learns to do good on his own, not only on command.

What about the other regulations, such as fasting or vows?

Fasting has the same purposes. One is that the tongue, the ears, and the eyes abstain, so to speak, from evil speaking, evil hearing, and evil looking. Another aim is the cleansing of the body for our health. Last year I observed it for a while, but the eating at night didn't do me good and I broke it off.

A pilgrimage may prompt me to do some good for another person, but otherwise. . . . Once I told a rich man in a neighboring village who was about to leave for Mecca, "Every year five or six children die in your village from the filthy drinking water. If you spent your money for building a water pipeline, it would be worth more than making the pilgrimage, even if every year only one child would be saved." But others told him, "This teacher says a blasphemy." So he travelled to Mecca.

Vows have the same intention. If, by means of this belief, a hungry man gets bread, it's good. Otherwise, it's nothing.

The aim of all these rules is to encourage human beings to realize humanity.

6

The Young Teacher: Rationalism and Orthodoxy

The Young Teacher is a well-respected young man in his late twenties who has been teaching elementary school for about ten years. He did not grow up with his father and got neither land nor support from him. There are marked hostility and ill-feelings on both sides. His mother was divorced early, and in a quite unusual arrangement he grew up with her. Influenced by his very pious and religiously knowledgeable mother, the modern rational ideas he picked up as a student in the Teacher Training College became firmly embedded in the conservative moral values of traditional religion. Combined with his belief in the intrinsic good of education, these values create a paternalistic attitude towards his wife, mother, and three children, and give him the reputation of a circumspect and no-nonsense master of his house.

With an as yet small family to support, his salary seems to provide him with a better than average living standard. This impression is intensified by the unusually tidy and well-kept appearance of his house. (1971/76).

Do the schools have an influence on the character of the people?

Potentially they could have a very great effect, but up until now I can't see very much of it. The reason for this is that the teachers are only transmitting knowledge—this, admittedly, they do very well—but neglect to teach the children good behavior, concern for others, truthfulness, honesty, respect for elders, willingness to carry out orders—in short, fail to give them a true education. They cannot give it because they have no true education themselves, and also because the word of us teachers doesn't count much in our community. This is a great shortcoming of the schools here. If it could be corrected, the character and morals of the people would gradually improve.

The people here say that if a child has a bad character, it is because his parents ate unlawful food (*luqmah harām*), that is, food obtained by stealing, oppression, and so on. But this is not true. It's not the food that causes a bad character, but the education the child receives. Also, one's character is not, as they say, written on one's forehead, that is, predestined. If a child is educated well, he will become good; if he is educated badly, he will become bad, and he will have troubles later on, for a person without true education is disliked and has enemies. He may be literate and knowledgeable and even be a government official who more or less fulfills his duties, but if he lacks a true education and is, for example, abusing people, these will eventually become dissatisfied with him and refuse to follow his orders.

So, a person's fortune is influenced by his conduct?

Yes, definitely. The people here say that every person has two agents assigned to him in heaven, two angels. One of them is writing down what the person does, the other pleads for him at the court of God. This heavenly angel is called the good fortune of a person. People say that when somebody has good fortune—many new lambs and kids, let's say—his agent pleaded well for him with God. When a person has ill fortune, when, as they say, his good fortune is asleep, it means that his agent in the court of heaven has forgotten his duties.

I think this is nonsense. Our religion tells us that God will set things right for anyone who is doing good but that He will send evil upon a person who is doing wrong. Thus, if I do not encroach on the property of my neighbor, do not look at his wife and daughter, do not walk through his field and squash the crop, if I wish from God that he may prosper, and if I am really pleased when I see that God provides well for others—if I have this kind of attitude, and work hard, God will undoubtedly provide well for me, too. But if I am violating the rights and property of others, if I am displeased when I see the health, happiness and prosperity of others, then God won't give me a good life, He won't give me His blessings. No matter how hard I will work, nothing will come of it and my possessions will vanish.

I have seen this verified in my own life. When I was in the Teacher Training Institute, I had a classmate who was well off. He had a father, fields, sheep and goats, a good house, everything. Then, when we came back and he took up his job he started an affair with a married woman and took to gambling. I urged him not to do these things, but to no avail. Now he is in debt, his possessions have vanished, his life is unpleasant, his reputation is bad. Not that he simply lost his wealth in gambling—he just has no blessing.

But I had nothing, absolutely nothing. My mother provided for me by doing needlework and by weaving for others. We had one small room and, for sleeping, a small rug and one quilt under which we slept together before I went to the Teacher Training Institute. But the night I came back, I no longer could sleep beside my mother. I stayed awake all night and in the morning travelled to the town where I knew a trader, borrowed some money, and bought bedding and other small things we needed. We also had debts from earlier years and then we ran up more debts because I married soon. My marriage wasn't based on love. My mother was sick and lonesome, and I thought of having children soon because we didn't have anybody by way of family. Ever since things have been going well with us. As you know, I have bought land, animals, a car, and our house is well-furnished.

As another example take my three uncles. When they divided up the family possessions, the two older brothers took the larger land shares, and the best from everything else, and fought with each other. But the youngest was content with whatever he got. Now God has given him a better life than the others. This I have seen myself.

Fortune has nothing to do with why somebody is poor. In my view there are two possible reasons for poverty: either the person doesn't understand what he has to do to be doing well, or else he does not gain things the lawful way. In this case the Lord does not give him anything because He is displeased with his attitude or because He knows that if He were to give him riches he would use them to do evil.

One cannot see the moral inside of a person. I may refrain from stealing only because I am afraid to do it. Since God knows that I am, in fact, a bad man—that I am a thief at heart—He is not providing for me, no matter what troubles I may be taking. But the people don't know what kind of person I really am. They say, "He is a good man, but he has no good fortune." This is not so. The poor are either lazy, or their character is bad, or their moral inside is not good.

This means that people are punished for their evil deeds in this world?

For every deed, every single act a person does he will in the end receive his requital, be it in this world or the next. There is no doubt about this. But in my opinion punishment is being exacted mainly in this world. Certainly, there is also the next world, but the point is that in this world we actually see it happening. Indeed, the fact that we can witness the punish-

ment of evil-doers in this world is one of the evidences for the existence of
the other world.

But I do not believe that God punishes somebody for the sins of his
father, which is what people mean when they say, "The father sows, the son
reaps." There is one thing though: children will pick up the evil habits of
their parents and so become themselves liable to do wrong and get punished for it. This is the true meaning of this saying.

Nor do I believe that a person can get his sins forgiven by doing
repentance. Every evil he commits he has to pay back. Or should he be able
to do all kinds of things and then be forgiven just because he says before
dying, "Oh God, I repent"? No. But these mullahs were a bad kind of
people, liars, thieves, adulterers—everything. Such a character would go to
a person and say, "You have done all these evil deeds . . . you must repent
them . . . in the Qur'ān it is written. . . . I will put the words of repentance
into your mouth." He would say something in Arabic for the person to
repeat, words the latter wouldn't understand—in fact, he wouldn't even
know what Arabic is—and then say, "This was your repentance. Now go,
God will forgive you." And he would receive a fee. The whole thing was a
trick they played on the people to get money.

What about the requital in the next world?

After a person has died, it is said, he will first be questioned in the
grave, in the same way as when the gendarmerie is making an inquiry. If,
for example, two people had a fight, the gendarmerie will interrogate both
parties, put everything on record, and send the file to the court. In the
meantime, the one who has been beaten up and is innocent will be told to
go home and take it easy till things are ready for court proceedings. But the
guilty person will be locked up in a bad place, maybe even beaten, until he
is sent to court.

In the grave it is the same way. First they come and do the questioning. Then, if he has been a good man, they will give him a comfortable
place and tell him to stay there in peace and happiness until he would
receive the reward for his deeds. If he has been an evil-doer, they will . . . I
don't know . . . it is said they will put him up with snakes and dogs in a
tight, bad place till the day that is said to last for 50,000 years will come
and he will receive his punishment. The mullahs are saying this wrong.
They say that this day will come after 50,000 years. This is wrong because
the earth has existed for millions of years. Rather, that day itself from
morning till sunset will last as long as 50,000 years. On that day all the
dead of the world will be summoned to be judged. All the good and bad
deeds will be weighed. If the former weigh more, the person will go to
heaven; if the latter weigh more, he will go to hell.

So sins can be redeemed by a proportionate amount of good deeds?

No, no, there is no such thing. Evil deeds cannot be redeemed; they have to be atoned for. For his sins a person will be punished and for his good deeds he will be rewarded; good and evil deeds will be requited separately. It is also said that on the Day of Judgment the sins of the people will be forgiven for the sake of the blood of the Imām Husayn. This is a lie. Should the Imām have sacrificed himself for the profit of evil-doers? If this were so, the people of all religions would already since a long time have become Muslims to have their sins redeemed in an easy way.

What do you then consider part of the true religion?

Not to lie, not to steal, not to slander, to give help when you see someone in misery—this is what I understand as religion, and what I want to teach my children. I believe that a person who is abiding by this won't fare badly on the Day of Judgment.

As to saying the prayers, that's nothing special, that's something we do every day as a matter of course just as eating. The fasting is good, too. Its purpose is said to be, for one thing, that by going hungry, one experiences the sufferings of the hungry, feels pity, and is moved to help the poor, and, for another, that it betters one's health. I agree to this; it is true. But I get ill when I am fasting. I fasted in earlier years, but quit when I saw it was impossible.

As to the Muharram celebration, when you put your hand on your chest, call the feat of the Imām Husayn to your mind and for what sake he did it, and your heart is filled with compassion for the Imām, that's the right meaning of the mourning for Husayn, and that is what I am telling my children. I do not want them to go to the mosque and stay awake all night beating their chests. The chest beating has no good reason, it is not in the Qur'ān. Once in the mosque a gendarme wanted me to take off my shirt and join in the breast beating. I refused and he became angry and a fight arose. I left and never went there again. Shall I go there and watch things, like in a show? Some of it is outrightly absurd, such as the women who go there to see the bodies of men, and young men who bare their chests and beat themselves madly because they want to make an impression on the women and girls.

In short, I agree to what is the original religion, but not to what the mullahs say, not to the kind of religion that consists in going to the mosque and sitting there, with prayer beads in hand, to see what the mullah has to say, while at home one's wife and children are in need of food and clothing; or saying twenty units of prayer instead of the regular four and doing additional fastings but robbing one's neighbor should the opportunity arise. I don't like this kind of religion. In fact, most of the people I have seen perform rituals in overly devout ways did so to cover up some evil, in the same way as I would use a thousand devious words to hoodwink a person I robbed without his knowledge.

What about vows and written prayers?

I do no longer believe in vows. Five years ago I still promised one-fourth of the offspring of my mare to the Imām Husayn if she foaled all right. But now I would rather say that helping a brother or cousin who— God forbid—is in need, is also a kind of vow, and I don't believe any is better. Nevertheless, I did make the pilgrimage to Mashhad recently, but more so because I had to take my mother there who, when I was a child, had made a vow to make the pilgrimage when I would be grown-up.

People even used to make vows like saying, "Oh Imāmzādah so-and-so, one hand of this child shall be dedicated to you, so that he may grow up hale and well," and then, every year, bring one-fourth of the boy's estimated earnings, that is, the equivalent of one hand, to that Imāmzādah. Worse yet, they would even give a daughter as an offering to an Imāmzādah, that is, give her in marriage to one of his descendants without asking for a bride price. This is, of course, very wrong. She is a human being and has a right to her own life and future. But people did these things because they did not know what else to do. They were oppressed by their landlords, afflicted with innumerable diseases, had no doctor. So they took recourse to these things.

As to the written prayers, I think they are effective only if one believes very strongly in them. For someone who has doubts, like myself, they are useless. I do, however, approve of the damband against a wolf. Just recently I had one made for one of my cows that got lost. Of course, I could make it myself, too, but we believe that God approves of it more if it is made by the descendant of an Imām.

What about the other things people believe here?

The people here do not have much education or reason or wisdom. When suffering some harm or distress, they do not say that it was brought about by nature. Instead, they resort to all kinds of explanations. When, for example, a child dies, they don't say that he had not been taken care of in a proper, hygienic way. Rather, they say he died because a neighbor put a curse on him, or because the harvest of a wheat field was *navaruzī*, that is, beyond the limits of the ordinary. These things have not been proven. They are just said.

Or when a rash appears on the skin of a child, people will take him to somebody who, they believe, has received the gift from the jinn to heal this disease by spreading his saliva over it. This is, of course, also nonsense. It may be possible though that this kind of rash can be soothed by saliva.

I do, however, believe in the custom to wait a while before going someplace if someone just sneezed. Not that this were written anywhere or that it were really true that sneezing portends evil. Rather, I think, the effect is due to the strong belief that has been attached to this.

As to good and bad dreams, in earlier years I believed in them and gave alms to the poor to ward off the evil when I had a dream of such portent. But now I do no longer think it's true. Neither do I believe—in fact I never did—in auspicious and inauspicious days. Every day is as good as any other to accomplish some work. Such beliefs have nothing to do with religion: they are propagated by the mullahs.

The mullahs can write whatever they want—there is nobody to prevent them—and call it *risālah,* a treatise, a book of religious rules. Then a mullah goes to a peasant here, an uneducated, plain, simple, upright man who has worked hard all his life and tells him, "I have seen it written in the risālah that you will die or God will send His wrath on your children if you do not give me a goat." And the peasant gives him a goat. It is all superstition and lies.

Take our Mullah. He wears this Arab cloak, talks much about religion, preaches to the people, and so on. Why is he doing this? To draw some money out of us. He is like a fruit vendor: the more he advertises his goods and the more excited he gets about them, the more customers he will have to profit from. If the Mullah were hired today by a government office, he would dress up with a neat shirt and a crease in his trousers and talk no longer about the religion at all.

Do you approve of artificial birth control?

Someone who believes in the religion and in God will say that killing a child, a sperm a night old in the womb of the mother—which is what the pill is doing—is the same thing as killing a grown-up person; it is murder. If the Lord wants to give children to somebody, He will give. If He doesn't want to give, He won't give. If He wants to give few, He will give few. If He wants to give many, He will give many. Birth control means to interfere with the order of God. Therefore, I think it is not good and I don't let my wife take them. The natural way is better.

Yes, they say that bearing many children isn't good for a woman. But again, I believe that if God wants to keep a woman well and healthy, He can do so no matter how many children she is bearing. But if He doesn't want to, she will become ill even if she doesn't bear any children at all. There are now many women in this village who were perfectly healthy, but have become ill since taking the pill. It is obviously not good.

7

The Craftsman: Modernist Purism

The Craftsman, who is from a large, well-respected local peasant family, is in his late fifties now. As a young man in the 1930's he had stayed in Tehran for several years, where he acquired some skills in carpentry. These now make him the most professional carpenter in the village. Although he does own some land, he considers himself a craftsman rather than a peasant. For this reason and also because he has hardly any help from others—all his children attend school, and from his brothers he is separated by discord—he devotes most of his time to his craft while his agricultural activity is rather low-keyed. He does not make use of all his land, little as it is, and he does not operate a herding outpost, partly because he does not have enough animals to make this necessary or even feasible, but mainly because he thinks it would be wrong to involve his children in herding and thereby to deprive them of schooling.

Although he had no chance to go to school, he taught himself to read and write. His literacy, the experiences in Tehran and a lifelong lively interest in intellectual matters and the world at large make him a knowledgeable and highly individualistic man, and a kind of non-conformist who likes to keep to himself. Most days he can be seen working in his simple workshop, fashioning with relentless diligence window sashes, doors, baking boards, baby cribs, and agricultural tools with his partially self-made hand tools. Rarely is he seen standing around with other men at the village's informal meeting places, nor does he socialize much at other occasions. Despite his diligence, however, his living standard is low. He does manage to support his oldest son in secondary school in town, but only with great difficulty, and what remains for himself, his wife, and his other five children is bare survival. Especially his non-involvement in village affairs makes him politically weak and vulnerable to transgressions by more dynamic villagers. He claims that his brothers usurped part of his inheritance, an accusation they refute by saying that he had been loafing around for years, totally neglecting his land, and that therefore the fields he now owns must be considered a gift they gave him. (1971).

What is the meaning of life?

The meaning of life is to recognize God's power and His greatness. Man was made to admire the works of God, such as the change of the seasons or that a tree branch planted in the ground begins to sprout. God has established all this once and since then it is so, just as I have made this plane once and since then it works for me as a plane.

Religion for me is the knowledge of God, the knowledge that God is the being which has greater power than all other beings; that He is the power which can make something out of nothing and nothing out of something; that He has created us and He will kill us again, and that therefore we must behave in a way that pleases Him so that He may be merciful to us and ease our life in this world and in the other world may forgive us so that we may fare well; and that we must not do evil, so as not to incur His wrath. If I stole something, for example, or said a lie, then for sure God would become angry and send down misfortune on me.

This, to me, is religion. But what they say about wine and the veiling and the chest beating is without substance, for it is not written in any book, not in the Torah, nor in the Gospel, nor in the Book of Abraham, nor in the Psalms, nor in the Qur'ān. Religion means that man worships God, not that man worships man. Therefore, I won't worship anything man-made. Only God, who is the power, the force that created us, is worthy of worship.

A Pakistani, Muhammad Ali Iqbāl, in his *White Book,* said:

I did not see a dog before a dog to bow its head.
It is from blindness man did render slave himself to man.

That means, everybody must think for himself to find the truth, like Jesus, or Muhammad, or Abraham, or Moses, or all the other prophets. They found it, so you will find it, too. Why should you need those mullahs? Only a blind man has to follow others. Open your eyes yourself, and see the good, and see the evil, and don't do the evil, but do good—so that you, too, become Jesus, you too become Muhammad, you too become Husayn.

For what reasons do you do good to others?

I know God to be the One who causes dry grains to become green wheat, to grow to a certain height, and to yield ten man for every man of seed. God does not need us to kill a chicken, His own creature, for him to be pleased. Rather, we make offerings out of kindness by way of charity, in the way of God. If someone has and another has not, then the one who has must give to the other. Especially if somebody has much he should share it. For example, if one has a rich harvest, he should slaughter an animal and distribute the meat among his neighbors, so that they won't become envious, but become his friends. This is the old Iranian religion. But I don't approve of offerings to be made as vows, for example, by saying, "Oh God, give me this or that, then I will give something to the poor." And I also disapprove of the belief that a person will be carried to paradise if he makes such offerings or will be damned if he does not.

I do believe that God gives blessings. He gives blessings to your possessions if you share them with others. He does not give them in return for the animal you killed. Rather, God is pleased by my sharing and so He may give me a good harvest, good health, and keep away misfortune. And this is what I wish from God: well-being and lawful possessions. Whenever I sow a field I say, "God, you are powerful, and I am powerless, give blessings to this seed, so that I won't become a thief." If God does not give His blessings, one's possessions will decrease.

Why are people doing evil things?

It is said that the devil deceives and misleads people, but this is not true. People do evil things for two reasons. First, for lack of a livelihood: if somebody is hungry, he will steal. And secondly, out of desire and greed: if somebody has nothing, he wants a donkey, if he has a donkey, he wants a mule, then a horse, then a truck. And he desires status and power to dominate others. So when people lie, it is either because they are poor or because of politics. But it is not true that Iranians lie more than other peoples, as some say.

By and large, the people of this village are bad. There are so many quarrels between brothers. If people want to increase their crops they should clear their own fields of stones rather than plow into the field of their neighbor. Take this man who came here yesterday to persuade me of his rights in the dispute he has with some others. He lied. He lied by the Hazrat-i 'Abbās so that his lies might pass as the truth. Of course, there are always two views in a dispute—as in the case of Genghis Khan. When they told him that future generations will say he brought bloodshed to the world, he said, "I have purified the world with blood." But people must tell a man that his perception of a case is mistaken—to do so has merit and to neglect doing it is sinful. This man knows he is in the wrong. There are witnesses. But the people cannot persuade him to acknowledge it and make peace. Maybe you will be here still when God sends him a misfortune. My own brother who has stolen part of my land even goes to the mosque so that people may say he is innocent. The devil comes in disguise, and therefore one should not shake hands with everybody.

For what reasons don't you do evil things yourself?

It is for fear of God. I fear God. I fear that God would send me misfortune if I did something evil as, for example, eat the property of others, or be untrustworthy, that is, not return something I was entrusted with. For example, whenever I find something, I have it announced by the barber all over the village so that the owner may come and get it. I would be ashamed of evil deeds on the Day of Judgment. Also, I could not walk around freely and raise my head among the people. I would have to be ashamed and hide myself.

Believers are those who don't lie and don't steal, those who fear that God may send a misfortune: disease, or pain, or death; those who won't go into a garden to steal, fearing that God may make a snake bite them from a bush if they did so. The religion exists for the purpose that people have fear. If there was no religion, everything would fall to pieces.

I call God the Great Judge who has everything in his hands: to give life and to take life, to give possessions and to take possessions, to send disease and to take away disease—it is all in the hands of the Great Judge. A wicked life He will punish. Evil and ill-fortune in this world are consequences of sinful behavior, as are diseases. Who really knows that a sick person has no sins? If, however, a truly innocent person suffers some ill-fate, like poverty, then it is his own fault. He should do something about it, like work in a city where he earns more. On the other hand, well-being may be seen as a reward from God. God is like the master of a good and bad servant. He will be pleased with the good one and praise him and reward him, but punish the bad one. About an evil-doer we say, "Eventually God will send him misfortune." It really has happened. There are many here who were robbers and now are very poor. Our Former Landlord did a lot of evil, and now look at him, in what misery he lives.

But then his innocent son will go hungry, too. Isn't this unjust of God?

We say, "The father sows, the son reaps," that is, every poor son is poor because of the misdeeds of his father. This is not unjust. The father's semen was unlawful (harām) because of his misdeeds, and therefore the son must suffer; so that I am aware that if I act like this man my son will become like his son, and that I must act better.

What about punishment in hell, what about paradise?

I'll tell you after I have been there. . . . I don't harm anybody and so I need not be afraid of anybody, not even of God. Those will go to hell who have to be afraid already in this world because they did harm to others. But none of this will be really known until that time. In the meantime, as I have said, the punishment takes place already here. One villager was the greatest robber around here. Now his sons don't want to support him any longer and recently one of his grandsons threw a stone at him that blinded one eye. This man is in hell right now. And our Former Landlord is, too.

Is it possible to obtain remission of sins?

All this is a lie: that sins will be forgiven by special prayers, or a pilgrimage, or fasting, or repentance, or by the blood of Husayn. If this were true one could steal a lot and then make a pilgrimage and it would be forgiven. Or, for example, when people steal from a garden and say, "We will fast to get rid of this sin"—is this possible? The mullahs tell them this. They tell them to do anything they want and then say, "Repentance!" to be forgiven. Take the case of another villager. He brought home three or four huge cooking pots and other stuff from a raid and gave something to our little Mullah who made it all lawful! Nevertheless, this man is burdened with the debt now, and on the Day of Judgment the rightful owner will get his property back from him, we say. But it is the mullahs' fault if the people's faith gets weak. A thief like this man is encouraged by the mullahs and so he will steal again. This is wrong. The Prophet said, "Cut off every hand that has stolen!" But our Mullah says, "Come, I will make it lawful for you."

They say that the Imām Husayn drank the Cup of Suffering and for this has received the privilege of interceding for the sinners. This is non-sense. He was a man, a good one though, in his attempt to fight for the rights of the people. But if he could not defend himself, how can he help me? If it were true, the Westerners, who can go to the moon, already would have come a long time ago and carried away all of Karbala for their own profits. Even if they should hold a knife to my throat, I won't say that Husayn will hasten to my help after death. He can't do it. He was a man like all others. To shed tears over him avails him and us as little as shedding tears over anybody else.

They say that his blood, which was shed on the plain of Karbala, will wash away the sins of the believers. But this is a lie; it is neither in the Qur'ān nor in the Hadith. He was killed in a family dispute, a fight over land and water, that's all. To weep about this is meaningless. Besides, according to the Law itself, Husayn's death was justified because it was the Imāms who started the war. The story is told that once, in a battle, Ali killed one thousand men! Because of these killings the Imāms were liable to be killed, too. The Qur'ān says, "A head for a head, a nose for a nose." So their death conforms to the Qur'ān, the Law, nothing else.

So, the mullahs are corrupting the religion?

They impose upon the people. They want to swindle them of money. Take our Mullah, for example. How many times a day does he cut off the head of the Imām Husayn by reciting his passion for five or ten toman? They tell us, "Take this road to go to heaven," but they themselves aren't taking it. The Mullah takes ten toman on every ten toman he lends, but he keeps telling us that it is unlawful to take interest! And then this Mullah tells me, "Make your possessions lawful and pay the khums!" So I am to saw this tree-trunk into boards and with pains earn one toman—only to pay him a fifth of it? All their possessions are unlawful! If the religion of Muhammad ever was good, then those surely have corrupted it, those mullahs!

The people followed them because they were afraid of them. The mullahs were allies of the landlords—our Landlord even forced us to fast— and so they had power. They also could be bribed. They would take bribes from both sides and then use their influence in favor of the one who gave more.

I don't agree with what they say. One of their books, for example, tells the story—and there is also a picture of it—that the Imām Ali struck his sword at a certain Khaybari with such force that it split him and his horse in two. When God saw that even the earth would be split into halves, He sent Gabriel to hold his wing under the sword, but the sword cut through his wing, too, and through seven layers of the earth. And this should be true? It's impossible! The mullahs say this, not the religion! But when I say so they call me an unbeliever.

And those dervishes and Sayyids! Did you see these two dervishes with their painted screen depicting scenes of Karbala today? They are imposters. They recite the events of Karbala and handle a snake to show how blessed they are—which is ridiculous. In the city they couldn't do this, but here they collect money for it. People gave them money so that the Imāms would intercede for them on the Day of Judgment. It is stupid of people to do this. I commit no sins and need no Imāms.

And I don't approve of those begging Sayyids, either, who imagine themselves higher and better than the villagers. Their religion is of no value whatsoever. They should work. Once I was working in another village and such a Sayyid came. He was invited into the house, but when he was offered the waterpipe he declined and asked for cigarettes instead. The people told him they didn't have any. So the son of this Sayyid went outside and after a while started to shout, "Oh, Oh, the Imām sent us cigarettes!" With this trick they wanted to impress the people and cheat them out of their property. I took a stick and chased them away. I can tell you many stories of this sort. One day a Sayyid came along begging for bread and a place to stay. So I invited him. At night he got up and left, taking my shoes along with him. Such are the descendants of our Prophet!

What did the Arabs really have? Wasn't what is now called the House of God, the Kaaba, an idol temple? It was we who were worshipping God! It was we who had the places of worship. We had temples in which God and Jesus and others were perpetually venerated. Also, the moral rules, the knowledge, the science was ours. History says that when the Arabs conquered Iran, they fired the bathhouses of Arabestan with the books from our libraries for seventy years! Then they brought us the Qur'ān. Now, when I say I have a headache, the mullahs, instead of telling me to go to the doctor and get a medicine say, "We will write a prayer, tie it to your head, and you will get well." Is this possible? Of course it is not. We had to accept it because they were our conquerors. At first the Iranians defeated them. Shāpūr, one of our kings, killed and killed and killed the Arabs until he was persuaded to stop, and then he seized the rest and dislodged their shoulders so that they could not strike a sword any longer. But then the Arabs subjugated us and brought this over us. By the Messiah, by God, I am well-disposed towards all Europeans and ill-disposed towards the Arabs because the Europeans didn't harm us, but the Arabs did.

The Twelve Imāms too?

About the Twelve Imāms I say if they were good men, God may have mercy on them. But it's not so that they can do me any good or that I can do them any good. They were men and they are dust now, and they just can't make, for example, a sick person well again. And if I beat my chest, shall this be good for them? So I am saying, "God have mercy on them." Likewise, to those who say, "Umar be damned!" I say, "Don't say that so that they won't say 'Ali be damned' either!" I have nothing against the Sunni, we are brothers.

Do you say this about other religions too?

Certainly, I don't say that Islam is more true or better than other religions. It's not until the Day of Judgment—if it exists—that we will know. Then I will say to whoever will be the superior, "You are the king." Do we know who will be king? No. So what's the use of us beating each other up over this now? Besides, it is known that part of the Qur'ān is from the Gospel. How can one approve of the Qur'ān then, but not of the Gospel? When I say such things, our Mullah calls me an unbeliever. But I accept everything in the Qur'ān that's from God. Only what is not from Him, the man-made stories, I do not accept, like the one that God made man out of dust. This wasn't so. It was just as a chicken comes from an egg: a natural process by the order of God.

What is the meaning of saying the Five Prayers?

It serves to show submission to God, and to remember Him, the Creator, the force which brought us into existence. It's also healthy. But one cannot base a claim on it, as many people do. They believe that if they say the prayers, castles will be built for them, that on the Day of Judgment they can claim something by saying, "We said the prayers, we have beaten our chests for Husayn!" I know that there is absolutely nothing to this claim. Why? Because nobody came back from there who could have testified. It's only the words of the mullahs, words they say to gain an income. Likewise, it is absolutely meaningless to say the prayers if one's behavior is evil, if one has, for example, eaten someone else's property or been untrustworthy, which I consider the gravest offences. But the prayers are good. I say them every day. I disapprove of the fact, though, that they include the name of a man, Muhammad. This looks as if he was equal to God.

Are you observing the Fasting?

No. Formerly I did, but now I can't anymore. And anyway, its real meaning is to fast with the eyes and the tongue, and to do so always. The eyes should be blind, that is, one should not look at another's wife; and the tongue should be dumb, that is, one should not talk badly about other people. If this isn't done, abstaining from food is of no value. God does not approve of such fasting.

Fasting is also a matter of health, and also a matter of something Shāh Salah al-Dīn of Iran—or was it Shāh Hūshang?—has said. In his time there was a drought, and he said, "Whoever eats three meals a day eat only two and give one to those who have none!" Now we do this, too. At the end of the Month of Fasting we give a special alms (*fitrīyah*) to the poor, to those who have less than we do—but not to the Sayyids. Even if one is not fasting, he must give it. But most people, deceived by the mullahs, are perverting it. They are fasting without giving anything to the poor. They believe that one who dies while fasting will go straight to paradise. I believed it, too, when I was young. Once I was bitten by a snake in the Month of Fasting. My foot swelled up horribly and people wanted me to drink milk that would draw the poison out from my blood. But I refused, believing I would go directly to paradise if I died! Such nonsense!

What about the Muharram celebrations?

They are nonsense, too, at least the mourning, the chest beating, weeping, the sitting around smoking cigarettes, chatting, and gossiping. I do not participate in that. As I have said, it's of no use—neither to the Imām, nor to us. Rather, we should weep about not having made another Husayn out of ourselves.

The day of 'Ashūrā, when they killed the Imām Husayn, was about 1300 years ago. But these mourning celebrations did not exist until about 700 years ago. Then a certain Amīr who was on good terms with the group of Arabs who followed the Imāms propagated them in Iran to show his allegiance to this group. He wanted to do something to attain a place in paradise. The mullahs fabricated these things for their own profit. Our mullah here got 170 toman every day during the past Muharram celebrations for going from one congregation to another and cutting off the head of the Imām Husayn.

Does it earn merit to make a pilgrimage?

No, it doesn't. Instead, one should give the money to the poor. A story tells that once 600,000 people made the pilgrimage to Mecca, but God approved no one's. He did, however, approve of the pilgrimage of a man who never made it. This man had given all the money he had set aside for the pilgrimage to a poor woman who, with her child, was sitting beside the road, in her misery roasting a piece of a dead donkey. Similarly, to travel to Mashhad is not a sign of true believing. Most travel there only for the honor of being called "Mashhadi" afterwards. These people have debts and should pay them off first. Besides, they possibly do some evil afterwards and then will swear "by the road I went" that they didn't do it. Sa'dī said that even a camel that went to Mecca is a Hajji.

It earns merit, however, to help in the building of a bathhouse, for example, because this is a charitable work. It is for the benefit of the public.

Did you attend the fātihah khvānī *(prayer for the dead) for the boy who was killed yesterday?*

No. But here at home I said it for him. Why should I go there? Does he perhaps come personally to receive the *fātihah?* If the *fātihah* reaches anything at all, then it will reach his soul—if it is true that a soul exists—from any place I say it.

What does it do for the dead? Will sins be forgiven?

No. If this was so, one could do any bad thing. It's only to console the living, his father and mother. People come to their house and say, "Let's say a fātihah so that his soul will be happy." It's like this: After you have left this village, we'll say whenever we speak of you, "Blessed be his memory!" Will this be of any use to you over there in your country? "Blessed be his memory" we say regarding a living person; "God have mercy" we say for a dead one.

But his relatives don't know you said the fātihah here alone; so why did you say it?

Well, it's a custom—like, when we pass by a graveyard we say, "Oh, people of yonder, the Judgment is near!" Is this perhaps true? Did they write us a letter telling us that the Day of Judgment will come soon? It is a custom, a local custom.

What do you think of the other prescriptions?

The wine they forbade because it was something we Iranians had and we had given the Arabs a lot of troubles earlier. But wine is good. I drank it, too—yet I didn't lie and I didn't harm people. Eating the meat of boars, snakes, bears, and so on has been made unlawful because it is too dangerous to hunt these animals. The washing of the dead is, of course, for hygienic reasons. The veiling of women is not based on the religion: the mullahs say that. Aisha, Zaynab, and Shahrbānū fought battles, riding on horseback. Could they have been veiled? Also, that girls shouldn't go to school, as the mullahs say, is wrong.

What is the correct behavior for girls and women?

A woman should stay around the house, do her work there. A girl should obey, study, be diligent, not sit with strangers so that these won't seduce her—as it has happened recently, as you know. She must not associate with just anybody, only with her own people, for her own safety. She must not be out alone after dark because it may happen. . . . There are all sorts of men! But all this doesn't mean that a woman is lower than a man. A woman likes to have a husband who provides a livelihood for her because she is weak. But to tell the women to wear a veil, to sit in the back of the mosque, to walk at the end of the procession—that's wrong, that's a lie. The religion does not say that.

What about the evil eye?

If a very beautiful thing gets damaged, people say, "It's the evil eye, go to the mullah to have a prayer written." Or these beads around the neck of my young son: this, they say, is against the evil eye. But it's a lie. Isn't everything that happens the wish of God?

By coincidence though, certain things do happen. Once, in Tehran, a motorcyclist harassed us. A person said, "Let's give him the evil eye! By

God, look how fast he is going!" The moment he said it, the cyclist was lifted up as if by an invisible hand and was thrown onto the road. People say that a certain villager, who died recently, had the evil eye. Once he even said to his own cow, "Look, how fat the cow has become!" and it dropped dead. They say, it's in his family, it's in their nature.

But it is not true that it happens inevitably, as people say. Otherwise one would need no hammer to smash rocks in the fields. One only had to say something by way of the evil eye and the rock would shatter. It is possible to talk about coincidence, but I would say, the evil eye as such does not exist.

Do written prayers (du'ā') have any effect?

No, the prayer-writing is a fraud. As I have said, the Arabs burned our books and then brought us these prayers instead. God gives and takes life and health according to His wish, and these prayers have absolutely no bearing on it. It may happen, for example, that one gets a prayer for rain and another one gets a prayer for no rain at the same time. When they speak a du'ā' over a sick person and he gets worse and starts shaking, they will say, "The force of the du'ā' is shaking him; he is recovering."

Once, when I was in a certain village, a woman came to me, all desperate, and said, "My daughter is dying, please write a prayer for her!" I refused, but she implored me, and so I wrote one. The next day I received a big basket of fruits as thanks for the effective prayer. Her daughter, she said, had recovered immediately. Isn't this ridiculous? It wasn't because of the du'ā'. It was either the force of God, or nature, or of whatever governs the course of this world, but certainly not that paper.

I say that if du'ā' ever had any effect at all, they had it through the word of prophets like Jesus and Muhammad, who spoke with the Creator—be this now true or not—but the prayers that are written now by people who live by thievery have no effect because those people themselves are unlawful. I know they are thieves. They have all been attached to the khan and kadkhudas, and from eating the stolen food they got from them their whole bodies have become unlawful. Besides, if you take that tiny piece of paper, write a line on it, and then ask for a hundred toman: Isn't this stealing? Isn't this cheating? Isn't this unlawful?

The damband against the wolf seems to work, though. I have seen a spellbound wolf myself. His jaws were slack, he couldn't bite. Then the man took a jack-knife and, not thinking that it was the knife upon which the spell had been spoken, opened it to kill the wolf. At this moment the wolf charged and got three animals.

But not the *gurāzband* against boars! One year wild boars were destroying the crops in this little valley over there. A villager got a gurāzband from one of the Sayyids in a nearby village who claim that their du'a' are very effective, and buried it in his field. When he came back the next day, he found that a boar had dug it up and shit on it! It's laughable, isn't it? It's a lie. People who believe in it are stupid.

How does one become a good man?

By fearing God. Someone who wants to better himself must repent the evil he has done, and resolve not to do it again, and say to God, "If I do it again, send me a misfortune!" In fear of this he won't do it again. But only a livelihood enables him to avoid evil. If he has taken pains, and made a life for himself, and if he also keeps in mind that God gave it to him— God says, "From you the effort, from me the blessings,"—then there is no need to do evil. If I did not have this occupation, with which I earned about thirty toman today, I would be forced to steal to provide a dinner for this child.

I was still young when I realized that a man must know a trade. I had read books—literacy I had picked up myself, I never went to the maktab— and I was a believer. I wanted to eat a lawful (*halal*) bit of bread and not to steal—at that time people here were raiding and plundering up to Isfahan— and therefore I wanted to learn a trade. So when in 1930 the government was taking the tribal chiefs to Tehran, I managed to go with them and to learn this craft. With it I can earn a lawful living. If I did not have it, I would be forced to do what these people do: one plows into my land, another one plows into someone else's land.

Was it in Tehran that your ideas changed?

Yes, my beliefs changed there. I saw Reza Shah bringing factories and machines to develop the country, despite the mullahs' complaints. About a flour mill, for example, they said, "The water from the heavens is God-given. What evil have we done that this man, having turned away from the religion, went to Europe, and brought a motor mill which deprives people of their rest at night?"

When I was young they told us that hell was made for the Christians and that paradise was made for us. In Tehran, I understood that this was a lie. If paradise was made at all, it was rather made for the Christians. Their faith is stronger. I learned a lot from them. I went to the American College with the Former Landlord's uncle, who learned English there, and we also went to their church. From what the ministers said and did to us, our beliefs changed. We realized that the true road wasn't the one our mullahs had shown us. Of course, the Christians, too, have to believe whatever their priests and ministers tell them, but these don't tell them lies as ours do. The ministers in the College gave things to us rather than taking things away from us. They offered us tea, gave us bread, taught us. And aren't you a Christian, giving us your medicines when one of us is sick? But our Imāms and mullahs neither gave us anything, nor will they give us anything.

Do you think that the religion will disappear?

No, because everybody, whoever he may be, will at least agree that a creator exists, a creator who causes trees to sprout, rain to fall, and so on. No, I don't think that the religion will disappear. Only the obsolete is now being dropped. The religion is being purified of the things that were not part of it, that are not found in our books, the things that the mullahs introduced for their own profit. It is purified by those who have travelled to Europe and America and now make us aware. Our own people ruined the religion and our own people are restoring it again. There are many villagers whose beliefs are still the same as those of the Mullah—although even the Mullah himself can't say any longer what he said thirty years ago; nobody would believe it. These people call me "modernist," and "Europe lover," that is, one whose views are like those of the Europeans. I only say, "Be that so!"—better anyway than be like the mullahs who approve of stealing and an unlawfully earned livelihood. And, by now, there are many who think the same way as I do.

8

The Representative of the People: Islamic Activism

The Representative, a tall, impressive man in his late fifties, is a peasant by birth and vocation, and one of the most literate, articulate, and outspoken villagers. With few animals and not much land, his living conditions are rather modest, especially because he also supports a son in the university and another one in high school. Only his wife and the youngest of his seven children still live with him. His fields are taken care of mostly by his sons-in-law and other villagers, leaving him relatively free to pursue his political missions.

Above all, the Representative has been the dynamic and highly charismatic spokesman for the villagers for many years. Indeed, his personal history is the history of the political and economic development of the village.

As a young man, he became one of the Former Landlord's retainers over the bitter objections of his parents. His father, a dervish and follower of Shāh Ni'matu'llah, already had fought the landlords' rule himself, supported by his wife. During a traumatic illness, however, the young man resolved to quit the Landlord's service and to take up the just cause of the people. Appalled by the coercion, oppression, injustice, and personal misconduct of the chiefs, he started to complain at various government offices all the way to Tehran with such resounding vehemence, that the local landlords and their ally, the paramount chief (Khan), alternately tried to bribe and to frighten him into silence. They had him imprisoned on trumped-up charges, exiled him, denounced him, threatened his life, and had him beaten up—he lost vision of an eye on one such occasion—but he did not yield.

After the Khan was killed in 1963 and the land reform started, his fight shifted to convincing the land-reform officials that the Landlord's claim was unfounded. By that time the Landlord's power had waned, but he had still enough clout with government officials to bring it about that in 1971 the Representative was sentenced to another prison term and then, on legalistic grounds, removed from his position as elected head of the Village Council, a position he had held since 1966. Nevertheless, the Representative continued to act as an astute speaker for his people, and dealt with the bureaucracy in such effective ways that the land issue was never settled in the Landlord's favor.

All the while, the Representative strove also to improve economic conditions. He cajoled his fellow villagers into cleaning up and modernizing the village and relentlessly pressed government agencies to provide schools, roads, a clinic, and a bathhouse. With the help of a government loan he built and is now running a gypsum factory in which he employs local men on a quasi profit-sharing basis and produces all the plaster necessary for the booming local building activity. Thus, he became one of the first entrepreneurs of the village. Although from a relatively small peasant family and not wealthy by any standards, he is one of the most influential and most highly regarded men in the village. (1971/76).

Why have you been fighting oppression?

The religion tells me that the landlords[2] have no rights to the land. The religion says that whoever cultivates a wasteland is its owner. We have done this here, therefore the land is not their property. When they claim the land, they are robbing the people. It is a violation of the laws of the religion. Therefore the religion says, "Fight it! Don't submit to oppression!" No religion whatsoever permits it that one should be the servant of the other. Or has God perhaps created you to become my servant? Once, when the Amīr al-Mu'minīn arrived someplace and one of his men wanted to take his horse to look after it, he didn't permit it. He said, "You look after your own horse, and I look after mine. People must be free and equal. Nobody must be higher than another."

So you do it for religious reasons?

There are two possibilities. Either I am doing it to say, "Look what a great man I am." If I am doing this, I am committing a sin—the sin of haughtiness—and I shall have to burn in the fire of hell. Or else I am doing it because of the religion: if, between myself and God, I do it for the satisfaction of God, and to help the people, then there is nothing better; it's better than all worship.

And you are doing it for this latter reason?

I can't say. Everybody says about everything he does that he is doing it for God. God Himself knows. It has to be between myself and Him.

What is the purpose of this life? What was God's aim in creating us?

God created us so that we may reach That Place. Everything is there, not here. As to here, we are told that there is first one world in the father's loins, then another world in the mother's womb, and then you come into this world. In this world you remain for a while, but then you have to go— just as we'll go home from where we are sitting now. When God created us, He said:

> I created to make divine,
> Not to give an eternal soul and then to annihilate.
> I did not create for my own benefit,
> But to do some good to my servants.[3]

And this good, He says, is not here. Here we are tested—as you are testing your students—and God tells us to live so as to pass that test. The good is there. This life is hard work, want, grief, tears, fear, and death. But *there,* there is no death, there is plenty, pleasure, peace, and ease. This world is fleeting. Or is there anything permanent? How many thousands of people have lived in Shiraz since Sa'dī and Hafiz? Where are they now? Even their graves have vanished. This you have to realize: all this here will come to an end. If these houses were not built of mud but of plaster, not of plaster but of cement, not of cement but of steel—they would still vanish. Things are built to go to ruin. Men are born to die. And when we die, everything here has to remain behind.

So what is the meaning of all this? What are we here for? Just to eat and shit and go again? And the universe should have been created just for that? No, there is something behind all this. All these stars and planets and men and things of the creation—these aren't just a joke. Or are we here to pile up things, to amass riches? Even if you had the riches of the whole world, what would they do for you there? You can't take them along. Or are we here that God be worshipped? If He were a God who needed me and you, what good would He be? Or are we here to sit in a corner and, muttering a *zikr,* pass prayer beads through our fingers while people are being oppressed? No, no, all this is nothing. If it weren't for doing something good to another and helping him, I wouldn't know what has meaning. If Hazrat-i 'Isā, the Prophet, the Imām Husayn, had not served the people, what good would they have been? This is what we have come here for: to work for the good of other people and in the love of God. To serve the people, which is to serve God, is in essence the meaning of all religious rules. This is what makes a person's faith right and true. And such deeds are the only riches that remain with him when he dies, the only thing he can take along. For these deeds God will give him a place there. Those who invented the car, made better medicines, built factories, have all been serving the people. If I am doing anything around here, it's service to the people. But all service to the people has to be done in the love of God and in the knowledge of God. These three are one; none is right without the others.

What does it mean, to know God?

It is to know: Who has made all this? What is God? What is the soul? What is man? For what has he been created? What is his duty? Where does he come from? Where does he go to? What is true faith? What are the true riches? And so on. If one doesn't know God, he may even lead a faultless life and it would amount to nothing.

Whoever has knowledge (*ma'rifat*)[4] won't do any evil. He will do good and God will give him a high place there. Once Hazrat-i 'Isā asked his disciples, "Do you want riches?" They said yes, and he left them. He came to the house of an old woman and her son, a poor brushwood collector. The son looked grieved, and when Jesus asked him why, he confessed to be in love with the daughter of the king, but given his position, he stood, of course, no chance of ever marrying her. Jesus told him to go to the king and ask for her hand. Hesitantly the youth went to the palace, was—as a joke— admitted to the king and stated his request. The king laughed at him and said, "Bring me first a tray full of jewels." The young man went back home and told Jesus. Jesus produced a tray of jewels and gave it to him to take to the king. When the king saw the jewels, he became wary, looked at the man, and said, "Bring me three more of these trays." Again Jesus provided the young man with what was requested. This time the king ordered seven more trays, and the young man brought these, too. At the sight of the seven trays of jewels, the king said, "Who is in your house? Bring him here!" Jesus came. The king recognized him, was filled with great joy, and agreed to the marriage. After that he died. Jesus made the young man king. Then he turned to leave. The young man asked him where he was going and why he did not make all this for himself. Jesus answered, "There is a greater kingdom where there is no death, and its king is the highest of all. It is he whom I want." At this the youth said, "Take me along, I want to go there, too." Jesus said, "Can you? Then you must leave all this behind." The youth got up, took off his crown and robes, left the throne, his wife, and his kingdom, and followed Jesus. Jesus returned with him to his disciples and said,

"This is a man who knows the true riches. He has knowledge of the divine (ma'rifat)."

Some people have reached very high levels of knowledge. Take Rumi, for instance. What wonder of knowledge is his Mathnavi! When you read it, and understand it—I must say I understand only a third of it—you sense the most profound pleasure and become drunk with God. Yet, the 'ulamā' touched it only with fire tongs, saying it was harām, and sinful to read. That shows you how they were suppressing true knowledge.

But no matter what knowledge we attain, we never shall come even close to understanding God, His greatness, His power, His wisdom. It is written that once, when Moses became haughty and thought nobody was like him, God ordered him to go to a certain place. Moses did, and there, on the shore of the sea, he met Hazrat-i Khizr. They started to talk about knowledge ('ilm)[5], each giving an account of what he knew. As they talked, an eagle came and scooped up a beakful of water from the sea. Khizr said, "Oh Moses, you should know that your knowledge is like this beakful of water, while mine, in comparison, is like this ocean. But after you others will come, and compared to their knowledge, my own is only like a beakful of water from the ocean. And yet, they have got only a beakful of the knowledge of God. And you presume to know everything?"

In a sense, we are like the fishes who once asked their chief in the assembly, "What is water?" Living in it, they didn't know what it was. In the same way God is everywhere, but we don't recognize Him. We see certain appearances, but we don't know what their essence is. Take the story of the devil.

He was originally an angel by the name of 'Azāzīl. Of all the angels in heaven he was the one nearest to God and had been worshipping God for thousands of years. Then, it is written, the Lord created Adam and ordered all angels to bow before him. All said, "We hear you and obey you," and bowed down except this 'Azāzīl. Haughtily he said, "I am made of light and this one of earth," and refused to bow. At that, the Lord placed Adam into a hall with an especially low doorway, and ordered 'Azāzīl to go in, expecting him to bend his head in the doorway. This He would have accepted as a bow and so forgiven him. But as the angel was about to enter the hall, he saw Adam sitting inside, stopped, and turned back. After that he was damned. The Lord asked him, "Do you want the reward for your worship in this world or the next?" The devil, wanting to have companions in hell, said, "I want it in this world. I want to have access to all the veins and nerves in the bodies of the offspring of this Adam. Then, on the Last Day, do with me whatever You like." Now the devil has this access to us, he can seduce us and lead us astray.

Well, what's now the wisdom (*hikmat*) of this? We can't say. Why has God given the devil this power? If there were no devil tempting us by means of our passions and desires, there would be less evil in this world, less oppression, violence, adultery, stealing, and so on. So, why? We don't know.

Does science give us knowledge of God?

Science lets us understand better God's power. For example, in the past, people said the religion tells a lie when it insists that we say the prayers: wherever God is, He is too far away to hear us. Now we see that the religion was right. Someone may talk in Tehran and at the same time we can hear him here in the radio. If man can do this, how much more can God who created us! Or when the moon turned black, we used to say a dragon wants to devour her, and we made a lot of noise with cans and bells and by shooting guns to scare it away. Now we know what an eclipse is and have recognized God's power a little better. After all, science itself comes from the Qur'ān. The Europeans have learned how to build machines and airplanes from the Qur'ān. For some reason that I do not know we here have failed to do this. We only took from the Qur'ān the knowledge about the Prophet, the Imāms, the prayers, and so on. However, science as such is blind. How much science do the Americans have—they can even go to the moon—and yet there is so much unbelief and injustice in their country and they are the oppressors in Vietnam.

And besides knowledge, you said, there has to be love?

Yes. Some are acting out of fear, others out of love. Acting out of love is better, much better. Mind you, there are two types of love, untrue love (*'ishq-i majāzī*) and true love (*'ishq-i haqīqī*). The former is the love of passion, like being in love with a girl; the other is love of God, the Prophet, the Amīr al-Mu'minīn, and so on. Untrue, profane love fades away after a while, but true love does not: it gets greater day by day until it becomes one spark of light. This true love can't be given to you. You have to want it, to will it, to find it inside your own self—that's the Sufi way. Look at Rumi: he became drunk with love toward God, but so can also quite simple people.

Once Moses heard a shepherd crying, "Where are you, oh God, that I may brush the dust off your feet, that I may kiss your feet, comb your hair, give you food?" Moses said to him, "Don't say such things; that's blasphemy." But the shepherd, drunk with God, continued, "Where are you, oh God, that I may sweep your room and put your head in my lap?" At that, Moses chased the shepherd away. Then God said to Moses, "This shepherd has true love. His love is greater than yours." Moses went after the shepherd and as he entered his hut, he saw the room filled with light and the shepherd, enraptured, thrust back his head and die. And he heard a voice saying, "This evening he will be my guest."[6]

When Hafiz talks about being drunk, he means being drunk with God. In this state of love all the things here lose their importance; one's heart is detached from the world. But it is out of this love that comes the will to do good. Never does it mean to submit to oppression. It means to fight it.

This is what the Imām Husayn has done?

Exactly. But to understand what he did, you have to know God's design behind it. The religion tells us that in the Miniature World ('ālam-i zarr), after the creation of Adam, all men who were to come into this world issued from Adam's side in miniature form, like small ants—in the same way as from one fly masses of other flies come forth (now that we know about the flies, we see that God can indeed do this and so understand Him even better). Then God said, "A prophet will come, the Prophet of the Last Times, and the people of this prophet will commit sins. Is there anybody ready to buy up these sins with his suffering?" All the prophets came forward, but to accept all sins proved to be beyond their strength. Each could take up only a tiny bit and the afflictions he suffered later in his life were in proportion to this. Finally Husayn, the son of Ali, got up and said, "Oh God, I want to buy up all the sins of my grandfather's people." God said, "But do you know the stipulations? Do you agree that you yourself shall be killed, that your sons shall be killed, that your brother shall be killed, that your sister and daughters shall be carried into captivity?" Husayn agreed. After that, all the miniature creatures returned into the body of Adam.

Then our world was created. Man came into being, all creatures came into existence, 124,000 prophets came and went again. Then the Last Prophet came, and Husayn, the son of Ali, was born. When Husayn was seven years old, Gabriel appeared to the Prophet and said, "God sends His peace and says He made an agreement with your Husayn in the Miniature World. Ask him whether he is still ready, and if he is, write it down." Again, Husayn declared himself ready. The document was written, sealed by the Prophet, Husayn's grandfather, the Amīr al-Mu'minīn, his father, and Fatima, his mother, and given to Gabriel, who took it to heaven. The Prophet kissed Husayn's throat, saying, "They will cut through this neck."

We are told that in Karbala, on the morning of 'Ashūrā, while the Imām Husayn was saying the prayers, Gabriel descended from heaven and again offered to him to withdraw from the agreement. And again Husayn, the son of Ali, declined. So he agreed to his own killing. This we do not fully understand; we say it, we read it, we hear it, but we do not grasp its inner meaning.

In the battle, all of the Imām's men were martyred. Two of the Imām's sons were shot dead in their father's arms. It is written, however, that as long as the Imām himself kept fighting, Yazīd's army could not harm him. It was only when he stopped fighting and sheathed his sword, that they could move in. Then they attacked him till, covered with innumerable wounds, he fell. They all, however, were afraid—or maybe ashamed—to cut off his head. They knew he was the grandson of the Prophet.

Right then, a Christian happened to come by. Yazīd promised him rich rewards here and in the hereafter if he would cut off Husayn's head. The Christian agreed, but when he stood in front of the Hazrat, the Hazrat said, "Christian, didn't you have a dream last night?" At that, the Christian remembered that the night before in a dream Hazrat-i 'Isā had said to him, "Tomorrow, don't disgrace me in the eyes of the Prophet!" Then, it is said, the Hazrat lifted the veil from the Christian's eyes so that he could see all the prophets. Hazrat-i 'Isā came forward and said to him again, "Don't disgrace me!" The Christian became a believer, drew his sword, and fought Yazīd's army till he was martyred. Now his grave is in Karbala and the Shiites make the pilgrimage to him, too.

Finally, Shimr went to cut Husayn's head. But no matter what he did, his sword would not cut through the Imām's throat. This was because the Prophet had kissed him there. At last, the Imām said, "You have to cut off my head from behind." Thus, Shimr cut the Imām's head from behind. After the Imām's death, his sister, Zaynab, his last son, and his daughters were taken as prisoners to Damascus. His wife Shahrbānū was ordered to flee to Iran where she escaped her pursuers near Rey by riding into a mountain which closed up behind her.

For the sake of this suffering, the Imām Husayn has the privilege to intercede for the people of Muhammad on the Last Day. This Last Day, it is said, will last for 50,000 years. The earth will tremble, the sun will turn into fire, and children will become old from fear. When fear will be beyond bounds, the Prophet will call Hazrat-i Fatima. She will take the Imām Husayn's blood-stained shirt to the throne of God and say, "Oh God, you have given me and my son a promise. For the sake of his sacrifice, have mercy upon the people of the Last Prophet!" Then, for the sake of Husayn, the son of Ali, God will forgive them, there will be peace, and the fire of hell will turn into a rose garden.

This then was the purpose of Husayn's martyrdom?

Yes, he agreed to his martyrdom to be able to intercede for the people on the Last Day. But also, if Husayn had not done this, where would be Islam, the pulpits, the mullahs? This religion would have been extinguished. Husayn established it, he drove it in like a nail.

But, as I said, here again is something which we do not fully understand. Why did Husayn go to Karbala? Did he know he would be killed there or didn't he? If he didn't know, then why are we beating our chests for him? But if he knew, he should not have gone there. Reason doesn't allow one to endanger one's life. Reason tells you that fire burns and, if in spite of this, you hold your hand into the fire, it is not a merit, but a sin. Thus, if Husayn knew he would be killed, reason forbade him to go there. Why did he act against reason? It was love that carried him there. He knew what would happen to him, but he did it out of love toward God. As one gets drunk with wine and then is carried away by his passions, so there is another drunkenness, the drunkenness with God, the love of God. If it hadn't been for that love, the love which is higher than reason, Husayn, the son of Ali, would have done wrong in Karbala.

But when I say that love is higher than reason, we are getting into another problem. For the Prophet is considered supreme reason and Ali supreme love, and when I say that love is higher than reason, this could be taken to mean that Ali was greater than the Prophet, which, of course, is not true. Some consider it a blasphemy to say that. But I say, the two together are one. Sure, Muhammad was supreme reason and Ali was supreme love, but that reason was also love and that love was also reason. Only those on the lower levels of understanding argue about whether, for example, Jesus was greater or Muhammad. Those with greater knowledge know that both are of one light. It is only you and I, or rather, the priests and the mullahs, who corrupt this truth and fight over it. Tomorrow, on the Last Day, both of us—I who said Muhammad is greater, and you who said Jesus is greater—will be told, "You both lied; you didn't understand." Thus, Husayn sacrificed himself for us for the love of God. But, mind you, whatever we say about his deed, we are only speaking about its outer form; we don't know its mystery.

You said if Husayn hadn't done this, the religion would not exist. Why should there be a religion?

If there were no religion, everybody would run after every woman and everybody would steal and rob. There would be sheer chaos. Life would be impossible. If the prophets and Imāms had not come and told us God's rules, we would be just animals. We would be nothing. We would know nothing. How would we know God? We would be savages. This doesn't mean, however, that everybody abides by the religious rules perfectly. In fact, only very few people are doing so. Most of those who carry out the rules do so because they are afraid of other people or because they want to show how pious they are.

Why is this so? How do you explain good and evil behavior?

There are two forces in man, 'aql (reason, intellect, spirit) and *nafs* (passion, carnal desires, drives). Reason tells us what is right, what God has told us through the prophets: to have faith, to help others, not to be haughty, not to steal, lie, commit adultery, and so on. It also tells us such things as that it is bad to do to others what you do not want anybody to do to you. Passions are the desires to eat, to sleep, to have sex; the greed for possessions, status and power; haughtiness, avarice, and so on. We don't know the roots of these passions. When you were a boy, you didn't desire women, but when you grew up, you did. Where did this come from? We don't know. When I am plowing my fields, I have the urge to plow over into the field of my neighbor. Why? God provides for man and yet he wants more and more. What does he want it for? I know that inevitably I shall have to die and yet I am trying to heap one thing on top of the other. Some say it's for their sons. Unfortunates! The God who provides for you will also provide for your sons. Our Landlord wants all people to walk behind him. When he sees one not doing it, he wants to slit his stomach in rage. There is something that makes man behave this way. Is it haughtiness, desire to rule, or what?

Now, God gave man a free will to choose between reason and passion. He can follow his reason or his passions. His actions are not decreed by God. If they were, and I committed a sin, God would be liable for it, not I myself. It is exactly because of this free will that God has granted man a very high place in the universe. Animals are pure passion: they have no reason. They can only do what God has determined as their task—carry loads, give milk, watch herds, and so on. Angels are pure spirit; they have no passion. Man has both reason and passion. When he follows passion in an unlawful way and does evil, he is worse than an animal, for an animal at least fulfills its tasks in the service of man. When he follows reason and avoids evil and does good, he is better than the angels. For angels, having no passion, can inherently do no evil, but man, to avoid evil and do good, has to overcome his passions.

These passions make a very, very heavy load for man. But if there were no passions, how should one be good? If there were no darkness, we would not know the value of this lamp. So, God has decreed that man in order to reach the high place granted to him, must first come into this world and prove himself. When he fights his passions and conquers them, when he shoulders his heavy load and carries it all the way home, then he will be given a place higher than all angels. Rumi said:

I died as mineral and became a plant,
I died as plant and rose to animal,

I died as animal and I was man.
Why should I fear? When was I less by dying?
Yet once more I shall die as man, to soar
With angels blest; but even from angelhood
I must pass on: all except God doth perish.[7]

That means, when I die, I shall become something higher still—I shall be higher than the angels.

But the struggle against passion is very hard. Recently, a boy hit my son for no reason and injured him badly. When I saw it, rage welled up in me and filled me with violence. I had to use all my strength to hold back. Then I told my son it was nothing, took him to the doctor, and hushed it up before my wife so as not to upset her. There is constant conflict between reason and passion. Passion tells you, "This is a beautiful woman: sleep with her!" Reason says, "No, she belongs to someone else; it's forbidden." It is like a fight between two men: one goes down, comes up again, and the other goes down, comes up again, until finally one wins. Thus, desire tells you, "Go and steal a rug!" Reason says, "No, don't do it; it's sinful." So you restrain yourself. Suddenly passion comes with full force from another direction. You start thinking, "If I don't steal a rug now, I won't have one tomorrow for my guest, and he will think I am nothing, I am poor, I am not a man." Such thoughts don't leave you alone. Reason gets weaker, it is pushed aside. You say, "By getting a rug, I am doing something good to myself and my family, and this is not forbidden by the religion." Finally, passion prevails and you say, "What is said about the Last Day is a lie. And so what! I don't care. Let's go!" When passion is thus in command, it governs man like a rider governs his horse. He knows it is a sin to steal. He knows he will have to pay it back on the Last Day. Yet he is doing it.

Are there methods for reason to gain the upper hand in this struggle?

First, one has to think. People do not think much before they do wrong because of their vanity. They just go ahead—and passion has won. But one has to be aware of what one is going to do, and realize the consequences. For example, the landlords have been offering me land and money if I stopped fighting them. But I know I'll have to die. The land and money will remain here, but I shall have to go there and answer for it. This is it. There is absolutely no talking around this, not even by the mullahs. In the past, when people came back from a robbery, these impostors would say, "Give me something and I will make the things lawful for you." Any uneducated person knows that it is impossible to make stolen goods lawful. The mullahs knew it, too, but their passion, their greed, got the better of their reason.

When I first decided to fight for the rights of the people, it was out of vanity—so as to be esteemed, to be considered a good person. Then I saw that this was bad, that this was haughtiness, and so I decided to do it for God. But even now, I sometimes catch myself thinking, "Look, you're great!" Suddenly I realize that it is passion that tells me this, and I say to myself, "No, no, no; haughtiness brings a person down on the Last Day. The haughty will vanish before God." Haughtiness is one of the greatest sins. The devil, the highest angel was cursed by God for his haughtiness. If you were to pray and read the Qur'ān day and night, but you were haughty, it wouldn't count a thing.

Besides, you have to control yourself. This is hard, indeed. You have to tighten your belt, and by force constrain yourself, and want the good: then you will do it. You have to really want it. And you have to want it from God. The Imām Husayn and God will help you, but simply asking them for help is not enough. They won't go by your words, but by your will. If you will it, firmly resolve to do it, then they will help you. When man takes one step towards God, God comes 100 steps his way. You asked me once from where I had the power to fight the landlords. God gave it to me. I wanted it, and He gave it to me. I wished from Him to be able to serve the people, and I wasn't afraid, just as God has told us not to be afraid, and went to face the landlords. I said to myself, "If they kill me, so be it. Even then it will be to my benefit and that of the village." But this didn't come all at once. Little by little it grew and got better. One has to practice; step by step and bit by bit one gets to improve. One must train oneself and gradually make it a habit to do good. It must become part of oneself. Once my father was given a shirt by the Landlord. At night I saw him getting up and taking it off. I asked him why he did so. He said, "This shirt is burning on my body. It doesn't let me sleep."

The religion forbids to kill passion, as by castrating oneself, but it is good to suppress it. Eating moderately, for example, weakens passion. I think, however, it is more important to build up habits in other regards, like carefully respecting other people's property, or controlling sensual desires. Whenever I notice a beautiful woman, I make it a habit to force myself not to look at her. When passion is weakened, reason gets stronger and it is less likely that one will sin. On the other hand, if one yields to passion, it will become stronger, less controllable, and eventually make you miserable. If you are used to eating stew, what will you do if you haven't any? You must go and steal. And what good does the stew do you anyway? If I eat bread for lunch and you eat stew, after a few hours, what's the difference between our two bellies? None. God has told us not to attach ourselves to this world. Sure, it is good to have this rug here in the house. But I don't attach my heart to it. If I lost it now, I wouldn't care. I don't love it. Whatever one loves most, that is one's God. Some people's God is their belly, others' their sheep. I tell you, if these people here were loving God as much as their sheep, they would be perfect Muslims.

So, the reason why one person becomes good and the other bad . . .

. . . lies essentially with themselves. It's like the difference between this teapot and that brick in the wall. Both are of earth. But to the material of the teapot something has been done: it was refined into the more precious porcelain. In the same way, all men are of the same material, that is, earth, and God has given all the same power to become good. If God gave it only to one and not the other, He would be liable for their deeds. But the one resists passion, forces himself, trains himself, teaches himself good habits, and makes himself into porcelain or even a jewel. The other doesn't do this and remains plain earth.

In this endeavor to make oneself good, is it useful to practice a zikr?

It depends on the kind of zikr. If it only consists of sitting in a corner and endlessly repeating "Allah-*hu*," it is entirely worthless. But there is also a zikr in the sense of keeping God in mind at all times, in all you do. One goes after one's affairs, cares for his wife and children, works and takes pain, but, as one is doing it, one's mind is with God.

Are you practicing this type of zikr?

All the time. Sometimes I may forget, but then it comes by itself again. Sa'dī said:

When the breath goes in, it prolongs our life.
When it comes out, it cheers our nature.[8]

This means, breathing has to be in remembrance of God, that is, God should be on one's mind all the time. You see, the only thing I know for sure is this: that one day they will carry me out of this house and I will face God. Our real home is there. All these stars, all these heavens and earths, all these religious rules we have been told, all these things show us that our real place is not here.

When I decided to work for God I attached this love to Him. This engraved a pattern (*naqsh bast*) in my heart, like the pattern, the zeal you have in regard to anthropology. But don't think I am completely innocent. I am not always saying the truth, and once, when I was still more of an ass than I'm today, I stole some money which I still have not restored, though I am determined to do it now. But as far as I can, I train myself, and my love is with God. It is out of this love that I have the zeal to do something that pleases God. But the power to do so comes from Him. In the morning, when I get up, I say, "In the name of God the merciful and compassionate. Oh God, let me do today something that pleases you."

To fight oppression and to better the conditions of the people, this was my goal, because God has told us to do so. The plaster factory I am running now allows people to build better houses and provides the workers with an income. Anything you do must be for the benefit of others, too. If Hazrat-i 'Isā or the Prophet had worked only for themselves, what use would they have been? As you know, I pay higher wages to my workers than anybody else here. Recently I suggested to my partner that he should pay the same wages as I do. At this he said, "Then I'll have only very little profit." I said to him, "Don't talk like this. Should these people perhaps work for our benefit? They ought to have a share in the profit, too." No, God doesn't want me to enrich myself at their expense. I consider myself just another worker, all of us sharing in the profit—like sitting around a tray of food and eating from it together. That's the way the Prophet has ordered it.

If you love God, you will do everything for Him, even the smallest thing, like lighting a lamp, moving a rock aside in the road, driving a straying cow out of a wheat field, whatever. To do something for someone else means to do it for God. When I get up at night to stir the fire or give water to a child, I do it for my children, but also for God, because He entrusted these children to me. When I clear stones out of a field, or plant a tree, God likes it because after me someone else will benefit from the field and eat the tree's fruits, and so I will forever have merit from my work— even if someone only sits in the shadow of a tree. In this way, you can do everything for God, all day long. This is the knowledge (ma'rifat) regarding all work. One who doesn't have this knowledge is like an animal. He eats and sleeps and shits and runs and runs from morning till sunset without understanding.

Inevitably everybody will sin; only the Imāms and the Prophet were without sin. What one has to do under these circumstances is to try every day to do more good deeds than bad ones, so that when the bad deeds are taken off from the good ones, one still has good deeds left. Ali said, "When you get up in the morning, you should think you are going to die this evening, but you also should think you are never going to die." This means, you should do so many good deeds that day as if it were your last day, but you also should work so hard as if you were never to die. And Sa'dī said: "Do you remember when you were born? All laughed and you cried. Make it so that when you go, everybody will cry and you'll laugh."

What happens when a person dies?

When a person is on the point of death, an angel, the angel 'Izrā'il, comes into the room. Only the dying person notices him and he may think it is his doctor. The angel asks him, "Where does it hurt?" and then, beginning at the feet, starts to pass his hands over him, like a doctor examining your body. Wherever he touches him, the person feels well and his pains stop. The angel moves his hands up and up until he reaches the throat and mouth. At that, he takes his soul. Suddenly the person, or rather, his soul, sees his body lying in the room and all the people sitting around it, wailing, and he realizes that he has died.

After the burial, when the grave has been filled, and the people have left, the soul re-enters the body. Two angels, Munkar and Nakīr, come into the grave and ask the person, "What is your religion? In whom did you believe? Who is your God? Who was your Prophet? Who were the Imāms? and so on. And they give him the record of his deeds in which all his actions are written down in every detail. If, on the basis of this record, it appears that he was a good person, then the earth around him will say, "Welcome, I am delighted that you give me the honor," and the grave will become large and wide and a houri will come to him and say, "I am your good deeds; God has made me from your good deeds," and he will be taken to heaven. If, on the other hand, it turns out that he was a bad person, he will see his evil deeds in the form of a frightful figure and will be taken to hell.

You have dreamed of being in far-away places, haven't you? What goes there and sees these places is your soul. When it leaves this mortal frame for good and goes to the next world, there is no more death. One is as alive there as one is here; there is no difference. Death means only moving to another place. Now you are living here in this village; after a while you will go back to America. After you have left, it will be as if you had died here. Yet you will be alive; you will only have returned home. Thus, when we die, we return to· our real home. It's exactly the same thing, exactly the same.

This life appears so sweet to us, and we hold on to it so fast. And yet, it is there where it is good, not here. Here, we have to take pains; there, we are at ease. Here, we have no desire for two or three days after intercourse; there, pleasure never ends and a paradisical houri is with you. Here is fear of death, sorrow over the death of others, fear of others' evil intentions, oppression, injustice, dirt, pollution. Over there is nothing of all this. Dying is as if someone led you from a miserable hut in the mountains to a fine apartment in the city, or as if someone freed you from prison. Once you are there, and you look back at this life, you say, "Oh, how could I have ever liked this life so much?"

*But if one goes to heaven or hell right after death, what is then the signifi-
cance of the Day of Judgment?*

On the Last Day the world will come to an end, the dead will come to
life again, and the accounting will be done. There are always two angels
with us, one writing down our good deeds, the other our bad deeds. On the
Last Day, which is said to last for several thousand years, this record of our
deeds will be produced, and we'll be unable to deny even the slightest
offence.

It is written that on this Last Day a sinner will look for excuses. One
will say, "Oh God, it was the devil who seduced me." The devil will be
called. He will ask, "Have you ever seen me?" The person will say no. Then
the devil will say, "How come that you disobeyed all those prophets who
were with you and told you what is right and wrong, and yet me, whom
you have never seen, you have obeyed? Come along with me!" Or one will
say, "Oh God, what help did you give me?" To this, God will answer, "I
gave you mind and reason. Did you ever want anybody to steal your property?" Or one may say, "Oh God, how could we have known you?" Then
God will say, "How come you have the intelligence to find your way to the
moon, but you don't have the intelligence to know who created the moon?
You know that when you drill four kilometers into the earth, oil will come
up, but you say you don't know who has brought the oil into existence?"
No, people will have no excuses on the Last Day.

How then will the accounting be done?

Every offence against other people will have to be paid back. If I have
harmed somebody, merits equivalent to this harm will be taken from me
and given to this person. Such merits are earned by serving other people, by
helping them, not simply by fulfilling religious obligations like saying the
prayers or keeping the fast. A servant who carries out all orders perfectly
well nevertheless commits a crime when he steals something, and has to
make up for it. If one has plenty of merits, he can pay off his creditors and
will still have merits left. If, however, one has no merits, he has to assume
tortures of his creditor in proportion to his offence. This is shown in the
following story.

A person going on pilgrimage to Mecca entrusted all his savings to a
learned man. When he came back, however, and asked for his money, the
man denied ever having received anything. So the pilgrim went to another
learned man, told him what had happened and asked for his help. This
learned man listened, thought for a while, then went to the fraudulent man
with the pilgrim. There he told this story: "Once I borrowed some money
from my grocer, but put off repaying it. When I finally wanted to pay it
back, it turned out that he had just died. Immediately I sent my servant to

his store, instructing him to give the money to the grocer's heirs or else simply throw it into the store. The servant went there, found the store closed, and dropped the money through a slit in the door. That night I had a dream. I dreamed that I had died and an angel was just leading me into paradise when behind us somebody called after us. I turned round and saw the grocer. His whole body was on fire. He demanded his money back. I said I had given it to him. He said he hadn't received it and wanted it now. I said I had no money with me. So he said, 'Then you have to take over some of my torments. The money you owe me corresponds to the torment in the three joints of my index finger.' And he touched my chest with that finger. Instantly I felt a sharp, burning pain on my chest and woke up. There was a wound as from a burn. Now, after ten years, I still have it." At that, the learned man opened his shirt and showed a festering wound on his chest, saying, "Whatever medicine I have applied, it didn't help. The wound is still burning like fire." Presently, the man who had embezzled the money got up, produced the money, and handed it back to the pilgrim.

Thus, if a debt of any sort—from stealing, embezzling, cheating, borrowing or whatever—has not been settled in this world, one will have to pay it off in the next, either by giving merits to one's creditor or by assuming torments from him. It is in this sense that Ali said that every morning one must make the intention to end up in the evening with more merits than sins. If one has more merits than sins, one can redeem his sins, and will go to heaven. If, however, one has more sins, one will have to go to hell and pay everything back to the last tiny bit; one will have to be in hell in proportion to one's offences, like in a prison.

But isn't God merciful and forgiving?

There are two types of sins, sins against the right of God (*haqqu'l-lah*) and sins against the rights of man (*haqqu'n-nās*). Drinking wine or not saying the prayers are sins against God. These sins God will forgive if one repents them and resolves not to do them again. But God cannot forgive sins against other people, such as oppression and stealing. If He forgave such sins, He would not be just but unjust. Such offences—and if it were only the theft of a sunflower seed—have to be paid back entirely, unless the harmed person himself waives his rights. If one is a good person though, God will give him merits in case he should run short of them, so that he can pay off his creditors. If one loves God and the Imām Husayn, one will have plenty on the Day of Judgment.

And if one is bad and has no love?

This I can't say. But God and the Imāms are great, and great ones have forgiveness and mercy. God doesn't look for a pretext to punish. He looks for a pretext to forgive.

What about your Former Landlord? Can he be forgiven?

No, never. There is no forgiveness for his crimes. God cannot do that. That was oppression. And it wasn't one or two or three or a hundred or a thousand acts: it was all these villages and all that time. Everything he possessed was stolen from the people. Everything he ate was taken from the people's own livelihood: the butterfat poured over his rice was the blood of the people. I can't tell you all the things he did. Whenever he went to a village, every woman he wanted had to go to him. When she wasn't willing, he had her husband beaten up and imprisoned and their household raided. He took the people's food away and at night gave rawzah ceremonies in his house with it—with food taken away from the people! Once, when a peasant came with sugar from the town, he took it all from him with the promise to pay for it. When the peasant later reminded him to pay, the Landlord abused him and took ten kilograms of honey from him saying, "Why have you said that?" We were all forced to attend these ceremonies. We had no choice but to eat from that food. Yet it was unlawful food. On the Last Day we shall have to pay for everything we ate in his house, for we knew it was obtained by oppression.

Maybe the Landlord himself didn't consider his acts oppression. Maybe he believed that it was his right to collect land rents and that it was good to hold rawzahs?

No, no, he knew it was oppression. He knew it. He knows the religion better than the Mullah. But his desire to dominate didn't allow him to abide by it. His passions had the upper hand. No, he knew exactly what he was doing. Once, when the earth was still trembling under his foot, I told him to repent his adulteries, and he said, "I repented already three times; but I have done it again." He said the prayers like no one else, and he still does, spending much time on them and saying special prayers as well. They are all worthless because the prayers of an oppressor are worthless. And he knows it: he knows that Umar's prayers were worthless. Yet he says them. He says to himself, "God will forgive." But God will not forgive. Never, never. If you drink wine and repent it, you may be forgiven. But if you take away others' property and you take and take and take, it's impossible to repent and be forgiven. Even if I steal the smallest trifle, I will have to pay it back on the Last Day—even if I were a prophet. This is written in the Qur'ān.

But didn't you say that on the Last Day the sins of the people will be forgiven for the sake of Husayn's martyrdom?

Yes, Husayn will come to the help of all who are of Muhammad's religion, and God will forgive their sins. But there are a number of people

who cannot be forgiven: those who are fundamentally bad and depraved.
Haughtiness is such a sin. There is no way that haughtiness can be forgiven.
The devil was thrown down for his haughtiness. If I committed that sin and
it were forgiven, the devil would claim forgiveness, too. And so it is with
oppression. Only sins against God can be forgiven by the blood of the
Imām Husayn.

Aren't these sins forgiven anyway by simply doing repentance?

Yes, this is true. But the Imām can intervene with the harmed person
so that the person himself will forgive his wrong-doer. It is written that a
man used to cause his mother great harm and trouble. Once, when she
quarreled with his wife, he flew into a rage and threw her into the bread
oven. When this man died and was buried, a flame of fire came out of the
grave. The Prophet and his companions asked what had happened. When
he learned about the man's misdeeds towards his mother, he sent Ali to ask
the woman to forgive her son. Ali did so, but she said, "May the fire burn
twice as strong!" Nor did she forgive when Hazrat-i Fatima and then the
Imām Hasan asked her. But when the Imām Husayn went to her and told
her who he was, she was moved and forgave her son. Yes, I would do the
same. If I were killed, I would forgive my murderer because I know that the
Prophet and the Imām Husayn would be distressed if I didn't.

Yet about oppression I don't know what to say. They are a very noble
family. One cannot say no, they won't forgive; nor can one say they will
forgive oppression. I don't know what to say. Once the Prophet was stoned,
he didn't curse the people, he forgave them. Their heart is full of mercy. In
fact, we are afraid that maybe even Shimr, the man who cut off Husayn's
head, and the murderer of Ali might be forgiven. They don't want people to
burn in hell. They have no hatred and vengefulness in their hearts, as we
do. Take the story of Yazīd.

After the Imām Husayn and his companions had been killed, Yazīd
became sorry for his misdeeds and sent for Hazrat-i Zayn al-'ābidīn, Husayn's son, to ask for a prayer by which the Lord would forgive his crime.
Out of mercy, Hazrat-i Zayn al-'ābidīn told him the prayer ghufaylah. But
whenever Yazīd wanted to say this prayer, he got such strong stomach aches
that he couldn't do it. Eventually he became sick, and one of his doctors
pulled a scorpion out of Yazīd's stomach. When the doctor saw it, he said
in horror, "You must have killed a prophet or a prophet's offspring. There is
no cure for your disease." Later, Yazīd went hunting, and a coffin of fire
came down from heaven and carried him off.

So he was not forgiven after all. But if by the Imām Husayn's intercession
evil-doers are forgiven on the Last Day, wouldn't it be an injustice and
wouldn't it then make no difference whether one sins or not?

No, no, till then they will be in hell. Till the Last Day there is a lot of time. But, if I think about it, this would mean they won't be forgiven after all. Because if they are going to stay in hell, they will pay back their sins anyway and by the Last Day nothing will be left that needs to be forgiven. I don't know what to say to this.

Also, when does the good person who, as you said, is taken to paradise right after death, benefit from the Imām's intercession?

Immediately in the grave. Besides, the good ones don't need it. Husayn helps them already in this world, so that they become good and don't need his intercession.

How can God, who is all love, create a person whom He knows will go to hell?

God knows what a person will do, but that person has a free will. If God would not create those persons whom He knows will sin, man would not be free. God could prevent me from doing evil. When I want to steal something, He could make my hand lame or He could make me blind. But then I would not be free. He laid down an order. Either we are free or we aren't free. If we are free, then it has to be this way. If I were not free, everything would be on Him.

God created us with a free will. That much we can say. Beyond that we don't know. We don't understand why God created one to do wrong. Either God knows or He doesn't know. If He doesn't know, what good is He? But if He knew that I was going to do evil, why did He, who is all love, nevertheless create me, so that I would do that evil and go to hell? Here it gets narrow and we cannot go on. This is something only He knows.

But why did He give us a free will if this meant that ever so many people would suffer in hell?

If we were not free and we were created in such a way that everybody would do good and go to heaven, what pleasure would heaven have? If there were no night, what pleasure would day have? If there were no bitterness, what pleasure would sweetness have? If there were no death, life would not be dear. If there were no evil, good would not be known. If there were no hell, heaven would have no pleasure.

Would you say the same about suffering in this world?

The meaning of this-worldly suffering is difficult to tell. We don't know God's wisdom. This is shown to us in the story of Khizr and Moses. I told you already how Moses was sent to Khizr, and Khizr said to him that, compared to his own, Moses' knowledge was as little as a beakful of water from the ocean. Then Moses said, "Take me along and show me your knowledge!" Khizr said, "I will, but only under the condition that you'll never ask why I am doing something." Moses agreed. So Khizr took him along. They travelled by boat. As they were sitting in the boat, Moses noticed that Khizr was digging a hole into the bottom of the boat with his cane. Astonished he asked, "Khizr, why are you doing this?" Khizr said, "Didn't you promise not to ask why? You can't go with me any longer." Moses begged forgiveness and asked for another chance. Khizr consented. They got off the boat and entered the city. Suddenly Khizr took hold of a boy and cut his head off. Shocked by this, Moses could not restrain himself and asked again, "Khizr, why did you do that?" Khizr wanted to send him away, but Moses entreated him, saying, "Give me one more chance; it shall be the last one." Khizr granted him the wish. After a while they reached an old wall. Khizr stopped and said, "Moses, help me take down this wall." They took down the wall, but then Khizr said, "Now, let's build it up again." Moses held himself back, but when they were done, he said, "Khizr, I can't help it; I have to ask. I will go, but tell me why you did all these things." Khizr said, "Very well. The hole in the boat I made because I knew that the shāh's agents will come to confiscate boats for a war at sea and would take the boat if it were undamaged. This would deprive the man and his family of their livelihood and they would become destitute. This way, however, the boat will not be taken, and the man can repair it and go on earning a living. As to the boy, I killed him because I knew that he would have become an unbeliever and committed such outrageous deeds that his parents would have lost their honor and faith. This way, however, they will get a daughter in his place and she will bear two prophets. Finally, as to the wall, I rebuilt it because I knew that a treasure is buried underneath it. Its rightful heir is still too young to take possession of it, and if the wall were to collapse, the treasure would be discovered and stolen. So, however, it will be preserved for him and he will do many good and charitable deeds with it. And now that I have told you this, go your way."

Thus, if Moses didn't know the wisdom in what he saw, how much less can we know God's wisdom in the misfortunes that happen to us. Why did our neighbor's child die last night? He was innocent, only a few months old. Why all the trouble? Why did my own son die when he was twelve? I don't know, but there is a wisdom in it. For sure there is a wisdom, but I don't have the knowledge to recognize it. There are different degrees of knowledge just as there are gold, rubies, and diamonds, each precious to a different degree.

This son of mine was quite a son, so good, so well-behaved, so bright. I loved him more than words can tell. When he was twelve, he fell ill with measles. His condition became very bad. Many people came to sit with us. The boy was lying in front of me, faint and lifeless. I raised his head and said, "Son, how are you?" He said, "Father, I am dying." When he said this, I was overcome by something I cannot describe. I leaned back against the wall. His mother said, "What's wrong? What did he say?" I said, "Nothing." Then I bent over him again. I raised his head and saw that he was about to die. I placed his head into my lap and held him in my arms. So he took his last breath.

I told the people to keep calm and to get the Mullah. When he came, I said to him, "My son surrendered his soul in my arms. It was the will of God. God gave it, God has taken it. Whatever God wills is right. He went to a place we'll all have to go to." The people got up to take the boy and carry him out. But I said, "No, whatever has to be done I'll do myself." They didn't want to let me do it. But no matter what they did, I said, "No, he has to be at my side." I carried him to the bathhouse for the dead and I performed the ablutions on him. Then, despite their objections, I took him in my arms and carried him to the graveyard. There they said again, "Now give him to us." But I said, "This is my son. I want to put him into the grave myself." I crawled into the grave and as he was handed down to me I placed him in the right position. Then, as is the custom, I opened the part of the shroud that covered his face. I looked at him, and he seemed to smile at me. After this I don't know what happened to me. People say I passed out in the grave. They said I showed great endurance. God has ordered us to have endurance; a father has to have endurance at the death of his son. But we mustn't ask, "Why has God done this?" It would be vain to do so. We cannot even see the back of our heads, and we want to know the reasons for God's ways?

Can an affliction also be a trial?

Certainly, you may be sent illness, pain, misery, hardship, and in this way you may be tried. Hazrat-i 'Isā was thrown into a pit, carried into captivity, sold, and made a slave. That was a trial. But again, we don't know. It may also be, for example, that a person who dies young would have done evil had he lived. Look at this cripple who has to go around in the village begging for a livelihood: maybe, if he had been born ablebodied, he would have committed some wrong. Also, we say that suffering an affliction takes off some of a person's sins. But this has one condition: he must be content with the will of God, and not ask, "Oh God, why have you brought this on to me?" The affliction must, however, come from the favor of God, not from His wrath.

What is the wrath of God?

If one is doing evil and the Lord inflicts evil on him, that is the wrath of God. But it is not possible to say that any affliction is the wrath of God.

It can also be the favor of God. There is something involved here that we do not know. But someone who does no wrong will not suffer the wrath of God. Was it perhaps the wrath of God that Husayn, the son of Ali, was killed? No, it was the favor of God. Looking at it now, we see that if Husayn hadn't been killed, this religion wouldn't exist. There is some inner wisdom which we do not understand.

But there is also the wrath of God. Remember, I showed you those dead poplar trees below the village. All other trees there are green. Only these are dead. The man who owns them stole land from his father and brothers, he took a false oath on the Qur'ān, he is abusing God 400 times a day, he committed adultery with the wives of two men, and he killed a man at the saltwell over a bag of salt. He didn't sell those poplar trees when his father wanted him to; he wanted to wait till his father had died and then pocket all the profit. Now his father is still living and the trees have dried up. He lives well, but recently has started to sell things and he keeps on selling. Slowly he is being impoverished for his misdeeds. One of his sons is feeble-minded and keeps failing in school year after year. The other son cannot find a wife—a young man his age usually has five children already. And his unmarried daughter, as you know, is said to be pregnant. As yet, nothing definite is known, but sooner or later this will happen to him. If you commit adultery, the same thing will be done to you, unfailingly—either to your daughter or your sister or your wife.

Is it also God's punishment that the Former Landlord has become destitute?

Yes, and now the people say it, too. But while he was the powerful landlord, they said, "God wanted it this way. God has made him great." This was nonsense and unlawful to say. His misery now, yes, that has been made by God. But that he was landlord wasn't made by God. He made himself landlord. But the people said, "If God hadn't wanted it, He would not give him so many sons." To this I said, "Woe to you; don't say this! God is giving him these sons now so that later they will pay for the injustice of their father." But, as it is, now he is paying only a tiny little bit, only a token. Afterwards, in that world, he will really pay.

But it's not only he who has been afflicted. Everyone who served him as agent and participated in his oppression has become destitute. One has no children; another lives in dire poverty, unwanted by his sons and deserted by his wife; and still others, a group of brothers, are constantly fighting with each other, stealing from each other, beating up each other. On the other hand, those who didn't cooperate with the Landlord and rather suffered oppression now are doing all right. We all have seen this.

An evil-doer, however, is not necessarily afflicted in this world. God may let him go—till then. The religion teaches us that God gives ease and plenty to some of those who commit oppression and do not heed the religion. They get everything they want: beautiful women, the best houses, servants, money, plenty of goods. God says, "They want the world: they shall have it. But there is nothing for them in the next."

Nor does the Landlord's fate mean that poverty always is the wrath of God. We don't know God's reason for giving more to one and less to another. Whatever we think about it, we don't know. Ali tilled the soil with his own hands. The Prophet didn't have anything either: he gave everything he had in the way of Islam. Nor did Jesus or Moses have anything. On the other hand, didn't Pharaoh, who claimed to be God and who was God's enemy, have all the riches of the world? And didn't Shaddād, who also claimed to be God, possess so much that he wanted to build paradise? These things are not known. Did God perhaps not love Ali or the Prophet or Jesus? Jesus turned stones into jewels, yet he was poor. Why? Because wealth is nothing.

If God sends punishment in this world, does He also send rewards?

There is blessing. When a person's fields prosper or he and his family eat and eat, and their provisions last far longer than those of others who had much more, we say he has blessing. The man I just mentioned who is getting poor despite his hard work has no blessing.

Do you think you have blessing?

Last year, we harvested ten loads of wheat, 120 kilogram to a load. One load we set aside as seed grain and two or three more we took to the store in payment for other goods. From the rest we have been eating bread till now in late spring, and there is still enough left to last us through the new harvest. Whatever we eat, there is still more. God gave us blessings. But don't tell this to anybody. The Landlord's younger brother harvested nine loads of wheat and in addition has been buying a lot of wheat in the store over the year; but now, his wife tells us, they are out of it again.

Two years ago you introduced the use of scourges to replace the traditional chest-beating at the Muharram celebrations. Why did you do this?

Because the chest-beating isn't right by the law of the religion. A man may do it just to show off in front of the women, and a woman looking at a bare-chested young man may be filled with desire: it may please her, which is very sinful. Thus, wearing the black shirts and flagellating with the chains is better. But black shirts, chains, cymbals, banners, and these things are of no importance in themselves. One could do without them and still be a very pious person. They serve the propagation of the religion. If they were all discarded, the religion would become weak. How else should the young people learn the religion? Also, maybe among all the flagellators there is one who is really beating himself out of love for Husayn, out of grief, goodness, and knowledge. Maybe, by virtue of the ritual, two people in this village will become good men. Otherwise these things are not needed.

It takes a lot of power to flagellate oneself with knowledge (ma'rifat), to beat oneself really for Husayn himself, to beat oneself with fervor, love, a burning heart. I know most people aren't doing it this way. They are joking and laughing during the ceremonies, and from this I know that they are not serious. And when I ask them what Husayn was doing, why he went to Karbala, what the purpose of his martyrdom was, they don't know. They weep at the celebration, but it's not genuine. If put to the test, they would all run away.

So it is with the other rituals. People do observe the prayers, the fasting, the ritual bathing after intercourse and so on, but not the way the Qur'ān says. For the prayers to be right one must not steal, lie, commit adultery, harbor ill-feelings or be angry at others; above all, one must not be haughty or submit to oppression—otherwise the prayers are nothing, mere gestures without meaning. And fasting doesn't only mean to abstain from food, but that the eyes, the ears, the tongue are fasting; that is, that one doesn't look at the wives and daughters of other people, and one doesn't gossip, slander and cause enmity between people.

But the people do all these things. Even the poorest man here will say haughtily, "Why should I sweep the village lanes?" They plow into their neighbor's fields, and, if they can, even steal land from their brothers. They are reined and ridden by their passions like horses by their riders. So, their prayers and fasting aren't right. Besides, if the truth be known, most people do not perform the ritual for the sake of God. They do it so that their neighbors may say they are good men. And they do it because it's the custom. Just as they have learned to say greetings, use titles, make compliments, so they also say "God." They do have faith, but the faith is not strong. God says, "Do not submit! Fight! Do not allow others to oppress you! If you do, you are their accomplice and your crime is no less than theirs." Yet they let themselves be robbed and beaten.

What is the role of the Mullah in all this?

He accepts it all to have an income. At first, when he came back from his studies in Qom, he vowed that even if he had nothing but plain bread, he would spread the religion among the people. Then he married a sister of the Landlord and ever since has taken the Landlord's side in any conflict. Once he came to me and offered me a large amount of land if I recognized the Landlord as landowner. I never told the people about this. They would have judged the religion by his behavior, and the religion would have become discredited.

He did, however, other things that had the same effect. While the raiding and plundering was going on, he tricked people into giving him all kinds of gifts so that he would, as he said, make their loot lawful for them. In this way, he encouraged them in their robbing, deceived them about their sins, and made a profit for himself. When the Landlord gave those rawzahs with the goods stolen from the people, the Mullah held the ceremonies. He would say special prayers for the well-being of the Landlord and we all had to say 'Amen.' Once I said to him, "Don't you see that for these ceremonies he takes the people's possessions away?" He said, "Yes, he does, but he spends it for the people again." He knew that what he did was wrong. His knowledge is far greater than mine. But—like most others of his kind—he doesn't abide by it. The knowledge of these people is like a load of Qur'āns on a donkey. They don't benefit from it.

In recent years he has made it a habit to leave the village exactly when he would be needed most, that is, in the months of Ramadan and Muharram. He goes to a town where he earns more. I told him these uneducated people here would need him more than the town people. He said, "Why aren't you paying me?" I said, "You are materialistic." He said, "What shall I live on?" I told him how much he is earning from his various incomes. He said, "The more there is the longer a way it goes." I said, "Tomorrow, on the Last Day, you won't be able to give this answer."

There have to be mullahs and 'ulamā'; without them the religion wouldn't be spread. They have studied; they know the religion; they can teach it. But one mustn't look at their behavior. It's like with a dog that holds a jewel in its mouth: you take the jewel and forget about the dog. But there are many different kinds of mullahs. Some use their cloak to damage the religion. In fact, they use the religion to deceive the people. Mullah Rumi in his Mathnavi tells us of a bird—I forgot its name—that used to recite the Qur'ān. As it sings, all the birds gather around to listen because it has such a good voice. They draw closer and closer, and the bird, while reciting, watches them slyly. And when they are well within reach, it suddenly grabs one. Some of the 'ulamā' are this way. But there are others who are very good. They live withdrawn from public life and are not commonly known. I know some of them, but as they live in the city I do not have much contact with them. I think that now there are more of the really good ones than there were twenty or thirty years ago, as quite generally I think that the religion and faith of the people have become better and stronger. True, in the big cities today there appears to be very little faith. But it is in the ruins that you find the jewels. It is only in the upper classes that you find this irreligion, not in the lower ones. Among these there are some very, very good people.

What about the younger generation?

The young people have changed over the last years. Earlier, children used to follow their parents' example, be it good or bad. That's different now. The boys who have gone to study no longer listen to anybody. They go around saying the religion is superstition, there is no God. They disregard the religion. With this kind of people it is impossible to talk. The reason for this unbelief is, more than anything else, that they follow their passion. They run after the easy money that has become available now, burning over a few toman. I have told my son who goes to the university, "If you leave the order of God, if wine passes your lips or you start gambling, then go and do what you want." You know how much I love this son. But the love of God is much, much greater. I and my son are mortal. But God is eternal. I cannot abandon God, I cannot abandon the Last Day.

9

The Prayer-Writer: The Problem of Efficacy

The Prayer-Writer is a literate peasant in his late forties. Although he is from a rather small lineage and does not have much land, he is economically doing a little better than the average peasant, mostly because he turned most of his land into orchards and vineyards and tends them with utmost diligence. With the help of his oldest son, who is married but has not yet separated from his father, he cares for a household of six people. Quiet and withdrawn, he is seldom seen in public places in the village, but unfailingly can be found working in his gardens summer and winter. In the evenings, people often come to his house with requests for written prayers. Indeed, he is regarded as the best local amulet writer. This judgment is based on the alleged success of his amulets, but also on his reputation as a trustworthy, upright, and honest man. (1976).

How did you happen to become a prayer-writer?

In former times my uncle, who was a very pious man, did the prayer-writing. I studied with him. When he died, I was the only one familiar with the Qur'ān and the prayer-writing. People started coming to me, saying, "My child is ill; write a prayer for him," and I did. So I took it up little by little, and, after a while, I couldn't give it up anymore no matter how much I would have wanted to. It was a matter of people being in need and tugging at my sleeve asking for help.

I do this as a service for the people, not to make a living. I never charge a fee. The people themselves may bring something, one may give me ten toman, another an egg, and another 100 toman. This I take, except when I see that the person is poor. It's not wrong to take something, but it is wrong to fix a price. We say, the words of the Imāms cannot be sold. Some men in other villages and in the towns make a business out of it. This is not right. I am not doing this. As you know, I am out working in the gardens and the fields all day long: that's how I make a living.

There are some people, some Sayyids, who say that prayer-writing is sinful. These have no reason in their heads. Is it good to serve the people, or bad? And after all, these Sayyids do not know more than the Imāms.

How do you find the appropriate du'ā' in your book?

You saw this man with me the other day. He came and said, "Look up a du'ā' for my son, he has the measles." First I figured out the boy's number. I wrote down the numbers corresponding to each of the letters in his name and his mother's name, and added them up, omitting all full twelves. The resulting number was two. This indicated that the boy belongs to the second sign of the zodiac, the sign of Taurus. Every person belongs to one or the other of these twelve signs, the twelve states of nature. Then I looked up this sign in the book. There are listed a number of questions which I asked the father: Are the boy's bones aching? Can he sleep well? Is he coughing? Does he have a fever? Does he have a sore throat? and so on. On the basis of the answers to such questions the book indicates what the disease is due to—a cold, the stomach, the evil eye, and so forth—and what the proper du'ā' for it is. In the case of the boy, the disease was due to a cold, and three du'ā' were indicated. I wrote them on three strips of paper and gave them to the man, telling him that one should be covered with wax and worn by the boy on his body, that the second should be dipped in water and the water given to the boy to drink, and that the third should be burned together with seeds of the wild rue underneath the feet of the boy so that the smoke would drift over his body. I also told him that it did not matter if the child wasn't eating anything now, because for a certain time a sick person is not disposed to eat.

All diseases also have their medicines (*davā*), which are also stated in this book. For example, for a toothache you dissolve some sugar candy in boiling water and drink it. This will soothe it. If not, take part of an egg plant, the skin of a poppy-head, and camomile flowers, boil them in water and wash your mouth with it or drink it.

Where does the knowledge about these medicines come from?

From two sources: one part comes from Luqmān, the doctor, the other part from the twelve Imāms. Luqmān lived at the time of Alexander the Great. Alexander once ordered his ship steered right into the center of a whirlpool in the ocean. There he was given a plant, and was told to have it put into his bread and to eat it so as to gain wisdom. Luqmān was his baker. He put the plant in the dough but burned the bread and so ate it himself, baking another one for Alexander. After Luqmān had eaten it, he began hearing the plants talk to each other and could understand their language. They told him what disease each plant was good for, and so he acquired this knowledge which he then wrote down in a book. This book came down to the doctors. The modern medicines the doctors give out are essentially made on the basis of this book. There might have been additions here or there, but in essence they are from Luqmān.

The other part of the medicines in my book comes from the twelve Imāms. In their times they were the doctors, they possessed the knowledge. When someone became ill, his family went to them and asked them for remedies and guidance. They wrote the du'ā', which are partly taken from the Qur'ān, partly their own sayings, and told them these medicines. The Imām Ja'far Sādiq even told us a medicine for cancer.

In former times, before there was a doctor here, I told people these medicines, too. But since the doctor came, I don't do this any longer. I tell them to go to the doctor for a medicine. As it is, a medicine may turn out to be harmful for a person. Then the government officials—most of whom do not believe in written prayers anyhow, possibly not even in God—would come and hold me responsible, saying, "Why did you tell him to eat this? Are you perhaps a doctor?" But, essentially, the medicines of this book are the same as those of the doctor.

From what do the written prayers derive their efficacy?

From God, of course, not from these letters on a piece of paper. It is like going into the house of God and imploring Him; it's an invocation of God. Its efficacy comes from God. But it also depends on the person himself. If he strongly wishes to come to you and have a prayer written, it will be efficacious. It's a matter of desiring it. If I desire to come to you and get a medicine, this medicine will do me good.

But people say your prayers are efficacious because you have what they call "efficacy of breath."

There are several men here who can write prayers. But when people come to me and have a prayer written, it is efficacious. I don't know why. God gives me efficacy. We can't say why this is so. I think it is the people's faith which carries me; that is, if I strongly believe, for example, that the medicine you give me has healing power and I take it, I will get well. Even if it is a bad medicine, I will get well. When someone is afraid while jumping across an irrigation channel, his foot will land in the water; if he is not fearful, he will get across all right. With faith it's the same thing.

But is it also related to your own faith?

Yes; I have to say, "Oh God, they want this from me, but I cannot do it. I am only writing something. God, they want this from You, not from me." This is the right belief. Efficacy of breath rests on right belief. Also, it depends on right conduct. For example, I never wish evil to anybody. Even if someone is my enemy, I do not wish him to suffer harm. If he hurts me, I'll say, "It lies with God; I have nothing to do with him."

And there is one more thing: you must never make a du'a' to produce discord and ill-will between people, like one to make a quarrel between a husband and wife. If you want your soul to be saved, never make such prayers. Written prayers are like guns. Guns are made for enemies, not friends; if you shoot your friend with it, it's wrong. Or like fire: your eyes see the fire; but if the fire enters your eyes, they'll be burned. Thus, there are good du'a' as well as bad ones. If you mix them up and do them both, it's bad, it's sinful, it will harm you, it wipes out the merits you gained from writing the good du'a', for a single bad thing wipes out a hundred good things. But evil has to exist, too: if there was no evil, would you be able to discern the good?

Is it possible to put these bad du'a' to some good use?

Sometimes yes. For example, your son wants to marry an unbeliever and you realize that if he did so, he, too, would become an unbeliever. You do not wish this to happen and have a du'a' written to make him want her no longer and come back. If you were to tell him outrightly not to marry her, he would quarrel with you. So you avoid this. In this case it is not sinful to make such a du'a'.

But never must they be made to create discord between your own people. If I were to write such du'a', the good ones would no longer be efficacious. God would no longer give healing. He wouldn't listen to the invocations of the du'a' I am writing. It is like if I went to someone and borrowed some money promising to give it back after ten days, but then didn't: if I asked him for money again, he wouldn't give me any. Thus the efficacy of the written prayers depends on my own faith, as well as on the faith of the person himself. The faith of that person must be in accord with me. My own faith must be in accord with the Lord.

But lastly it is the will of God. Lastly, when someone is not getting well, it is because the Lord wants to take him away, because his life has ended. If God wants to, He will make a person well—whatever the doctor and whatever the prayer may be—and if He doesn't, He won't do it. Look,

when one of the great men gets ill, a hundred doctors are brought to him—
to no avail, while someone else may become ill in the wilderness and get
well.

*Is the efficacy of a written prayer dependent on the person's moral
behavior?*

No, it may be that God wants an evil-doer to die so that others may
not learn evil from him. But it is also possible that an evil-doer may live
longer than a good person, or that a good person may be taken away by
God earlier so that he won't suffer. No, it's not a matter of good and evil.
Whoever he may be, if he implores God, God will help. The Lord doesn't
take vengeance this way. His works are not vengeance, but mercy and love.
If one has done wrong, he will be punished on the Last Day, when all men
will come alive again and judgment will be passed on them. It is written
that the prophet Esdras once doubted that the bodies of people can come to
life again. So God made him sleep for 300 years, until his body and everything around him had decayed. Then God woke him up and, opening first
his eyes, let him witness how his own body, his donkey, and the tree to
which it was tied, came into being again. Thus He showed him that He has
the power to make the bodies of men alive again on the Last Day. On that
day all people will be judged; then they will be taken to heaven or hell,
according to their deeds.

So there is no punishment in this world?

Oh yes, there is. Not all sins go into the next world. Some have to be
paid for back here—even if it is by the person's offspring. If I go to your
house and steal something, someone else has to come to my house, or the
house of my son, and steal from me. This has really happened, that someone who oppressed and harmed other people later had to suffer evil in this
world. We have seen it. These are things that show us that what the religion
says really exists, that God exists. So does the dreaming show us. When we
sleep we see ourselves in other places, far away: this is to show us that there
exists a soul and that this body is only its dress—otherwise the dreaming
wouldn't be needed.

Don't dreams also show us things that are about to come?

Certainly they do. This is proven. For example, if one dreams of
losing a front tooth it means that a close relative will die. Being attacked by
a dog means someone will start a quarrel with you. Seeing a gun or sword
means a child will be born. But dreams have significance only when the
mind of the person is at ease; otherwise, when his mind is worried or
preoccupied with something or restless, as in fever, they mean nothing.
Also, there is a relationship with the time of the dreams. Dreams in the

middle of the night come into effect after a long time, half a year or so later, whereas what you dream in the early morning you may see happening the very same day.

The evil a dream portends can be warded off—at least if it concerns yourself. If it concerns others, like the death of a relative, I don't know. According to the rules of the Imāms and the Prophet you have to give six kilogram of wheat, or its equivalent, to a poor person, and nobody must be told about it. That's the purpose of such dreams: that we shall remember God and be generous to the poor.

Thus, generosity is another way to deal with diseases and misfortunes?

Definitely so. The principle is this: if you have mercy on others, God will have mercy on you. In case of a serious disease, I even advise people to make an animal sacrifice (*khūn-rīzī*) and give the meat to the poor. This can be done in two ways. Either one can keep part of the meat for oneself and send the rest to six or seven needy households, or one doesn't keep anything for oneself, cuts the whole animal in seventy-two pieces, puts them into the skin and, without looking, takes one after the other out while announcing the name of the person to whom it should be sent. If these diseases and misfortunes did not exist, nobody would think of God. They come about so that man fears God, that he remembers God.

What about the evil eye and the talk of people?

The evil eye is the most dangerous of all things. It can bring harm and damage to anything: an animal, a house, a tool, a rug, a child. It makes people ill and causes them to have accidents, but it doesn't make one insane as some believe. It differs from person to person. There are some whose evil eye is so strong that when it hits something, this will die instantly and no written prayer can protect against it. We had one such person here in the village; he died recently. When he happened to look at a cow saying, "This is a good cow," the cow would drop dead. In this way he even caused damage to his own possessions.

The evil eye comes from avarice (*bukhl*), as when one says, "This man earns a salary!" while another simply says, "He works hard; may God give it to him." No matter how much the second person might say, "What a good house!" it would have no evil effect because his attitude is good. But the evil eye also comes from pleasure and happiness (*khushī*). Anything that strikes your eyes as sweet and pleasant, that you feel pleased with and happy about, may become afflicted. When a child gets sick, it is mostly due to the evil eye of the father and mother. The child smiles, they are happy and pleased, they feel joy, they love it, it is sweet to them. So they cast the evil eye onto their own child. And it is also hereditary. The people who have it strongest in this village and from whose evil eye people safeguard their animals and possessions—their fathers had it, too.

The talk of the people (*zabān mardum*) is something different. This doesn't come from any particular person but from being talked about by the people in general, as when they say, "He has built a house," or, "He has bought a car," or, "He has five sons." This is bad. It has a very strong effect. It is also said, "You can go through the fire of bullets, but never through the fire of tongues."

For protection against the evil eye there is a written prayer and a ritual, but if you are afraid that the evil eye might be cast on something, simply say three times *"Allah-hu akbar"* and it won't do any harm. Against the talk of the people, however, the best thing is giving alms (sadaqah), especially when you get something, and to remember God always and in everything. If you do not forget God, the talk of the people won't affect you.

You said insanity is not due to the evil eye?

No, insanity has different causes. It may come from the belly, from a cold, from fear, or from the jinn—from these four. Most cases of insanity come from the belly, either through overeating or eating food that does not agree with you. When a person overeats, his intestines fail to work and this affects his head. The remedy consists of shaving the head, making small incisions, and putting on a medicine made from lentils and the head of a chicken. When a person's condition is due to eating food that does not agree with his disposition, he has to follow a food regimen; otherwise his condition will get worse and he may end up vomiting blood. He must eat no "cold" food, like goat meat and sour things, and nothing that causes gases and indigestion. If his family takes care of him and only gives him the right kind of food and at the proper times, he will get well soon. But mostly they let him eat indiscriminately simply because he wants to. A cold may bring about insanity when it affects the head of a person and causes it to dry up. For this kind there exists a special medicine; written prayers would be useless.

As to fear, a person may become insane when he goes, for example, into the mountains at night and imagines something and becomes intensely afraid. For this type there is a written prayer. If, however, a person in such a state of intense fear happens to eat something sour, his condition may get so bad that it is incurable.

The type of insanity caused by jinn is rather rare, and the reason why it becomes very bad in some cases is only that the person eats indiscriminately. If he kept to a regimen his condition would be much lighter. To cure it there are written prayers and medicines. These latter are taken from a book by Sulaymān to whom the jinn told exactly how to recognize diseases caused by them and what to use as medicines. Certain cases are, however, incurable and I tell people so. Nevertheless, they go to prayer-writers in other villages who claim to have an efficacious du'ā', and pay as much as 500 toman for it. Of course, it doesn't help.

Why should the jinn afflict a person at all?

If they did not exist, nobody would remember God. It is because of them that we say, "In the name of God, the merciful and compassionate." If they didn't exist, people would say, "Nature has made everything; there is no God." There are many places where people do not say, "In the name of God," where they do not believe in God, but, instead, worship something they have made themselves. A god that is made by men: is this God? We consider God someone who has the power over earth and heaven and who has made this our body from a drop of semen. Some say, nature has made it this way. These do not realize that this cannot be so. Is a car made by nature, or an engineer? This house has a builder and heaven should have no builder? These 160 veins in our body: who has made them? God has made everything.

Do the jinn also give gifts (bahrah) to people?

Rarely they do. As far as I can remember there was only one man from another village who was given such a gift. He had a brother lying wounded from a gunshot in our village and travelled here to visit him. On the road he met someone who gave him a piece of bread and said, "Take this and eat it." He put it into his bag, but as he walked on there was a man from our village on the road asking for some bread and he gave it to him. So this man ate it and after he came back here he became fairly wealthy.

What does this mean?

It means that God who has created us will give us our daily bread, be it through our hard work or whatever. He cannot give no livelihood at all. You see it yourself. One is just sitting around, whereas another, like myself, is working very hard. Of course it's better to work hard and the Prophet also says so, but, as it is, we are both getting by.

Nevertheless there is poverty!

What is needed for one's daily sustenance is given by the Lord. One man cultivates his land and seven or eight people are living off it, whereas another, cultivating as much land and working as hard but having only two people to feed, is still not getting anywhere. This you have to understand: God is giving everyone a livelihood.

But what about that poor cripple who goes around begging?

In this way the Lord shows us that He gave us hands, that He gave us feet, that He gave us eyes; and that we could be like this man and he could be like us. No, it is not an injustice to him, and you cannot ask why it's he and not you. That's an example He gives us in this world so that we may know the value of our hands and feet; so as to show me and you that He could make us that way too. If this man wasn't this way, would we know the value of our hands and feet? If there were no poor, would we know the value of the things we have?

Some people here call you a dervish because of the efficacy of your written prayers and the morality of your way of life.

No, I am only the child of a dervish. My father was a dervish. I am trying to be one, but I am not making it. I have greed, passions, the desire to get more. I am not getting there. To be a dervish means not to cause harm to others, not to steal, not to be greedy, not to be preoccupied with plans for tomorrow or what to do or where to go. He must work hard—those who do not work hard and go around begging are not true dervishes—but he must not worry as to what will happen tomorrow and how this will work out and how that will work out. He must trust that God, who created us, will provide. A dervish is one who is entirely unconcerned with what he shall eat or drink or wear. Whatever happens, he will say, "Be it so," unperturbed, seeing day passing and night coming, day passing and night coming, in expectation of death. And, above all, a dervish has the true love, the love that consumes, the love that never becomes satisfied. Sa'dī, Hafiz, Rumi: these had the true love.

The real dervishes can see divine mysteries. They can see things we cannot see. They see, for example, what will happen tomorrow. But they cannot say it: if they said it, it would be harmful for them. If we, however, saw the future, we could not take it. A parable says that when a child is being born and sees this world, it says, "Why should I come out? The world I have here is much better than the world out there." So if I saw what is going to happen tomorrow—for example, if I saw that I shall die tomorrow—I won't be able to work anymore. But in this way I don't know when I shall die, and say to myself, "I shall live forever" and apply myself to my work. But the real dervishes know their hour. For example, if the Imām Husayn had not looked into his future, he would not have gone and offered himself as a target for his enemies. He saw the future and knew what was going to happen.

The method of becoming a dervish is first of all to do good, not to wish evil to anybody, not to steal, not to lie, and to worship God. A poem says: "Through worship you cannot become God or a Jesus, the Spirit of

God, but you can become a Moses, the one who spoke to God." But certainly it is not a matter of saying a zikr, of repeating endlessly, "*Ya-Allah, Ya-Allah,*" or sitting there and saying as one breathes in and out, "*Ya-hu, ya-hu.*" That wouldn't work. I may be doing that and yet be a thief or drink wine or do wrong. Those who are practicing this, meeting in their convents (*khāngāh*) in the cities and going around begging, are dervishes only by appearance. They think that by saying, "We are dervishes," they become dervishes. I will tell you a story. Once in the time of Shāh 'Abbās a man presented himself at the court claiming to be a prophet. Shāh 'Abbās, who was a great dervish, took him to a precipice and, making it appear to him as being only a meter deep, told him to step down. The man, imagining that it was only a meter deep, did so and fell 100 meters. At that Shāh 'Abbās said, "This is how you shall recognize a prophet: if one cannot even see what is in front of his own feet, how can he claim to be a prophet?"

Do you see any change in the faith of the people?

Yes, the belief of the people was better in the past. Belief means to truly live by the rules of the religion. This was better in the past. Now more people are coming to the celebrations in the mosque, but that doesn't mean anything. For we can see that the Mullah himself, who is preaching it, doesn't practice what the Prophet has told us. It's because of him that I do not go to the mosque. My father used to say that in the next world seventy mills are being driven by the blood of the mullahs.

In regard to the prayer-writing there isn't much difference between then and now. The prayers people always have been coming for were mostly prayers for their children, especially prayers against the evil eye and to cure diseases. These they want now about as much as they did before. As I have said, however, I am no longer telling them the medicines for the diseases. For those I tell them to go to the doctor.

10

The Mystic: The Secrets of Control

The Mystic is a peasant in his mid-forties with a large family of ten children. Although he owns a good-sized herd and a fair amount of land and occasionally works as a carpenter, his standard of living is just somewhat over the bare subsistence level. Because of his strained economic situation he feels compelled to involve his children heavily in his agricultural activities. The two eldest sons did not attend school at all but had to take over shepherding for him at an early age, thereby making it financially possible for at least the younger of his very talented children to get some formal education.

Bright, introspective and somewhat literate, the Mystic has a consuming interest in deeper meanings of existence. His preoccupation with spiritual matters, a guarded secretiveness about his thoughts and knowledge, and a tendency to keep himself apart from the others make him appear somewhat strange in the eyes of his fellow villagers. (1971/76).

When I asked you about the "road" five years ago, you said you couldn't talk about it.

Yes, because I wasn't sure how serious you were. "Matters of the heart must only be entrusted to the People of the Heart," we say. Now that you are on the search yourself, I can tell you some of it, though not its essence; this you have to find for yourself. You have to work on it and ask Ali, peace be upon him, to be your patron. You are doing well in your search anyway. If I had known then what you know now, I would have arrived earlier.

But five years ago you seemed to know a lot already.

I knew something, yes, but I didn't have the inner eye. For twelve years I was running after it. I ran and ran but I didn't know the road. What a master I knew at that time! The best teacher! But I didn't know how to ask. He came here several times and told me to follow the road and what the world is like and so on. I didn't know what he was talking about, I didn't understand the meaning of his very words. Oh, good God!

How did you then acquire the inner eye?

Someone told me the zikr. I'll show it to you in the Qur'ān. . . . Here it is:

Amman yujību 'l-muztarra azā da‘āhu va yakshifu 's-sū' [Surely He is the best who answers the prayer of the afflicted and relieves his distress. Sura 27/62.]

This is from the sura "The Ant." You have to recite it on forty-two Wednesday nights, repeating it over and over again. If you recite it beside a stream of water, it is even better. On the forty-second night, or maybe even earlier, by the grace of God, suddenly a child or an old man or a youth or someone will come towards you. He will say, "This has merit, this is good," and you have to ask, "What is it good for?" Then he will say something, and you will recognize him immediately. Whoever knows the inner secrets of your heart, that is he, he himself. Then you have reached the one you have to reach: Ali, peace be upon him! Then your inner eye will be opened.

Suddenly you realize that there is something in your heart. You look and see—oh, oh, how great, how great! There is a whole world, the life! Then you turn to the road. Your past, your life, your situation appear in front of you like in a mirror, and you think, "Ah, alas, why haven't I discovered this earlier? Where have I been? What have I been doing? What life have I led? Where is this road and where have I been going?" Suddenly one wishes not to have this body at all.

Your heart has to fill with love. No other love has to be there except the love of God and Ali. Then you have arrived. Then you will see for yourself whatever world, whatever place you want to see. There is no need to go to other places to see what it is like. You see everything, everything, everything. This is the greatest pleasure. Wonderful, wonderful, wonderful! No pleasure is greater than that! But whatever you see—about your children, your father, the world, whatever it be—do not say anything to anybody. Nobody must understand what is on your mind, nobody at all.

So it was by means of this zikr that your inner eye was opened?

Yes, this zikr is like the fire that one lights to cook food. If there is no fire, food doesn't get cooked. Yes, this is the zikr that lets you reach the goal. Do you see these pencil marks beside the sura? These are the tallies I made each Wednesday night four years ago. There are forty-one. That was when I arrived.

I have a lot of grey hair, haven't I? But not so my wife; hers is like that of a child. If a woman who has born ten children looks as young as a child, but I have grey hair, what does it mean? It means that her body and her mind are at ease, whereas I am burdened with two hardships. One you can see for yourself: you see how hard I am working. The other is a secret hardship—it is even greater than the first.

What is this hardship?

The secret one? Sleeplessness. It is worse than anything else. I find very, very little sleep. So my body is being worn out faster. For six entire years I have to bear this hardship.

Who told you to do this?

I myself agreed to it. I promised that during these six years I would never be inactive, never forget about my work, never let myself go, take it easy, go to sleep carefree. No, only fear of Him shall be in my heart and at night I shall say a special prayer that has to be said at night, away from the people. Sometimes I may doze off at midnight, sometimes just before dawn, sometimes not at all. But I want nobody to know this, so I get up quickly and go after my work.

To whom did you promise this?

To that holy existence, Ali, peace be upon him. It is a contract. When I arrived on that day, he said, "What do you want, what do you consent to?" I said that I wished he would not conceal himself from me for six years, and I agreed that in this period I would attend to my work, provide for my children, and accept the affliction of sleeplessness. After these six years, *insha'llah,* I shall be at ease. This was the agreement. Now four years have passed and my whole body has been worn out. Two more years I have to go. Then I shall receive what is due to me: no more hardship. In a quiet corner I shall sit and be at ease. . . . But then again . . . maybe I've been deceived in all this.

The hardships I have had to endure! If I told you, I don't know whether you would believe it. There are all kinds of trials, and when God wants to try a person, He does it by means of what that person desires most. Do you know how He tried me? He tried me with sexual desire, with the finest women of the most beautiful beauty. They would suddenly come close to me—this happened both in dreams and in reality—and begin to beguile me. Oh good God! I am nobody! I seized the skirt of Ali, peace be upon him, and implored him to take these temptations away from me. After the fourth or fifth time they ended.

You know how this is: you may be travelling someplace, or a guest may happen to come to your house, or someone comes to your house in all privacy and then starts to be very enticing and alluring to you. If you understand what is going on and you have the power to control yourself and resist passion, then you will win. Sure, these women wanted to seduce me. But why? To try me; for that purpose they were sent—for a trial. Such trials come without fail, absolutely without fail. God has to try a person from all sides. If you go and buy something, don't you first look at it carefully? In the same way God has to examine each person to see whether he is worthy or not.

Are you now practicing a zikr?

Yes, but this one is different from the one I told you, the one which you recite to arrive there. You know the zikr where you say "hu" as your breath goes in, and "Allah" as it comes out? Well, my zikr is of this kind. It is always with me, wherever I am, whether I am awake or asleep, at work or at ease.

Mustn't you sit down in quiet to practice this zikr?

No, sitting down won't do. The day Hazrat-i Adam was seduced by the devil and driven out of paradise, God said, "Go away, and neither you nor your offspring shall ever be at ease." Since then we have had to work and toil and sweat. If I didn't work, my children would have no bread to eat. But believe me, in the midst of all toiling, in the midst of all hardships we can do the zikr even better, much better. Only if you want your inner eye to work, to see, then you sit down. But not for this zikr. You may be at work, you may be in the mountains, you may be asleep, you may be awake, you may have any thought, but your zikr mustn't be lost; don't let go of your zikr! Now we are walking, our eyes watch the road, we are talking, but the zikr is with me, in the core of my heart. Of course, you have to learn practicing your zikr. It's like learning how to read. When you began reading, how much trouble did you have with a single word! But now you can read without effort and under any condition. In this search you go slowly. When you have gained a bit, you move higher up, step by step.

You can be sure, the Westerners, who take great pains in developing industry so that people can live in ease, will discover the road sooner than most of us. Once they have found it, they will not only be able to produce an even better industry, but also find a thousand times more pleasure. For this is the best road, the really true road. It gives you the greatest pleasure, immense pleasure.

Is this the benefit of going this road?

When the Sustainer has shown you this road and lifted the veil from your eyes, everything will be at your fingertips. Then you will come to understand this world and the mysteries of God. You will see beyond the outside appearances of things and discover their inner essence. When you have entered this state of seeing, oh, oh, oh! If the world were to catch fire, it would be nothing. There is only pleasure, and you go, and keep on seeing and seeing. But what you see must never be told. You may see that a misfortune is coming upon a person, or that a flood is about to come and destroy a summer camp, or that one is oppressing somebody, but you mustn't say anything; you mustn't have anything to do with it. If you have the inner eye and you see that a man of God is in distress, simply say, "Oh Sustainer, have mercy!" If you have efficacy of breath, your prayer will be heard.

When you have found it, then wherever you may be—far or near—we shall be as close together as we are now and talk with each other perfectly easily. Wherever you may be, it would be as if you were here. In this way I communicate with my teacher although he lives in another village. Whenever I need his advice, I get in contact with him. He knows much more than I do. He has reached a much higher state.

Those who have reached such a state understand all things, everything. . . . They see everything in this world as well as the next. They see so much, that they do not want this world at all. They have nothing to do with this world: if they get ill, it does not concern them; if the world progresses, it does not concern them; if another's possessions prosper, it does not concern them. They have nothing to do with anybody. They may be hungry—so they are hungry; they may die—so they die; they may have wealth or no wealth—it makes no difference. They may lose all they have, yet feel no grief at all because they understand that these things are of no consequence. Their heart is not attached to this world. They have completely abandoned the world. That's the road of being a dervish.

How is this with you?

My children want to live. I have to provide them with what they need. God has created this land so that we bring forth its riches for the children. In fact, the care for the children and the hard work for their future is a great pleasure. Thus, I agree to have these worldly possessions so that they may be provided for. But as for myself, I may have plain bread to eat or a full meal, it makes no difference. I need nothing. Death may come, hardship may come, anything may come, it makes no difference to me at all.

When my wheat crop failed this year, you asked me if God would give me a better crop in another field instead. Sure He will, absolutely. He does it every year. But you mustn't be concerned about this. You know what alone is necessary? You only have to do your hard work and ask God to provide a livelihood for those you are responsible for. Only this is necessary. You mustn't be concerned whether you'll get a livelihood or not, or whether you'll get it from this field or that.

Thus, worldly possessions are needed, they are useful, they are good; but they have to be spent in the ways ordered by the religion, that is, for your children, for your kinsmen, for those in need, for those who rely on you. "What is yours is part of others'," we say. And never must you attach your heart to them. You have to ask God for help and say, "Oh Sustainer, I don't want these things. I want the true road. I only want you." Nothing must separate man from the love of God. If you love a thing very much, God will destroy it.

How about acting against nature, like abstaining from food. Can you in this way ward off evil or get a wish granted?

No, eating has nothing to do with it. But when your inner eye has been opened and you have efficacy of breath, you will obtain everything you wish from the Lord. In a danger you only have to say, "Oh Sustainer, for the sake of the holy existence of Ali, peace be upon him, remove this danger!" That's all. Even in the greatest danger you will be safe. You need not fear. He knows about it and will come to your help, unfailingly.

How does one get efficacy of breath?

One gets it when one arrives. The inner eye and this breath go together. It is said, "One who knows the secret of making his breath a 'Wind of Yemen'⁹ can turn a stone into a brilliant ruby." That means, this breath is like the wind of Yemen. Whoever knows all about it and knows how to use it has such power that he could blow over this stone and change it into gold and ruby.

Take our Shah. He is exactly a true dervish and very, very good. If he were not, the Sustainer would not have given him such bounties. Look how much well-wishing he has for his whole country and what pains he takes to develop it: this is exactly because of his being a dervish. For the same reason he has never been hurt when they tried to kill him. His efficacy of breath is very great. As long as his breath is one with God, the Beloved, and his zikr is on his mind, he is perfectly safe. One hundred guns could be aimed at him and they wouldn't go off: the powder wouldn't catch fire. He doesn't need a *tīrband* to spell-bind a bullet, or any other du'ā'.

But you are using such du'ā', aren't you?

I used to. In this road you go step by step, haste is not good. My teacher guided me in everything. Whenever I needed a du'ā', he gave it to me and told me how to recite it. Oh, I had one du'ā', that was so good! It was to prevent all kinds of evil. Once we were in a summer camp in the mountains when it rained and a flood came down the valley. The people were paralyzed with fear. I recited this prayer, and the flood didn't reach us at all. It was because of the efficacy of this du'ā'. But I don't have it any longer. I gave it to someone who needed it.

Do you now use another one instead?

Well, by now I have passed that hard part. Now, when, for example, I am talked about by the people—which, as you know, is very dangerous—I merely say, "Oh God, You know what to do with them." But when I greatly desire God's help, I say this zikr:

> *Qul rabbī yā Fātimah adkhilnī mudkhala sidqin va akhrijnī mukhraja sidqin va aj'al lī min ladunka sultānan nasīra* [Say: Lord, oh Fatima, let me enter in truth and come out in truth and help me with your power. Sura 17/80, with accretion of "oh Fatima."].

And I add, "By Your greatest name, grant me this!" This zikr calms one's mind. Right after you have said it, you will feel relieved. With it you may ask for His help in an illness, in distress, to ward off evil, to catch a bus when you are late—whatever. God will grant you the wish for sure, absolutely for sure. The zikr may have no efficacy with you right now because you haven't reached that state yet, but it's good if you have it.

Five years ago you told me how you once warded off a misfortune that you had foreseen in a dream by giving alms to the poor, wasn't it?

Yes, I remember it well. I went with my son into the mountains to get firewood. The night before I had had a bad dream. I cannot tell you what the dream was—those things mustn't be told—but it meant danger and misfortune. In the morning I gave five toman to a woman who lives in dire poverty, so that God may ward off the evil. Then we set out. I wondered what was going to happen. We went to a place where there is plenty of firewood and started to work—I at one spot and my son at another one a bit lower down. After a while he called me and said he needed my help. So I stopped working and walked down. As I did so, my son started to walk up towards me. At this moment a rock came down the cliff—you know how they crack loose from the ice in winter. Oh Sir, only this Creator knows and only He alone! As this rock came bouncing down the cliff, it split into two. One of them, God is my witness, hit the ground exactly where I had been working and the other where my son had been. Then I knew. Only I knew and God knew. The people working nearby came and said, "There is no god except God!" I had to laugh. Then I said to my son, "Come on and work!" I knew that God had warded it off. This didn't happen because I and my son had left our places by chance, but because He wanted it that way and to waive the misfortune.

Whatever there is signifies something: it has a deeper meaning. When your inner eye has been opened and you see this meaning, you have won. Those people who simply think that whatever happens just happens don't know what is going on. They are like animals. But one who recognizes the signs and knows their portent knows infallibly. When you have a dream, you will immediately ascertain the circumstances, and you will know what it means. It will inevitably come true. I have seen this with my own eyes, and it is absolutely impossible that it be not so.

But if I were to have such a dream now, the misfortune would be warded off if I simply asked for it. Formerly, giving alms was necessary. Now what matters is to be well-esteemed, to have "breath," that is, to know Ali, peace be upon him. Today I would say to him, "You are held in high esteem with the Sustainer; for the sake of your honor, make it all right!" And it would be made all right; it would be warded off. Oh, how great! Yes, today is very, very different from those times.

Does this mean that you can ward off any misfortune?

If it is the right thing to do, yes; that means, if it does not interfere with the will of God. If God wants it that way, you must not do anything; you cannot do anything. This year my wheat crop failed. This had to be so. God wanted the wheat to grow to a certain height and then to send a pest. Likewise, if something is a person's destiny, you mustn't interfere. Everyone has to fulfill his destiny. You asked me why I didn't prevent my daughter from marrying that young man although I knew she would be unhappy in his family. I did tell her not to do it. I said, "Child, they have deceived you; it will not work out." But she said, "It's none of your business." When I saw that she would not listen, I did not interfere with her. Because she herself wanted it, I consented. It would not have been right to force her. The day she was born this was written down to be her destiny, and I cannot change it.

But how do you know whether God wants something, or it is a person's destiny?

How do I know?! These pains I am taking, these nights without sleep, this solitude in the mountains, this love: what should all this be for? It is exactly for knowing this, is it not? If I didn't know that, well, what else should I know? I just know; I see.

Do you also see the meaning or purpose of a misfortune?

Absolutely. But it must not be told. I know exactly why this happened with my wheat this year, but I can't tell you. You have to see it yourself. Or you mentioned the war in Lebanon and felt pity. If you had the inner eye, you would see where fundamentally they did wrong so that God brought this hardship down upon them.

God inevitably exacts retribution in this world, absolutely inevitably. If a person does something wrong, God be my witness, you will see that before long God makes him lame or mute or insane or sends some other misfortune on him. The Prophet said that for stealing a person will be made to pay in three ways. For one thing, he will get into a state of want and need. For another, he will fall into ill repute. And finally, on the Last Day, he will have to stand shamefaced in the presence of the Prophet.

Take the family my daughter married into. They deceived her. With sweet talk and lies they made her get very attached to them. Her husband's mother even got a written prayer for that purpose. Yes, such things exist. But since the marriage they have been treating her badly. They harass her and find fault with her for no good reason. Now—did you hear the latest?—a dispute has broken out between her husband's father and brother. Very bad fighting is going on between them. They are suffering such retribution that it is burning their fathers in hell. This happened precisely because they violated our rights. I have nothing against them. I only expect my rights to be acknowledged.

Five years ago you told me this daughter was cheated out of her wages by a carpet weaver for whom she had worked and you said you hoped that God would oppress him the same way as he had wronged you. Did it happen?

That same fall he came here and I asked him to pay what he owed us. He said he had lost 30,000 toman in a business enterprise. I said, "Wait till, inshā'llah, you will suffer the next blow." After that he had a car accident and broke his arm. I went to visit him, and he said, "Clear your heart of your misgivings toward me." I said, "I don't have anything to do with you, but be afraid of the sudden wrath of God."

Did you hear that a few days ago the doctor had all his things stolen? This was a consequence of my efficacy of breath. He had written an attestation that my daughter's father-in-law had some broken ribs—which was a lie—and it was implied that I had done it. They had bribed him with 400 toman to write this. That his things were now stolen was not simply God's retribution: with my efficacy of breath I had asked the Creator to punish him.

What about poverty? Is this also God's punishment?

No, this is the people's own fault. Whose fault should it be otherwise? It's all because of their own deeds. Yes, even in the case of the man who was born blind. If he were seeing, he would bring ruin and trouble on the whole creation. God prevented this on the day he was born. If he had been given eyes, believe me, maybe the greatest evils would have resulted.

Have you suffered any punishment yourself?

Punishment, no. There are hardships, suffering, anguish, as when a child gets very ill. These are trials. God wants to see whether I am worthy or not. But, by the favor of the Sustainer, I have seen no punishment. I am not doing anything that would deserve punishment. When I understand that someone has misgivings toward me, I go to him and say, "What's wrong? What's the problem?" I have nothing against him, absolutely nothing. You saw it the other day, when my daughter's father-in-law sent a boy to ask us for help with his harvest. I sent him my son. I had to help him. I mustn't remember these past events at all. When my daughter's husband comes back from his work in the city and sees how much help we have given his father, he will be ashamed and take the side of my child. I have to dismiss everything that has happened from my heart.

Do you, on the basis of your insights, also understand the nature of diseases?

Yes, certainly. You saw it yourself the other day when my neighbor became unwell and people crowded into his room and cried and wailed and said he had died. I came and felt his pulse and said, "What's the matter? There is nothing to worry about. He is all right." I knew exactly what had come over him. As you know, he soon got well again.

Once I was working in another village when I learned that someone was ill here. I came back as quickly as I could and found my oldest daughter lying here without life, without any life at all. The people were wailing and said she was dead. I paid no heed to them. I took her to the doctor. He said she would not make it to the clinic in town. I laughed. I fully understood her condition. I took her on the bus all the way to Shiraz. For six days and nights she was in intensive care on an automatic respirator. Every morning I went there, and no, she hadn't died, she was still there. Then, on the sixth day, by the power of God, she came to life again.

So you are not using medicines to cure diseases?

Why, yes, sure I do. We have the best medicines in the book of Luqmān. Do you know how this book came about? I'll tell you. A wise man once gave a sultan some powder and told him to put it into his bread and eat it. The sultan gave it to his baker who made a loaf of bread with it, but was careless enough to burn that loaf. So he baked another loaf for the sultan and gave the burned one to a poor orphan boy by the name of Luqmān, who ate it. That night, after lying down to sleep, this boy suddenly heard voices from the earth saying, "We are happy that you put your head to rest on us." And in the morning he heard the voices of the plants. He understood what they were saying and he could talk with them. Do you perhaps think that these plants and animals cannot talk? They can as much as we can and they converse with their Creator. Luqmān spent his life getting to know their wisdom. He asked, for example, each plant what diseases it could cure, how it had to be prepared for a medicine, and so on. All this wisdom he wrote down in a book. After his death parts of this book were lost and other parts were acquired by the foreigners. It's on the basis of this book that the foreigners built their science and could make such progress.

From this book we have wonderful medicines, medicines that effectively cure and remove pain. If I come to an ill or injured person, I will first immerse myself in thought. Then, when I know that it is the right thing to do, that is, that it does not interfere with the works of God and my remedy is exactly the one that is needed, I will treat him. If a bone is broken, I will set it—as I did with my son's arm a few years ago—and if he is ill, I will give him a medicine, trying to put him back on his feet as soon as possible. But first you have to know whether this is the right thing to do or not. I am not—like most people—just fooling around, trying this and that without really knowing what is going on. That's useless. Either I myself know or I ask one who understands better. Now, for example, this other daughter of mine has something wrong with her leg that makes her limp. The way to heal this would be to take her to the hospital in Shiraz. But if I go, nobody will bring in my harvest and it will be destroyed. In this case I do not have the efficacy of breath to decide the right thing to do. But I do know the master who can decide. His efficacy is even greater than that of my teacher, and I will ask him when he comes here. If he tells me to take her to the city, I will do so; if he says no, I won't.

People tell me you can cure a certain skin disease with your saliva and that this is a gift from the jinn. Is this true?

Yes, an ancestress of mine received it from a jinn. She was working around the house one day when she noticed a child sneaking into the room to steal some food. The child's feet looked like donkey hoofs. Immediately she realized that this was a jinn's child and quickly threw an iron bracelet around his feet. That caught him. After a while his mother came for him. But my ancestress said she would set him free only if she got something in return. At that, the mother said, "Open your mouth!" As she did so, the jinn spat into it and said, "For seven generations your offspring shall have the gift to cure a *sawdā'*." A sawdā' is a dry spot on the skin of the face. When people bring their children to me with such a disease, I simply spread some saliva on it, and after one or two treatments the rash disappears. Of course, my brothers and sisters and other members of our family have the gift, too.

How about written prayers, du'ā'—do they cure diseases, too?

Sure they do. I have tried them out myself. Once, in a summer camp, another daughter of mine fell very ill. At that time I was not yet in the world of the "road." We had a prayer written for her by the Prayer-Writer. With this she got well very soon. The prayers of this prayer-writer are very good, that is, his efficacy of breath is very good. He did so many good things for our children! If there is need for a doctor, he tells us to take the child to the doctor. If there is need for a written prayer, he writes it and— for whatever illness it may be—it will be very efficacious. But there is something better than written prayers, just as there are cars and airplanes. Both serve the transportation of travellers, but the airplane is, of course, better. When those who have the greatest efficacy of breath want to invoke God's help for someone, they have only to ask God for it in a short prayer—that's enough. Calling on the Sustainer they could blow over this piece of sugar, and the ill person who eats it would get well by the order of God.

What was the illness of your daughter?

It was caused by the fact that she has a spirit twin (*hamzād*) who did not get along with her. They were like water and fire. Everybody has such a jinn twin. If the two get along well with each other, nothing happens. But if they do not get along, this twin disturbs the mind of the person and he becomes odd. This was the condition the written prayer cured. But I can't tell you why they were not getting along in the first place. That's a secret. If only you could see, then you would understand all this! Oh, there are so many things, such extraordinary things! But the only way to know them is to see them yourself. And you can see them, you can! When, inshā 'llah, you will arrive, you will see everything, everything!

Your daughter is exceptionally intelligent. She completed the first six grades of school in two years and got by far the highest marks in the teacher-training entrance exam. How do you explain this?

It is due to that first moment. Do you know what makes the character of a child this way or that? I'll tell you. It depends mainly on your disposition of mind at the time of intercourse. Whatever intent you form at that time, whatever design you have in your heart, that is exactly the way the child will be unfailingly. My daughter's intelligence is due to that. But it is only the people of religion who do this, not everyone. Most people are carried away by their passion and are unmindful as to what becomes of the child and his future. With my oldest son it was like this: My teacher came here one day and said to me, "God wants to give you a son. Over the next fifteen days form an intent, and after completing ritual bathing have intercourse. Then, after the boy has been born, behave toward him this way: always let he himself decide what he wants to do. He will know what is right." This is what I have been doing. Recently, as you know, he went to work in the city and I let him go. If he goes to a city, it is all right; if he remains here it is all right, too. Inshā 'llah, he will do well.

When we do not know the true road, we are like the blind. We just wander about, and wherever it takes us, it takes us. Most people are like this. They do not even think of looking for the right way. But when you have found the true road and are ready to follow it—don't be suddenly afraid to!—you will go straight ahead and get what you want. Once the Sustainer has lifted this veil from your eyes so that you can see the inner essence of all that exists, you have made it. Then you can leave this world alone and indeed you must do so. But when you are back in America and you have a friend you know well, and you understand that it would be good if he knew, you may show him the way.

11

The Old Hunter: Familiar of the Jinn

An old man of about sixty, the Old Hunter prefers to live in very modest circumstances and all by himself, which the villagers regard as somewhat eccentric. He was once a successful traditional surgeon in the village, setting fractures, dressing wounds, draining abscesses, removing bullets, and generally treating injuries from warfare and hunting. Moreover, he is famous for his unusual skills and knowledge in game hunting and for this reason is still called *Mīrshikār*, master of the hunt, a title which was also given to his father. But these are things of the past. Now that the people prefer the new clinic, hardly anybody calls on his surgical skills any longer and the large herds of wild goats and sheep, which had fascinated the tribesmen more than anything else, have disappeared from the mountain sides. Yet the lore of the mountain is still alive and he recounts it with the humble dignity and quiet authority of the old and knowledgeable. (1971/ 76).

The jinn who visit you at night, are they making you trouble?

No, no, they visit with me. They are friendly. They come because they like me and I like them. We are familiar, we are friends. For generations this has been so, from father to son, from father to son. There are two of them, a Muslim and an Unbeliever—but you mustn't tell this to anybody in the village. The Unbeliever has two big teeth in front, one above, one below, and, it looks like, one eye here in the middle. The Muslim is very beautiful and pleasant to look at. They come at two o'clock after midnight,

141

once in a week or two; they stay for a while, but talk little. More I cannot tell you. It is a secret between me and them that must not be revealed to others. Otherwise, they would punish me. I asked them if you could come and see them, but they said, "No, this is impossible; we must remain hidden and secret." Also, the Muslim said if they were to show themselves to someone not brave enough, he would die of fear. Only to those with whom they visited for generations, and who are strong and brave at heart, can they show themselves.

No, the jinn are not troubling me. But they will cause trouble to anybody who is doing them some harm, for example, if one shoots one of their herd-animals when they appear in the form of wild sheep and goats. This happened to my uncle. He went hunting one day and came across a herd of wild goats. Spotting a big buck of seven years among them, he stalked it and, when close enough, took careful aim with his muzzle-loader, and fired. At this moment, a greyhound sped across and the bullet grazed its nose. The buck was hit in the thigh and took off. My uncle took after it and suddenly found himself in a camp—a camp of jinn. They looked like people and had tents and everything exactly like we do. An old woman was taking care of the wound of the buck he had shot, and the greyhound's wound was being dressed too. Then the greyhound changed into a young man and said, "Why did you harm the buck of the old woman? It was the breeding buck of her herd!" At that, my uncle fainted. He was later found and brought to the village and died after three days.

How do you explain this?

The Unbelievers among the jinn take on the shape of various animals: cats, snakes, mountain pigeons, and also wild sheep and goats, our game animals. We call them game of Abū Jahl, while the real game we call game of Abraham. They look exactly like our game. The buck that my uncle shot was such an Abū Jahl. The greyhound was a Muslim jinn. He knew that the buck belonged to the old woman's herd and that a hunter who shot it would be doomed. When he saw that my uncle did not know this and wanted to shoot it, he felt pity for him, turned into a greyhound, and tried to cover the buck with his own body, ready to give his life for my uncle. He didn't succeed and, once the buck was wounded, he couldn't save my uncle anymore.

Thus, when they make us trouble, it is because we have harmed them, either by shooting them when they appear as game animals, or by killing them as snakes, or bothering them as cats, or hurting their children when pouring out hot ashes. Before we do such things as shooting game or killing a snake or pouring out ashes, we have to say, "In the name of God, the merciful and compassionate!" This will cause them to disappear. If we do not say this and hurt them, they will send misfortunes, accidents, troubles, diseases, or they exchange our children, or strike a person with insanity. In most cases there is no remedy for these afflictions; but a Sayyid in a nearby village has a written prayer with which he cures insanity caused by the jinn.

Also, the jinn dislike it when a hunter kills too many animals. My grandfather had to suffer a lot because of this. Once, when he was sick, they took him to the mountains. They changed him into a buck and a buck that he had once shot they turned into my grandfather. Then they threw him off a cliff so that he was all smashed up, and the buck in my grandfather's form came and set his foot on him, cut his head off, and skinned him. Then they roasted his flesh over the fire. This and similar things they did to him because he had killed game excessively.

Some say that all these things are lies, that there are no jinn. But how come? Their position and power is greater than ours. In the battle at Karbala their chief came to Imām Husayn and offered to fight for him, but the Imām said, "No, this would not be fair because you are invisible." Certainly, they too are creatures of God; God, it is written in the Qur'ān, has created seventy-two peoples. Right now the jinn are present in the room and, believe me, they hear everything we say.

Are they also good to us?

Sure, they give gifts. My grandfather had the gift of being a successful hunter. A jinn appeared to him one night and gave it to him. He never returned from a hunt empty-handed. Several men in the village are said to have become wealthy after receiving a gift from the jinn. There may be others, too. I don't ask the jinn to whom they gave gifts; that's none of my business.

But in my case you have seen it yourself. Remember the man who came the other day with a broken leg, and I set it. This is a gift. The people of the village come to me for this. They think I am good at it. But it is not I who is doing it. I say, "Oh God, I will set it, but I cannot do anything. Oh God, make him well." And He does. He gave me this gift.

God or the jinn?

First God, then the jinn. God gave it by way of that Muslim jinn He has sent to me. In the past, when I started to work as a mason, I used to stand on the wall of a house and say, "Oh God, give me the skills to become the best of all the masons here, so that people will be pleased with my work!" And it happened. This is a gift of God.

What about wealth? Would the jinn give it to you if you asked for it?

They would, but I don't want it. What should I want it for? If they gave it to me now—a donkey, a horse, a car—what should I do with it? Put it in the stable and feed it? No, I am living the life of a dervish. I do not want the world. I have given it up. If in the other world I shall find some mercy, it is better. That is eternal. This world is like that door: we came in through it and we shall go out through it again.

You see how I am living here: the house of a dervish, the poverty of this room, these clothes, the food I eat, the solitude. I have turned out my son, not in bad spirits, but I told him I am an old man and can't live with others anymore. And my wife is living at my son-in-law's. Especially now that the jinn are visiting me, it wouldn't do with other people around. Dervishdom means poverty; it means to renounce the world, the way this first and foremost dervish, Shāh Ni'matu'llāh has shown us. It means to be content, to be pleased—rather than desirous—when you see one who has something to eat together with his bread, or has a new shirt, and to say, "Thanks to God; God may give him more."

The basic principle is that the dervish knows he will die, that is, we all know it, but he is aware of it and renounces the world, he is content, he resigns himself, he has no desire, no passion for this world. The world is nothing, it is transitory, it has to vanish. Even if I built this house of gold, would it vanish or not? Since the time of Shāh 'Abbās, how many people have come and gone? What did you eat yesterday? One ate the best food, another bread: what difference does it make? Both are getting by, so or so, good or bad.

No, for me the world has no value. What pleasure does wealth have? If a hundred worlds belonged to me, what would it mean except hardship, except trouble, except worries, except sorrow; sorrow that my donkey has died, that my horse has died, that my car has turned over, that my airplane has crashed, that my radio has broken? "Do not amass the things of this world, so you may never need to regret them," says a poem. Now I don't have a donkey that may die or be stolen, leaving me to say, "Woe to me!" I don't have sheep that may get killed by a wolf, leaving me to say, "Woe to me!" I don't have a house that may burn down, leaving me to say, "Woe to me!" The point is this: the less one possesses the better it is. Ali, peace be upon him, could turn a mountain into gold by glancing at it and yet he worked in his garden from sunrise to sundown. And it is no small thing to mention the name of Ali, peace be upon him, because our Prophet said, "You cannot say Ali is God, nor can you say he is separate from God."

There remains your body. But this can be controlled. You have seen it: the opium smoking. It kills the body. Indeed, it has two effects. First, it kills the body, makes it numb, weak, relaxed, passionless. And second it brings on thoughts, ideas, insights into all things. The learned men recommend to smoke half a *misqāl* a day. Be it now more or less, it has made my body weak and void of sexual desire. People do not understand why I smoke opium. I tell them I have a stomach-ache and it is doing me good, so that they won't understand.

What good is it to renounce the world, to become a dervish?

First, it is for the next world. God will have mercy, give a good place and ease in the next world. And second, a dervish will have efficacy of breath, that is, his prayers will be efficacious. I told you the story of the dervish who had killed his sexual desire and was so content that he ate only one almond a day. The efficacy of his prayer was so great that the wish of anyone he interceded for was granted. For example, when a girl came and wished to get a good husband who wouldn't violate her rights, he merely said, "Oh God, give her a good husband!" and she got one.

We had a dervish with very great efficacy of breath living in a nearby village. He could summon the soul of a dead person to ask, for example, why he had killed himself, or what his other-worldly conditions were like. He and his forefathers had had interaction with the jinn—the way it has been in our family—and he was given prayers by them. People from all around came to have prayers written by him and every year he wrote a sīmband for the fields of our village. To have such efficacy of breath one must renounce the world, withdraw from the world, give one's wealth to the poor and do no evil; one must pray, worship, go towards God and be content and of pure heart. Then one's efficacy of breath will be great. But as a true Muslim one must never write those prayers that create ill-feeling and quarrels between people. Some do write such prayers, and these are also efficacious, but this is sinful, it is unbelief, it brings damnation.

Do you think you have such efficacy of breath?

There are by now a number of people in this village who, with the grace and blessing of God, I could bring back onto the right road. They had done something wrong out of ignorance and I pleaded with them and said, "Let it be; God will be pleased," and they did so. My words took effect. That is a gift.

No, I am not writing prayers. I do, however, make the damband, a prayer that makes a wolf unable to attack a herd. One speaks two verses of the Qur'ān over a pair of opened scissors and then blows on them and snaps them shut; that's the damband. Many people come to me for that. Do you see all these tied-up scissors and jack-knives over there on the wall and in the niche? These are damband I have made. The people for whom I made them left them here because on their way home they had to cross a stream or canal, and taking a damband across water would void it.

Doing these things for others also earns merit, doesn't it?

Absolutely; without any doubt. When I set the broken leg of that man, it earned merit. He wanted to give me money. But he has nothing. It would be sinful to take money from him. I felt pity for him. I didn't take it. For the sake of such acts God will show mercy and take a person to paradise.

If I had all the gold of this world, I couldn't take a bit of it with me when I die. But if I give it away to others, it earns merits—100% it does. If I help the unfortunate, the poor, the destitute, the hungry, naked, weak, old, and blind—either with my wealth or my actions—my pockets will be full on the Last Day. This heart has to have compassion for others. If it does, one will have the blessing of God in this world and salvation in the next. But if one has no pity and compassion, then no matter how often one will make the pilgrimage to Imām Rezā, and no matter how much one will give to Shāh Charāgh—it will be for nothing. One must not gather everything towards oneself. That's wrong. One has to share, as this wise man, Sa'dī—may I become his sacrifice—has said:

Do not draw everything towards yourself, like an adze.
Do not push the profit of your work away, like a plane.
Take a lesson in economics from the saw instead,
Draw some towards you, and some scatter away.[10]

God gave us two roads to go, the straight road and the crooked road. The straight road means to recognize God, to earn a lawful piece of bread, to help other people, and never to cause harm to others, that is, not to steal, to commit adultery, to hurt others, to speak badly about them, and so on—as the poem says: "Drink wine and burn pulpits, but do not harm other people." If you go this straight path, the Lord will be kind to you, give you well-being, health, honor in this world and salvation in the next; your death will be good, your burial will be good, your answers to Munkar and Nakīr will be good, and your place in the next world will be good. Our real place is there: a good place with fountains, meadows, splendor, the smell of perfume, good fruits, paradisical virgins, good things. This world is only temporary.

But if you go the crooked road of evil-doing, thieving, killing, adultery, lying, slandering, and those things, you will be punished for it. Some people say that sins are forgiven by saying the prayer ghufaylah. But that's not true. I say this prayer every day—in addition, of course, to the regular prayers—but no sins are forgiven by it, absolutely none. If you stole a sheep, you have to do repentance and give it back to its owner; otherwise it is on your neck and you will have to suffer for it. Neither is wrong-doing something decreed by God. If one is sleeping and some fire falls on him from the fireplace and hurts him, this is destiny decreed by God. But if one commits a sin, like stealing, this is not decreed. He is responsible for it. He will have to suffer the punishment for it, inevitably and without fail, either in this world or the next. In this world he may become poor or blind or lame or sick. You know that old man here who has been bed-ridden for two years and can no longer take care of himself. God wants to prolong his life and so punish him to clear away his sins and prepare a place for him there. If he didn't pay back his sins here, he would have to suffer there. It is better here than there.

What did he do wrong?

Certainly there was something he did wrong. He was a hunter, like we were, and killed a lot of wild game; that's sinful. He was a retainer of our Former Landlord. Maybe he committed oppression; that is very bad: every bit of it has to be paid back. When a person suffers a misfortune or gets blind or lame or ill, we say for sure he must have done something wrong that this has happened to him. Nothing comes without reason.

Is then all suffering in this world because of evil deeds?

No, did the Imām Husayn perhaps commit a sin that he had to suffer so much? Suffering may be several things. It may be a punishment for sins. When I do something wrong and then suddenly become ill, we say this happened because of that wrong I did. It may be a test for those who are wealthy: whether they give help to someone living in misery and poverty. It may also be a trial of the person himself, that God wants to see whether he has endurance or not. In fact, if you want to know the truth, whoever is more virtuous will be sent more afflictions, more trials. That's the way the Lord is doing it. He wants to see if he has endurance, if he has patience, if he can put his hand on his heart and say, "Oh God, thanks. You made me blind: oh God, thanks. You made me deaf: oh God, thanks. Oh God, thanks!" No matter what affliction God sends a person, he has to be thankful, that is, he has to worship God and say, "Oh God, thanks; I have no eyes to see whether someone's shirt is new or old; I have no eyes to see whether someone's wife is beautiful or ugly; I have no eyes to see whether someone's sheep are many or few; oh God, thanks!" If he does this, for sure he will be given everything in the next world. He will have the best life.

But also, misfortune just goes round, just as it is night in America now and day here. It goes round. It hits the one or the other, it cannot hit everybody. When a rain comes, one happens to be safe under a roof, another gets wet outside. Misfortune has to be. This is the rule for us servants of God: misfortune and fortune, illness and health, good and bad, day—night, male—female, hunger—satisfaction. All things are in pairs.

Every day 70 misfortunes come for a person. They are warded off by doing some good: giving an alms, saying the *salavāt,* saying "In the name of God," greeting someone sincerely, and so on. Any good drives some evil away. How many steps have you just walked to come from your house to mine? Many; for the sake of each one some evil will be driven off, for I was alone and you came and talked with me; that was good, like the love between brothers.

What misfortunes did you suffer in your own life?

One is that my only son is an invalid. Another was that accident in the city in which my head was injured. I am having bad aches in the back of my head ever since. Now you will ask me what I think the reasons were, right? I think these things happened because of the sins I committed, especially those of killing wild game. I think God did it in return for that. Maybe it was also because of the sin of my father; the son must harvest what the father sowed—and for generations we have been hunters and have killed game. That is sinful. It is sinful when it is excessive and beyond our needs. God created the game for us, his servants. We can use it, but according to the law. In the same way as He created the woman for the benefit of man, but we have to abide by the law of God and the Prophet: your wife belongs to you and mine to me. But why do we kill these animals? They have lives too and their lives are dear to them. Why do we kill this chicken? Sure, God has created it so that we can eat it, but its life is dear to it. Not that it is forbidden (harām) to kill it, but it is sinful. Anything that does harm to other beings is sinful.

But in the case of my accident there was something else, too. At that time I was quite ready to kill someone. As it was, I wanted to marry a girl. In fact, I wanted to help her family. They were strangers here and owned no land and could have taken care of my land. But they refused. They thought I was mad and only wanted a second wife. Also the girl said she wouldn't marry me. But I said I wouldn't permit anybody to marry her, I would kill him. Indeed I was determined to kill anybody who married her. So they filed complaints about me here and there and finally took me to court in the city. In the street I was knocked down by a car so that my head hit the pavement and I became unconscious. For two days and nights I lay in the hospital where the wounds on my head and chest were stitched and bandaged. This happened to me so that I should be unable to kill somebody. God helped me. He sent this misfortune so that no blood should come on my head. Oh God, thanks! Oh God, thanks! If we didn't get ill, we would be unbelievers. But as we get ill, we repent our sins and say, "Oh God, You are God!"

And your son?

I think the Lord wants to try him. If he is thankful and content and does not complain, saying, "To others You gave health but to me You didn't," then it is good for his Last Day, for his next life. It is written in the Qur'ān that God gives the blind and lame and crippled a good place in the next world—but on the condition that they be thankful. It is also a test for me and you. God wants to see whether I take good care of him or not. He wants to see if you who are healthy will help one who is not. So it is good for us as well as for him—if he remains thankful.

How will the accounting be done?

First there is the questioning in the grave. It is written that after the burial, when the people leaving the grave are seven paces away, Nakīr and Munkar, who are two angels of God, come into the grave. The soul, which has been wandering around since the person's death, enters the body, and they start asking him, "What was your religion? Who was your prophet? Who was the first Imām? What good did you do? Whose belly did you fill? Whom did you clothe?" If your faith was true and good, if you gave help, if you were generous, if you took the hand of the destitute, if you did good, you will be taken to a good and pleasant place, like paradise, a houri of paradise will be your companion, and you will have a good time until the Last Day. And the Last Day will come soon: two thousand years will pass like one hour. But if you did wrong, committed sins, oppressed the people, didn't say the prayers, you will be taken to a bad place and given a companion who will torment and torture you till the Last Day when the accounting will take place.

Through all our life one angel is sitting on our right shoulder, writing down our good deeds, and one on our left shoulder, writing down our evil deeds. On the Last Day then, a single day which will last 50,000 years, all our deeds will be presented to us. Now, how can we determine whether this is true or not? I can tell you. Your tape recorder is the proof. Isn't it recording exactly what I say? When you replay it, isn't it exactly the truth? Well, cannot God who created us from a single drop of semen do the same? When we are thus faced with the record of our deeds, what can we say? Nothing, we have no excuse. Our deeds will be our destiny; our deeds will be our companion. We will have to cross the bridge *sirāt*, which is thinner than a razor blade. A good person will go across like lightning, and on the other side there is paradise. He will be given a good place; he will be given a houri, a good beautiful lady; all the best he will be given. Oh paradise! How wonderful, how wonderful! But a sinful person will fall down from the bridge into hell below. There he will suffer God's punishment. Ah, he will be burned, stung, tortured, tormented, and never allowed to rest.

How long will they have to suffer?

Only God knows. But finally and in the end, Hazrat-i Muhammad will save them. It is written that Muhammad, God's blessing and peace be upon him, will go to hell and ask God to give him the people there, and so bring them out—as if I were in prison for twenty or thirty years and in the end you come and pay some money and set me free. Thus the evil-doers will pay the retribution for their sins, but in the end Hazrat-i Muhammad will save all his people. No Muslim will remain in hell, that is, none of those who followed the religion, God, the Prophet, and Ali. They will all be carried to paradise. We Muslim are the people of Muhammad and the shī'ah of Ali. These two persons will intercede for us on the Last Day.

I know that all this is true because I have seen the other world myself.

When was that?

Once when I was ill. I was lying in bed when suddenly a big, old man came into the room. He had two large, protruding teeth that he kept clapping against each other, and a long beard that was plastered with dough. His feet were like the hoofs of donkeys. As he walked up to me, his beard was swinging from side to side and made rig-rig-rig.

He said, "Get up!" and carried me away, far away into the mountains. There was a closed gate. Part of it was full of small holes, like a honeycomb. He put my head against such a hole and said, "Stick your head into that hole and get through there!" Oh sir, may I become your sacrifice, I am trembling at the thought of this! He made me turn and twist and screw my head to force it into that hole. It was a terrible pain. He said, "Go on!" and his long beard with the dough in it made rig-rig-rig. I implored him, "Dear sir, feel ashamed before the Amīr al-Mu'minīn, before God, before the One who created you! By your religion, stop torturing me!" He said all right and left.

After a while—God knows how long it was!—he came back, and instantly, blessings upon Muhammad, the gate opened. He had gone and gotten permission. We went in and came to a place with fountains and flower gardens, a place of beauty and splendor. A group of people were sitting there. At that moment a hand appeared and gave me a cup of tea and a piece of sugar. Then I knew that I would be cured. I ate the sugar and got well. Hazrat-i Ali, peace be upon him, had healed me. I opened my eyes. The people were sitting around me, crying. I said, "Don't cry! I have been cured."

Before I was brought back I was told to call all people together and tell them what I had been shown. Oh woe! I didn't do it. God is great! I couldn't. I didn't have the courage. Should I tell them so that they would say, "He is lying"? But in the morning I went to the two most pious men in the village and told them what had happened: how I was carried off, how I was shown the Last Day and heaven and hell, and how I was cured. They were deeply moved and wept.

You said, you saw the Day of Judgment, heaven and hell?

That was the Day of Judgment, was it not? That was the Last Day when I was forced to drive my head into that small hole. That happened because of my sins. This suffering was punishment for my sins. It was equal to ten thousand years of torment in this life. On the other side of the gate, the garden, the fountains, the flowers, that was paradise; yes, that was paradise. Hazrat-i Ali, peace be upon him, this spender of good and healing in this world and the next, gave the permission for the gate to be opened. It was he who gave me the piece of sugar that cured me. It was his hand that I saw, handsome and beautiful. Yes, Ali, peace be upon him, healed me.

They showed me the worlds. At one place there was a deep pit, one hundred or two hundred meters deep. Evil-doers are taken up to the seventh heaven and thrown from there into this pit. At another place was a black dog with a chain around the neck. He said, "I am so-and-so," and implored me not to tell the people. I didn't. He has a family here and they might be upset. He was a man who had done wrong and now had to endure this trouble. Hard! Hard! There is a God. We are mortals.

Do you understand now why I have renounced the world? It's because of all these things I have seen.

12

The Deep Believer: Belief as Knowledge

He is a quiet, methodical man of about forty-five, a member of an established, large lineage, who is sociable and well-respected for his forthright honesty. Neither rich nor poor, he works hard in his fields with the help of one of his three sons. His oldest son left the village; the youngest and the younger of his two daughters attend school locally. He seems to have a special affinity for religious matters and, though illiterate, had participated in the informal religious educational circle gathering around the Representative in the past. (1976).

You once worked for the Former Landlord, didn't you?

Yes, in former times I was an agent of the Landlord, carrying out orders, collecting dues, exacting special impositions, and so on. This was a mistake, it was oppression. It is unlawful (harām) to serve oppression, absolutely unlawful. I knew that, but I had no other choice, I was forced to put up with it. But I kept in mind that these villagers were my religious brothers, of the same kind as I am, and I tried to ease things for them, for example, by taking only two eggs from someone when I had been ordered to take a chicken.

No, I did not do repentance. In my own mind I consider it better merely to form an intention than to do formal repentance. For, if I make up my mind not to do something and then do it nevertheless, it is not as great a perfidy as if I had repented an act and promised God not to do it again.

Will this be forgiven?

God's mercy is great. He may balance it with good deeds, but we'll see what He wishes to do. By myself I think that if I go ahead and do good as well as I can for the rest of my life, then this trespass of the past will be forgiven.

What do you think about the ways in which God punishes?

Personally I think that there is a Last Day when God will inflict evil on those who have done evil. But in most cases He will punish in this world. He won't leave it for the Day of Judgment.

Take the case of a certain woman. Her former husband first married the wife of his brother who had been killed in a battle. Then he took that woman as his second wife. From then onwards he neglected his first wife completely. He did not provide for her, nor did he sleep with her. Then, in another war, God killed him, and his second wife was married to the son of his brother. Now, this man neither sleeps with her nor does he give her the daily bread. She had caused her former co-wife's misery and now exactly what she had done to her co-wife happens to herself. This is God's retribution (*mukāfāt*). He took vengeance in this world; it does not go to the next world.

I have also done things for which God has punished me. At that time people said that one who did not steal had no right to live. Once I stole a cow, and then three of my own cows perished. Is this retribution or not? Another time I stole honey from someone's beehive in the mountains. Then, when I went to my own five hives, I found that a bear had emptied all of them. Whenever I stole something, the Lord took twice as much from me so that my eyes opened and I knew I had done wrong and had to burn and suffer because of it. This was the retribution. For this reason I say that retribution is given mostly in this world and that little goes into the other world.

Or, if I get up tonight, take my shovel, and cut off someone's water to irrigate my own fields, then, when it will be my turn to get the water, I shall find that five men have already taken it. That's then the retribution for my having taken another's water. Or, if a poor man comes to my house and asks for something and I give him nothing, God will make my son, or the son of my son, so poor that he will go to this man's house and the man will give him nothing. That's retribution.

In the case of adultery it's this way. Let's assume I see that the skirts of my neighbor's daughter have slid up. If I pull them down again to her feet, then my neighbor will do the same for my daughter. But if I trouble her,

God will give her a son who will fornicate with my daughter so that vengeance will be done. This is God's punishment. Now, with a woman it is possible to commit adultery; but is it possible with a boy? You would think not. But take our Former Landlord. He committed adultery with a woman of this village. In return, the son of that woman fornicated with the Landlord's son—which is an impossibility. This is this-worldly retribution.

Whatever one has done, be it good or bad, he himself will see the consequences for it. If he has done good, he will reap good and this will also reach his offspring. If he has done evil, he will be afflicted by evil and his children will be afflicted, too. Say, I steal something and my wife and son and daughter eat from it, then they are not liable for it—the retribution is on my neck. I shall have to pay it back. But this unlawful morsel (luqmah harām) will separate them from virtuous behavior, it will morally corrupt them, make them loose talkers, lead them into crooked ways. For instance, when my son sits in his neighbor's house, his eyes will look for something to steal. If he cannot rid himself of this evil through good works, he will eventually do bad things and become liable for retribution himself.

So God punishes in this world. We perceive it with our own eyes. But we don't want to acknowledge it. When I harm someone and then suffer some harm myself, I won't say that this is because I did some harm to someone and that I should not do it again. Rather, out of stupidity and lack of understanding, I will say that it simply had to happen this way, it was my lot (qismat). But if I consider my deeds and recognize that I did evil to someone and after a while saw evil myself, then I must realize that this evil was for that deed, that God exacted retribution for the evil I had done earlier; or, if I did good to someone and received plenty, that this plenty was for that good.

Is sickness such a retribution?

No, sickness comes because of my own neglect. To discover the reason why I am sick, I have to ask myself what I have done to my body. Did I get a cold, or eat too much, or sweat and foolishly drink cold water? God has made everybody the master of his body. If I am not taking care of it and it starts to ache—did God make it ache or did I? Only death is given by God.

Is death given as a retribution by God?

No, we all have to die. Only a person whose mind cannot discern what is true will say that so-and-so should not have died, he was good. If you have a field of melons, will you pick the good ones and eat them, or the bad ones? So God, too, carries his good servants away earlier. He likes them better and takes them away earlier so that they won't become sinners.

But the way in which a person dies may be a retribution. The young man who was recently killed in a car accident—he died instantly. This was not a retribution. But an old woman in our neighborhood lay dying for two years and was so old and weak that she had to be fed with a spoon. This was a retribution.

And so it was in the case of another villager. He was robbing and raiding and living off the spoils he brought home and did not work his fields at all. In the evenings, ten or twenty men would gather in his house and have a good time, playing the flute and singing. For about ten years he did this. Then the Lord threw him down so that he could no longer go and plunder. For thirty years he was so decrepit that he had to beg for a crumb of bread. For those ten years he paid with thirty years of misery and when he died, nobody knew about it, nobody sat at his side, nobody closed his eyes, nobody was there to do anything. Not even a regular burial did he have. One got a shroud for him and some men carried him out and buried him, but nobody went along to his grave. Is this retribution or not? All men must die. But when one who takes pains and so earns his bread gets sick, he gets sick for one month or ten days or five days, one gives him water, one tidies the place where he lies, one sits at his head—until the minute he dies; and then he will be buried the way you have seen it.

What about poverty? Is this a punishment of God?

No, poverty is not a retributive punishment. Worldly possessions revolve. Only a number of people get wealthy at a time. Now you are rich and another man poor, but later your children may be poor and those of the other man rich. The Former Landlord, however, is being punished by God. He has become destitute because of his ungratefulness towards God. God gave him wealth and power so as to test him, but he was ungrateful and oppressive. Now he suffers God's retribution in return. Sure, he claimed, and still claims, he was the landlord and had the right to exact dues and impositions because his grandfather made the place habitable. But could one man alone have dug the irrigation channels and made the village habitable? No. So his claim is a lie and he knows perfectly well that it is a lie. He knew he did wrong and therefore he has no excuse.

How do you recognize whether a person's poverty is due to retribution?

The Landlord didn't work himself. He lived off the toil of the people. And he was never satisfied, but by force exacted more and more. God punished him for the oppression. But if one is working hard and a crop fails, it's not God's punishment. Rather, it may be God's wisdom. Surely, next year it will grow all right, or He will let another crop do better to make up for it.

What is the reason for sheep and goats to perish?

This is the decree (*taqdīr*) of God. This has to be so because anything that is born must die. It may be, however, that when a misfortune (*qazā'*) is about to hit a house and kill a son or daughter or the man himself, the Lord decrees that the misfortune hit something else instead, such as a cow, a sheep, a goat, a donkey. Then this animal dies and the misfortune is warded off from the family. Certainly, such a misfortune comes from God. Of course, if I jump down from the roof and break my leg, that's not decreed by God. This is brought about by my own carelessness. But if I go and cut wheat and a snake bites me, or I go to a herding outpost and on the way a bear or leopard attacks me—these are misfortunes decreed by God.

Why would He send them?

It is said that God charged 'Izrā'il with the task of taking the lives of all created things. 'Izrā'il thought it over, then said, "Oh God, you have given me a hard task; the whole creation will become my enemy." So God said instead, "I will send everyone a fatality (qazā') to die of, so that neither you, 'Izrā'il, nor I, God, have to be mindful of men." So he kills everyone under a certain name. If someone dies, one does not say, God has killed him, but rather, one says, he got a cold, or a fever, or a snake bit him, or he died of cancer. But the final cause of death is God.

It is said that a long time ago a king was told by his astrologers, "On a certain day at a certain time the Lord will send you a fatality by means of a scorpion, and you will die unless the fatality passes you." The king consulted with his ministers as to what to do. Then, naked, he mounted a horse and rode into the middle of the sea. As he stood there, an eagle clutching a bone flew by. When it was exactly above the king, a scorpion fell out of the bone and down onto the horse and got caught in its hair. The king looked at his watch and praised God because the time would be over presently. He was happy that the misfortune had passed, put his hand on the neck of the horse, and the scorpion stung it. He rode home and said, "Prepare my bed." By the time they had made it, he had died. That is the decree of God.

So if a snake bites me, it is the decree (taqdīr) of God; it is the destiny of a person (*sar nivisht, pīshānī nivisht*). The day I was born, God determined a destiny for me, for example, that at a certain time I must die by means of a snake bite. But if a snake bites me and I don't die—only have pains for several days and then get well again—then I have to give thanks to God, reminding myself how great my torment would be if that pain were always in my body.

After our talk the other day a snake did in fact bite you. Do you think there was a connection?

No, no; nor was it a punishment by God. It was decreed by God, and I must be thankful to Him that I got to the doctor in time and did not die, and that the pains went away after twenty hours. It is possible, however, that it was brought about by the talk of the people. I started to build a house with four rooms this year, and ten people may have been saying, "Oh, he is building four rooms this year, out of stone and plaster!" Such talk may have brought about this harm of the snake bite. That's also possible.

What are the reasons for your crippled hand?

When I was born—this I think myself; it may not be so with God, but to me it's undoubtedly this—when I was born, my parents, having lost three sons before me, made a vow, saying, "Oh Sayyid Mahamad, the right hand of this boy will be dedicated to you if he does not die." This means that whatever my right hand would earn should belong to that Imāmzā-dah. When I was some twelve years old, my father told me about this and took me on the pilgrimage to Sayyid Mahamad's shrine. He gave one of the people there a cow to pay off the vow so that anything my right hand would earn from then on we could lawfully keep.

After several more years I travelled with a group of fellow villagers to that shrine. At night we stayed there and I had a dream. Next morning I said to my companions, "Boys, either I am going to be killed today or something will happen to me so that you will carry me home on your backs." They asked, "How come?" I said, "I had a dream." But they said, "No, don't worry, you were thinking of our journey." This was a period of strife and robbery and danger. We set out. On our way I saw several wild sheep. I and some others took after them and, as we climbed, I suddenly fell, my gun went off, and the bullet went through my right hand. This is how it got crippled.

Now, I believe that the offering my father gave to that man at the shrine was not approved by the Imāmzādah, otherwise I would not have suffered this harm. It may be that the man had no right to receive a share of the Imāmzādah—maybe he was a thief or an adulterer—or that he did not declare he was content with it; or, if he did, that his words, because of his immorality, had no effect on the Imām. If the man had been worthy and had said with a truthful heart, "Oh God, I pardon the rest," everything would have been all right. To me, this is the reason why the Sayyid Maha-mad has done this.

What happens after death?

The soul of one who was sinful will be in pain and torment till the Last Day. The one who did no evil, however, his soul will be at ease, safe and sound. The Last Day is then a day of reckoning. Everybody's soul enters its body—at the time of retribution the soul must be in the body—and he is asked, "What did you do? What were your actions? What was your conduct?"

And then?

Then. . . . Then only God knows. The Prophet said that everyone whose conduct and actions are good will have a good place, a good house; but whoever did bad will be caught in torment. Yes, that's the truth. There is no doubt, it is exactly the truth.

So you know it?

Absolutely for sure we know it. I will tell you this: Here in our village we have had men who in our view were good and men who were doing harm to others. When, after their death, you saw the good person in a dream, he was in the same state as on earth. But the evil man, who in this world, let's say, went about with a suit or necktie but did harm to others, when we saw him in a dream, he was fighting with a dog or a boar, or he was lying in snow or in water. Was this because in my sleep I had an animosity against him? No; my soul has no animosity against anyone that would make it go and see how he is while I am asleep. No. The reason for this is the work of God. He does it so that I may see it and won't do wrong to others. Yes, I have dreamed this myself.

Another example. We had here two brothers. One did no harm to others, but the other oppressed the people at the order of the Landlord. Once the latter climbed a walnut tree. He wasn't up higher than the mirror on that wall, when he fell down. For twenty days he was ill. Then he died. After he was buried the stench of his decaying body came out from the earth and all cursed him. Was this because the earth has an animosity against anyone? No. It was the wisdom of God, the power of God. The people said, "May God not forgive him," and for sure God won't.

For, according to the Prophet, if ten people say about somebody that he is bad, he is also bad in the eyes of God. But if over the grave of a person who did wrong to others—within limits, that is, a bit of oppression, not much—seven pious, just, God-knowing men say with a faithful heart, "May God forgive him, may God have mercy on him," God will forgive him. God loves His servants very much.

It is said that by the blood of the Imām Husayn sins will also be forgiven.

There is no doubt about this. On the Last Day, when all the dead are brought before God, the Imām will come and say, "Oh God, I have given my head as a sacrifice to your cause. You have to pardon those who are my people and who love me." It is absolutely certain that the Lord forgives everyone for whom the Prophet or the Imām Husayn intercedes. There is no doubt about this. All this is in the Qur'ān.

By myself I think this way: how many years ago was it that the Prophet left this world? One thousand three hundred years, and still his words exist, firm and true. For instance, he said that I shouldn't eat anything sour when I have a cold. If I really get sick when I eat sour things, it shows his words are right—and they will be until the Last Day. How many millions of people were in the world after the Prophet? Do the words of anyone else remain? And where is the grave of Umar and Yazīd? But to the graves of the Imāms Hasan and Husayn come thousands of pilgrims every year, and recently a millionaire gave all his fortune to the Imām. From this it is evident that these stand very near to God and they can intercede for their people.

What is then the difference between those who have sinned and those who haven't?

Those who haven't will be in peace and in the love of God for all those thousand or hundred thousand years till the Last Day, whereas the others will be in pain. But the Imām Husayn will not intercede for all people—only for those who follow him, who love him, or who repent their sins. If I do now, for instance, something wrong, but then repent it, saying, "Oh God, I didn't understand; I didn't know I was doing something wrong," I will have to pay the penalty for this offence by being caught in anguish and pain until the day the Imām Husayn wants to intercede; but then he will petition God, saying, "This one failed because of ignorance; he made repentance; he has been punished for thirty, or a hundred, or a thousand years. Forgive him the rest for my sake." That's the difference. When He forgives it for the sake of the Imām Husayn it is like being saved from complete perishing. But there is complete perishing. Hell will not be empty. And it's, of course, not so that those who led a virtuous life have no need for the Imām Husayn. They do need him for the mere reason of having been here on earth.

Are there sins that will be forgiven and others that won't?

Yes, for instance, if I am very hungry and go into your wheat field and take an armful of your wheat and bring it home, saying in my heart, "Oh, God, I had no other choice, I took it so as not to perish," this will be forgiven by God. Or if I did not know that what I was doing was sinful, it will be forgiven. Or in the case of fasting, if I cannot work while fasting and my family goes hungry, then I am not obliged to fast. Or if someone does not say the prayers but nevertheless keeps God always in mind, it does not matter as much as if he didn't think of God at all. However, if I lead a sinful life while also saying the prayers, my sins will not be annulled by my prayers. Rather, my prayers will be annulled by my sins.

But God will never forgive oppression, doing wrong to others, and adultery. In the case of murder there are two kinds of retribution. Suppose my grandfather killed someone and after fifty or one hundred years a grandson of the victim kills someone of my family, then God makes this happen to avenge him. This is this-worldly retribution. If, however, a murderer goes into that world without having received punishment, he will suffer the retribution there. There is no forgiving. Not even for the sake of the Imām Husayn will God forgive that.

Also for a thief who has not made restoration, the Imām Husayn cannot intercede. Do you know how restoration is made? Suppose I have stolen something from you. After some years I come and say, "Sir, I have stolen from you. Will you make it lawful (halāl) for me or shall I give you its price?" If you say you make it lawful—fine, you have made it lawful. If you say no, you want its price and I give it to you—it's also all right. But if you say, out of spite, that you will neither pardon it nor take its value, but you want God to take vengeance, then God will forgive it nevertheless. Why? Because I was ready to give it back and so made repentance.

And also for an adulterer the Imām Husayn will never intercede. Indeed, he absolutely abhors such a person. Adultery is unforgivable. Retribution in this world is in kind. For instance, someone commits adultery with my wife and God gives me a son who in turn does it to his daughter. If it is not paid back here, one will be tormented there. Again, there are two types, however. If one lives without a wife and so has no other choice but to commit adultery, or if a widow who for years was living without a husband commits adultery, it is not as bad as when an unmarried girl or I, who have a wife, is doing it. For sure, both types are unforgivable, but the former is a smaller sin and its punishment is lighter. Thus all acts that oppress or harm other people are unforgivable and God will not forgive them.

What if the harmed person himself forgives the offence?

Then it's forgiven. In the Qur'ān it is said that once a son caused a lot of trouble to his mother. Then he died and was buried. A few hours later, the Prophet happened to pass by and heard the sound of great clamor rising from the grave. In another grave was one who had died 300 years ago. The Prophet asked God to let him talk to the two men. When he called on the one who had died only hours before, the man could answer only in a very, very thin and weak voice. The Prophet asked him when he had died, and the man said, "Oh Prophet, more than a thousand years ago." But the other man, asked the same question, said, "I don't know, an hour, or an hour and a half ago." The Prophet asked God the reason for this and was told that the first man had caused great misery to his mother. So he went to this woman and saw that she was neither crying nor wailing but was rather happy. She did not recognize the Prophet, and when he asked her to forgive her son, she urged God instead to make his torment greater. The Prophet went back to the grave and saw a flame of fire coming out. He sent Hazrat-i Fatima to the woman to tell her she should be ashamed before God. The woman was moved by Hazrat-i Fatima and said, "Oh God, I forgive him for the sake of Hazrat-i Fatima." When the Prophet returned to the grave, the fire was out and the clamor had stopped.

Do you have to fear the Day of Judgment?

Yes. Whoever doesn't fear the Last Day is not a believer. Even if one has no sin, the very hour he stops being fearful, he will begin to sin. The Last Day must always be on a person's mind. Then he won't do evil. And this is exactly the meaning of the daily prayers, namely, that one always keeps God in mind, that one's heart is near God, and thereby one stays away from evil deeds. That's their purpose. Otherwise God does not need the prayers.

A person who always says the prayers will never commit suicide—like some women do when they feel bad about their husbands. A woman may be cut to pieces by her husband, still, if she always says the prayers, she will not kill herself. Why? Because the devil cannot get near anybody who says the prayers. The devil was originally an angel who was driven from the court of God when he refused to bow down before Adam, but was allowed to seduce men. However, a person saying the prayers cannot be seduced by him to do forbidden things.

But why should the religion say that something is forbidden? Let's take the case of wine-drinking. One who drinks wine loses his senses and it's possible that he may commit adultery with his own sister or daughter. When he gets sober again he sees that he has done something evil. Thus we recognize that what the religion says is not good, is, indeed, not good for us. So the benefits of what the religion had said 2000 or 3000 years ago still reach us today, and we see that it is true.

Whatever one does must be done according to the religion—actually first God and then the religion because, of course, the religion, like everything else, originated from God. If I lift up a stone when I build my house, or put my foot on the first rung of the ladder, or lay down to sleep, I say,

"In the name of God, I trust in You." I cannot make a single step without God and the religion.

What did God create you for?

To work hard; to worship God and to work hard; to work in the hope that the future will be better, without considering the fact that the hour of death is nearer to man than the hair on his head. The religion orders me to sow this wheat and I have to do it even though I don't know whether I will live long enough to harvest it. But if I won't eat it, someone else will, and that's the aim of it: that there shall be life in this world and that the world shall be made habitable.

Will this hard work be rewarded in the next world?

Yes, and the reason for it is this. For instance, I grow wheat. This gives others bread to eat, it gives them sustenance and life. This has merit. Although the others may pay for it, the merit from producing this bread belongs to me who has taken pains, who has sweated, who got thorns in his hands. The Prophet said that for the sake of the merit earned from hard work God will even forgive sins. But someone who works hard will have to answer for fewer sins than an idler on the Last Day anyway, because a person who works hard is preoccupied with his work. His mind does not turn to bad things, to lying, stealing, adultery. Therefore God likes him better than an idler.

When we raise a crop, worms eat from it, boars eat, sparrows eat, ants eat, everything eats from it. This earns merit for the cultivator. Those ants and boars and sparrows and mice—they, too, were created by God; they, too, must get something to live on. So when we cast out the seed, we say, "Oh God, I trust in you; let all beings eat from it and give me my daily bread, too!" These animals don't eat my livelihood. Rather, the Lord blesses my field so that it yields their food as well as mine.

God gives us all this bounty, so we too have to give to others—to whatever or whoever it may be. The Lord gave me hands, He gave me feet, and He has given me an ox so that I can cultivate wheat. An ant, after all, has no ox and no hands: it cannot cultivate.

If we give to others, God will give us His blessing in return. If we don't give, God will also stop giving us our daily food. When guests come to our house, we tribesmen say, their food comes along with them. Indeed, the Lord blesses our food so that there is enough for them to eat, too. We must not be displeased when a guest comes and think we'll be hungry. Anyone who goes into my vineyard and eats from the grapes may do so. I am content: if I were not, the Lord wouldn't give me much either.

On the other hand, if God gives riches to someone, it is not necessarily because this person is good. It may be a test. Men are like melons: you know their qualities only when you see their inside. And a person's inside is revealed by his actions. If he shares his wealth with others, he has dignity and worth and goodness, and it will be blessed. But if he doesn't, his possessions have no blessings and will vanish.

Yes, what I am giving earns merit. It's wholly impossible that it wouldn't. It is 100% certain that it has merit, both in the next world and in this one. Do you know how in this world? If you give me a handful of bread, I shall say to everyone I meet, "May God give him a good future!" And I shall always be thankful to you and always shame-faced. These are its this-worldly merits. What its merits in the next world will be, only God knows.

What we have is from the grace of God and we have to be thankful for it, whatever it may be: good and bad, sweet and bitter, blind and seeing. If He gives me a lot and I have rice and meat to eat, or bread and honey, or bread and butter, and I am thankful for it, the Lord will bless it and make it more. But if I am ungrateful, that is, if I don't appreciate what I have, if I belittle it and greedily desire more and more—as I said our Former Landlord did—then I shall incur God's punishment. God will diminish my wealth, He will take it from me so that I will only have plain bread to eat. As the Prophet has said, "Gratitude for wealth will bring you more wealth; ingratitude will take it away from you."

But even if He gives me only little and if I have to toil so that my body aches, I have to be contented and thankful for whatever I have: a healthy body, hands and feet to work, eyes to see. When I see a blind man stumbling with his feet against a stone, God wants me to give thanks to Him that I am not blind. If I am not thankful for my eyes and one starts to hurt, or if I do not appreciate that the Lord gave me these hands and one gets lame, that happens because of my ungratefulness.

You said that God would make up the losses of a crop?

Yes, for sure He will. If one crop fails, He will put the blessings belonging to this crop into something else instead—into the gardens, the vineyard, the animals, or another crop, so as to replace the loss. Unfailingly He will do this. This year, for instance, the heavy snow destroyed my wheat. But my vineyard, I figured out, bears two or three times as many grapes as last year. So what failed in the wheat came into existence in another crop. God gave me the daily bread anyway, so that I won't be in want in the eyes of the people.

Is this also true the other way round, that is, that a loss will occur if things prosper?

No, God is not an oppressor. He is just. If the wheat turns out fine and God would destroy something else instead, there would be no progress in the world. If things prosper, however, damage may come about in another way, namely, by the talk of people (zabān mardum). As the saying goes: "You can go through the fire of bullets but not the fire of tongues." This means that if your wealth is talked about by the people, it's more dangerous than if somebody would shoot at you. For instance, someone drives by in a car. Five people sit at the roadside and one says, "Oh, look how fast that car goes," and suddenly a tire blows: that's the effect of the talk. Or one has a very fat and beautiful cow, and a passer-by says, "Oh, look how fat this cow is!" and the cow drops dead: that's because of the talk. The damage comes by means of that talk, but that talk is a way of God to hit man. That's why the talk of people is also called "the scourge of God" and "the arrow of destiny," meaning that what happens through the talk is the decree of God (taqdīr Allah).

There is also what is called navaruzī, a sudden, unusually great increase, like a goat giving birth to three kids, or all goats in a herd giving birth to two kids. If this happens, either the animals will perish or a misfortune will hit the house, like the death of a child—unless an alms (sadaqah) is given. As I have said, God gives plenty to see whether a person is worthy and thankful to Him. If he is worthy and thankful and gives one of these animals away as an alms in the way of God, or in the way of the Imām Husayn, then the misfortune will be turned away. But if he doesn't do so, he will inevitably suffer a blow. You have, for instance, three shirts and I have none and you won't give me one, and at night you get up and see that your shirt has either been eaten by mice or burned in the fireplace: what's the reason for this? God has made it this way so that you will have pity on those in need and they, too, will have something.

Sometimes a twist forms in a wheat field (kākul). This happens when God blesses a person's wheat so that it gets heavy and twisted. In this case one has to sacrifice an animal over it. If one doesn't, people say one will suffer a loss in one way or another. To a certain degree I believe in this too, but not as completely as in the fact that God is free to do with the wheat whatever He wants.

What do you think about Ali and the other Imāms?

Once, when Adam was still in paradise and had not yet been seduced by the devil to eat from the wheat, he asked God whether anyone had come into existence before him. God ordered Gabriel to tell him, "There is one who will come into existence from yourself, but still, came already before you. This is Hazrat-i Ali." He was very great. Already when he was a child his wisdom proved greater than that of Hazrat-i Khizr. Hazrat-i Khizr was so astounded that he said, "I do not know him to be God, but I do not know him to be different from God either." Once, as a young man, he was with a caravan stopping at an inn. As he entered, the doorway rose above his head by the order of God so that he wouldn't have to bow down. The owner of the inn, a learned man who had foreknowledge of Ali's greatness, recognized him by this sign and rose and bowed in reverence before him. And so there are many deeds and miracles of Hazrat-i Ali.

Among all Imāms, however, the Imām Husayn became the most distinguished and best loved because he gave his life in the way of God. The people commemorate his death every year by beating their chests, but that's of no use. It is the heart that must do the chest beating, not the arms. The heart must be filled with love for the Imām Husayn.

Why haven't you made the pilgrimage to Mashhad yet?

It wasn't my destiny (qismat) yet. I have not been invited yet. It is not up to a person. One must be invited. If you watch, for instance, a group of singing pilgrims leaving for Mashhad and suddenly your heart is so moved that you, too, must go, then it means you have been invited. But first of all, to go to Mashhad requires that your actions must be right. When I return from the pilgrimage, I must not steal, not lie, not harm other people. But conditions do not allow me not to harm anybody, not to go through another's field and squash his crop under my feet, not to get into a fight. That's why I haven't gone yet. If someone goes to Mashhad and then acts badly nevertheless, he has only added a title to his name.

What are the reasons for making the pilgrimage?

Everyone has another intention. One is ill and seeks a cure. Another goes for his reputation. Another goes to see how much wisdom and wonders and love of God surround the Imāms and how close to God they were to have reached this position. And still another has so much love and affection for the Imām that he wants to make a pilgrimage to his grave.

The Imāms are the advocates of curing and giving favors. But it depends on the morality of the sick person whether an Imām will cure him. If the Imām recognizes that after my recovery I'll get busy doing wrong to others, he won't cure me. But if he sees in my heart that I shall abide by the laws of God, he will most certainly cure me; or rather, God will cure me for his sake.

In the same way, the foremost thing with a vow is not how much one gives, but rather, that what one gives has been acquired in a lawful way by one's own work. If one doesn't have much, but what he has is lawful, his offering may indeed be very small and still accepted. As we say, "Even the leg of a locust is an offering for Sulaymān." That is, when an ant going to see Hazrat-i Sulaymān, the ruler of all animals, takes the leg of a locust in its jaws so as not to appear empty-handed before him and this is all it has got, Sulaymān is pleased by it.

But the Imām Rezā doesn't need the money, or does he?

Of course he needs it. He now owns about 12,000 camels, 12,000 herds of sheep and goats, and a great many fields on which hundreds of people work—all from votive offerings. The dome over his shrine is built of golden bricks. How come? Why are people, who root out their lives for ten misqāl of gold, ready to spend 100,000 tons of it for the dome of the Imām Reza? Why do they not spend it on the grave of someone else? After all, many kings and many great men have died. The reason for this is the love of God—the love of God has made this so.

From the story about your hand it appears you believe in the forebodings of dreams?

Yes, I do. I have tried it myself. There are certain dreams which by general opinion are good or bad. For instance, if you would dream that I have died, this is a good dream; it is said to mean a long life. But if you dream of a wedding, or that a dog attacks you, or that you fight with a wolf or bear, that's bad. In principle, however, everyone must find out for himself whether a dream is good or bad. If I have a dream once or twice and something bad happens afterwards, I know it is a bad dream.

If the dream forebodes evil, you have to give some alms to a poor man or woman in the morning—two kilograms of wheat or so—so as to ward off the evil you have seen. That's an order the Lord has given to the Prophet, not something we people say. He told us this so that those who have give some of their wealth away and needy people get some food. If I give half a kilogram of wheat as alms to a poor family because of a bad dream, I won't become poor and the poor get some bread.

Yes, it's true, I didn't have a dream foreboding evil when I was bitten by the snake. If I had had such a dream, I wouldn't have gone out or would have given alms. But there is one thing: you cannot reverse the decree of God. What I dream is like a message, it tells me of the evil to come, and that I can take care of it. But what I have no information on, I cannot deal with: that's then the decree of God.

Do you also believe in the written prayers against the evil eye, illness, pain, and such?

In these I believe, too, but their effect depends on the prayer-writer. Only those who do no wrong have efficacy of breath. Such a person writes a prayer for a child that has a cough, and it is put in some water, and the child drinks it and stops coughing. My father could handle snakes after making a damband to bind their jaws. Once a calf of mine was lost in the mountains, and I had a damband made for it by someone whose efficacy of breath was very good. When I found it the next day, the wolf had scratched up the calf's skin all over with its claws, but had been unable to tear it up.

No, our Mullah has no efficacy of breath. He loves the world. Twenty years ago the people here paid him all respect, but he went after the goods of the world. In regard to such mullahs the Imām Husayn told us, "Follow their words but not their deeds." Despite the fact that he takes interest on his money we must not do the same. It is wrong because the Qur'ān forbids it, and he will suffer the punishment for it. In fact, it is said that on the Last Day 70,000 mills will be turned by the blood of such mullahs who did not abide by the laws of the religion.

But I do not believe in the jinn although the Qur'ān gives notice of them. For me jinn are people who are doing harm to others, who are lying, who are gossiping, who, when insulted, immediately raise a shovel or hoe and hit the other's head. These are jinn; jinn are in their bodies. A woman who does not like her husband but ten other men: that's a jinn, a jinn that appears in her shape, or the devil. Jinn and devil, that's the same thing. When they say a person is afflicted by a jinn, that's simply an illness. I think, when a child is told about jinn and wolves, he is made afraid of them and from this fear—not the jinn—he becomes sick. And as to the belief that jinn may give special gifts (bahrah), like wealth or healing power—these are the words of simpletons.

Neither do I believe that certain days are auspicious and others not. God has not made days differently. Of course, not every day can bring good. There are the days, however, on which we commemorate the deaths of Hazrat-i Ali and the Imām Husayn and the Imām Hasan. On these days one should not work out of respect for them. During the war I worked for the Americans in Abadan, and at first they wouldn't give us the day of Hazrat-i Ali off. But then a railroad accident happened in which millions worth of goods were spoiled. They asked us for the reason and we told them, and they were so convinced that they contributed 100 sacks of sugar for the celebration of the day.

What would happen if there was no religion?

The world wouldn't exist, either. The world came into being with the existence of the religion. The Lord gave the religion to Muhammad and Ali a thousand years before He created Adam, their ancestor. He created the world for their sake and the sake of the Imāms, so that His word will be spread and practiced. And as long as unbelief doesn't prevail, God won't send His wrath. But when some place the evil outnumber the good, God's wrath will come, as an earthquake, diseases, and the like.

This son of mine is twenty-one now and hasn't once observed the fasting. By the same age I had been observing it for years and under what hardship! At that time we had only acorn bread to eat. Why are they not heeding the religion? Because they don't earn their bread with their own hands and efforts. One gets to know the religion by doing hard work, for religion means hard work.

True, in the cities there are many more without religion. But for every 100 who drink wine and don't wear the veil, there are 10,000 who abide by the religion. Once they took me to the movies in Tehran. I am ashamed to tell you what we saw . . . women, all naked but for a very tiny piece of cloth . . . I was very much troubled. Some men even covered their eyes. On the way home, we passed by a mosque and walked in. There were about 400 people sitting there—four times as many as in the cinema. When I saw that so many more people followed the religion, my worries disappeared. As long as there are more good people than bad, the world will exist. Only when the evil ones become more, will the world be destroyed.

13

The Fundamentalist: Purist Orthodoxy

The Fundamentalist is a well-regarded member of a large, long-established lineage and a father of five children. In his late thirties, bright, outspoken and with some literacy, he is actively involved in many kingroup and neighborhood affairs and in economic enterprises like the building of a diesel-driven flour mill. His agricultural activities and especially his diligent pursuit of animal husbandry in his high-pasture outpost provide him with enough income to send his sons to high school. Without help from his sons, however, he feels herding is no longer feasible or profitable and so plans to give it up. (1976).

In what sense is there destiny and in what sense is man free?

Some people say that man has no control over most things he is doing. That's nonsense. When God created man, He gave him full authority over himself, that is, He gave him a free will. Otherwise, what would be the point of God sending the Prophet and showing us the right way and the wrong way? Evidently man should have a free will to choose between the two so that on the Last Day nobody can say, "Oh God, I had no power to choose," or, "I didn't know." In this way God is testing man. If, for instance, one of my goats dies, yet I don't turn away from the faith but continue to recognize God as the provider, that's good, but if I make the goat my god and say, "Woe to me! What has God done to me!" that's wrong. Thus, man has a choice. Or, when women take the pill, do they get children or not? No. So it is evident that this is not a matter of destiny, that they can choose.

The point is that man is free, as I was free to go to the religious school (maktab) or not, and as I can raise animals or go to a city and work there or start some small business. Whatever I want to do, I am free to do. The things I possess come from my hard work. If I hadn't raised these animals, would they exist?

But our daily bread comes from the hand of God. If He doesn't want these animals to live or give milk, then they won't. This is not under our control though it is in our power to take good care of the animals, to gather enough fodder for them, and so on. But when people say that the reason for a scarce livelihood is that one has no good fortune, then it is superstition, entirely superstition. These people do not understand that man is a creature of God. If God has complete power over us, what shall then good fortune be? Thus, in this case it is only right to say, "It is the will of God, God did not give," because in the Qur'ān God says that He has determined the destinies of all men. Not even a leaf can fall from a tree without His will. So I believe that everything that happens to man comes from God. He grants every person a certain station in this world. No person is equal to another, just as no finger on a hand is equal to any other. These differences are from God. He says in the Qur'ān, "Both greatness and smallness come from Me."

Are these sent as reward and punishment?

No, good and bad will be requited in the next world, not here. Well, of course, things gained in unlawful ways vanish quickly; and doing good earns God's blessing in this world. This has been proven. In fact, I believe that if we all paid the religious taxes (khums and zakāt) and practiced faithfully what God has ordered us to do, we wouldn't have these troubles, lose animals, suffer misery. Why? Because God would be pleased and He would set things right for us.

But I do not believe, as most people do, that it is God's punishment that, for instance, the Former Landlord has now become poverty-stricken and destitute. Understand it this way: when you walk through the mountains some of the paths are uphill and hard, others are downhill and easy. The course of life is the same way. Sometimes life is good and easy, at other times it is filled with trouble and hardship. Our Former Landlord is now in such an uphill part. To this we cannot say it is God's punishment. We don't know why it is so.

God created the fortunes of all men on the very day He created Hazrat-i Adam. On that day He determined the course of life of every single one of His servants, wrote it down and showed it to Hazrat-i Adam. This is now like a gramophone record: it turns, and turns, and turns, and everything on it inevitably comes. This is what is called destiny (qismat) and it is true. But only God Himself knows for what reasons He has made the destinies the way He did. We don't know. Therefore we can't say what it means that the Landlord has become destitute. Is it perhaps revealed in the Qur'ān? I, for my part, believe only what is written in the Qur'ān and the other sacred books. Everything else is hidden and unknown.

What about the Last Day?

About the Last Day the Lord has informed us completely in the Qur'ān, and there is not the slightest doubt about it. When a person dies, his soul is carried to heaven, to the place where it has been before an angel carried it into the womb of his mother. There it will remain till the Last Day. In the meantime the body decomposes in the soil. Then, on the Last Day, so God has informed us and all the prophets have told us, the soul will enter the body and the body will come alive again. The Lord will bring to life all the people who ever lived since the first day, as in spring dry seeds are coming alive.

After that everyone will receive his requital for the deeds he has done, be they good or bad. The Lord says in the Qur'ān, "Not the tiniest fraction of one misqāl I shall let go by." Whoever has done the least bit of good will be rewarded for it, and one who has done wrong will be punished. All these acts have been written down in the book of our deeds. They will be weighed on scales. It is said that if a person's good deeds will be heavier, God will send him to paradise; if his bad deeds are heavier, to hell. In the former case God will remit the bad deeds because the good ones are heavier.

Is it possible to remove through good works a sin like stealing?

No, these so-called sins against other people are unforgivable. The Lord says in the Qur'ān, "I will pardon offences against my own rights, but not offences against the rights of men." The former are faults in the worship of God, the latter are trespasses against other people's property, like stealing and oppression. These cannot be redeemed by any means; not by good works, nor by pilgrimage, nor by repentance, nor by special prayers.

So, how on the Last Day can God remit all the sins of one whose good deeds weigh heavier? Or will such a person have to go to hell for the sins he committed against other people?

These are things which are behind a veil, hidden, concealed by God. Nobody knows that. But it is known that God will requite good with good and bad with bad.

Will sins be forgiven for the sake of the blood of the Imām Husayn?

I don't have enough learning to know this. But in my view the Imām Husayn will intercede for those who are his friends. Or shall he perhaps intercede also for his enemies? That's impossible. If that were so, good ones and bad ones would be equally forgiven. No, never! Then all would be people of paradise and nobody would be in hell. He will specifically intercede for the people of the Shia. Or shall he intercede for those who do not believe and venerate the cow as God?

The Imāms and Imāmzādahs are said to work miracles, aren't they?

Yes, that's right, they do. If you want to know the essence of it, it's this: the Imāms, like the Prophet, were good and pure in their conduct and actions. They were men of this world, not angels. God did not create them this way. Rather, they attained their greatness by their own actions. They were good, they were virtuous, they helped others. When they had a dinner they gave it to the poor and slept hungry themselves. They guided the people on the way of God. For instance, on his way from Mecca to Khorasan, Hazrat-i Imām Rezā gathered the people and instructed them in the rules of Islam, telling them all conditions and stipulations attached to it. The people of the Shia flocked around him so much that the caliph of the time, Ma'mūn, the son of Harun al-Rashid, feared for his throne and gave the order to kill him. So he was poisoned.

When somebody is like this, God loves him and raises him to a high position. And that's the reason why these miracles happen. It is for the sake of these Imāms and their good actions that the Lord cures an ill person. These miracles have been proven. Many, many desperately ill persons have traveled to the Imāms and Imāmzādahs and gotten well. Take the wife of your neighbor. You saw yourself how badly ill she was. She went to Khorasan, to the Imām Rezā, tied a chain around her neck, and God had mercy on her and the lock sprang open. It is not possible, however, to find out why some people get cured and others not.

Are the written prayers (du'ā') also good for curing diseases?

Yes. These prayers are taken from the Qur'ān and the sayings of the twelve Imāms. They are not superstition. They are right. But they are right only for those who believe, for you have to take this into account: these prayers are extremely powerful. By their means one can do many, many things, good ones as well as bad ones. One can ward off the evil eye, cure diseases, soothe pain, protect fields from pests and wild boars. But one can also bring about discord between people, incapacitate a man so that he can't consummate a marriage, induce a young man whom one wants as a son-in-law to fall in love with one's daughter and to refuse the girl his parents selected for him, and so on. All the magic you see performed sometimes—a man handling snakes or piercing his tongue with a knife, or a thief blinding a person to empty his pockets—all these things are achieved by written prayers. These things are evil and unacceptable. Therefore these prayers mustn't be told to people who do not believe. Persons who have written such prayers for evil purposes have been brought to nought and their children did not fare well either.

But the other du'a' are all right. I myself make the damband to protect the animals against wolves. It consists of two pieces from the Qur'an, the sura *va 'sh-shams* [sura 90] and the verse *ayat ul-kursiy* [sura 2/255–257] which the Prophet himself told us are good for this purpose. These are said over a pair of scissors or a jack-knife, then you blow on it and snap it shut, and you define the region and time period for which the damband should work. I believe in this. It may be simple-minded or superstitious or what not, but its efficacy has been proven again and again. Just the night before last I made a damband for two calves which did not come home in the evening. I told myself, if a wolf gets them, it will have been the last time I ever made a damband; but if not, it will be another evidence of its efficacy. Then, yesterday morning, I found the two calves well and unhurt.

Why should there be a religion at all?

If there were no religion, man would eat man. The religion exists to control man. God has given us these rules so that we do no harm to others. What, for example, prevents a man from leaving his family? The religion; the religion tells him it is his obligation to provide for his family. But then again, maybe it's only because he wants his wife for his sexual desire.

What about the future of the religion?

The religion will exist forever. Even if the people desert it, it will still exist. Its rules have been ordered by God. Shall He now reverse them? Besides, they have been given for our own benefit. If one abides by them, it is good for one; if not, one is only harming oneself. It doesn't affect the religion itself. Take the rules regarding correct slaughtering. It is not simply that the Prophet has said that animals that have not been properly killed— like those frozen chickens from abroad—are forbidden as food, and that somebody who eats them will go to hell. Rather, the point is that eating the meat of such animals will cause illness because their blood has not been properly drained. That is why the Prophet forbade it. Of course he knew that; not on his own though—he was illiterate—but God told him. Thus, it is a hygienic regulation which is good for us, the same way as the rule to bathe after intercourse or to perform the ablutions three times daily.

God is now giving us Islamic countries this wealth of oil. What value this must be when the big countries like America and the Soviet Union are coming to lift it with their own equipment, by their own efforts, and paying for it on top of it! This shows that God loves us. But our moral behavior is not getting better.

Twenty or thirty years ago people had a stronger faith and consequently practiced the religion much better. Women did not go unveiled. People had a greater brotherly concern for each other, even though we lived under a régime of oppression. And they used to observe the fasting and say the prayers. But today, if today the Imām Husayn personally came to the mosque to perform a rawzah, nobody would come. If, however, a band of musicians would play, they would all come in crowds. Certainly this has to do with the modern education. The illiterate son of my neighbor earns here a lawful living by his own hard work. But the boys who go to school go after the miniskirts and start drinking and gambling. My oldest son, who is in high school, doesn't fast or pray, the way I did when I was his age, and have done ever since.

In fact, it is written that the morals will get worse and worse, and that a time will come when blasphemy and unbelief will abound—until the Imām of All Time will appear. There is no date given for his coming, but there are signs to this effect, and some say his coming is close.

14

The Doubtful: Reason versus Tradition

The history of the Doubtful's family is filled with tragic violence. An elder brother died just before marriage. His parents, more or less obliged to keep the bride, imposed on him to marry her. Although he had ardently hoped to acquire an education, he had to drop out of school to provide for his household. His first child was still young when his wife committed suicide. Soon afterwards another brother was shot dead in a fight with some robbers who had stolen a couple of donkeys. The killer offered him a daughter as blood payment, but he refused and married the dead brother's widow. Then his mother killed herself.

In his mid-forties now, he has to provide for his wife and five young children at home and a son in high school in town, with rather meager resources. Although he owns a moderate-size herd of sheep and goats, he has little land due to the land divisions between brothers in his and the preceding generation. To improve the situation, he is wringing land from the mountainside for more fields, removing tons of rocks and piling them up in broad walls, smashing unmovable boulders, hauling loads of dung to enrich the thin soil, and digging an irrigation channel—a back-breaking job to which he applies his full vigor over hours without a minute's break. All this hard work he performs on the customary diet of a few thin flatbreads, tea, and a little sugar in the morning; the same plus five or six walnuts and a couple of small onions for lunch; and in the evening, a tray of rice with some melted butter on it and more bread. Luckily, in all his activities he is assisted by his shot brother's son, a strong young man, who—although married and a young father—is not yet pressing for a division of the common property.

Literate, outspoken, vigorous, and from a large, important lineage, the Doubtful is a well-known and respected man, although he is not one of the better-situated villagers. (1971).

Why do people make the pilgrimage to Mashhad?

The pilgrimage to Mashhad is made so as to contribute to the well-being of the Imām Rezā who was killed there, and to say prayers which will be salutory for him. In return for this beneficent act and the trouble that one has taken to get there, the Imām Rezā will intercede on your behalf with God. Also for miracles people are going there. The wife of one villager, for example, went there and was cured of her mental illness. God is working these miracles for the sake of the compassion of the Imām. But only for one whose heart is pure are these miracles made. People even believe that sins will be forgiven there, but this is impossible. God cannot forgive theft, for example, unless the stolen goods are returned to the owner.

It is the mullahs, the 'ulamā' who contrived these things. The 'ulamā' adulterated the religion so that the people remain ignorant, and so that they can reap a profit. They claim, for instance, that adultery and theft can be redeemed by saying a special du'ā'. Or, as judges, they will decide in favor of the person who bribed them. In reality the religion tells us, "Go, take pains and work hard!" Also, reason tells us that one must work hard to acquire means, and then help other people. But the 'ulamā' urge us to observe the daily prayers and the fasting and so on even if a man may be so poor that he goes naked and is hungry all day long. They say God will give him paradise, that the world is nothing.

What was the meaning of the Imām Husayn's death?

The purpose of his death was that the religion of Islam may be spread. He knew that he would be killed, like all Imāms knew everything about each man and each place. But actually his death was decided upon already in a former world, the Miniature World ('ālam-i zarr), in which all men appeared in very tiny form. But you won't believe what I am going to tell you now. In that world, the Prophet, Hazrat-i Fatima, Amīr al-Mu'minīn, Imām Hasan, and Imām Husayn stood before the throne of God—in fact, God created this present world for the sake of these five persons—and God asked, "Is there anyone who is ready to drink the Cup of Suffering?"

At first the Prophet drank a bit and his suffering was realized when his uncle knocked him some teeth out. Then Hazrat-i Fatima drank a bit;

this meant that Abū Bakr was going to kick her in the abdomen, causing a miscarriage. Hazrat-i Ali also drank a bit, which was the sign for his being murdered; his head was to be split in half by the stroke of a sword. The Imām Hasan drank a bit: he was to be poisoned by his wife. But when it was Imām Husayn's turn, he took the Cup and emptied it to the bottom. This comprised the passion of Karbala: that he himself, two of his sons, his brother, his nephew, and all the rest of the seventy-two companions were to be killed, and that his third son, his two sisters, and the other women were to be led into captivity.

For the sake of this passion of Husayn then, on the Last Day all sins will be forgiven. This is the merit of his suffering.

What happens after death?

During the night after a person has died his soul enters the body again—so they say—and there in his grave he is questioned by the two angels, Munkar and Nakīr. "What is your religion? What did you do? Tell us, let us see!" During the questioning an angel will stand beside a good person, but an ugly being, a ghoul, beside an evil one. If a person's life has been good, then his soul will be brought to a pleasant spot—which is not the paradise, however—and a beautiful girl will be his companion until the Last Day. This period passes so swiftly for him that on the Last Day he will think he died only yesterday. If, however, a person's life was evil, then time passes in the normal way—so they say—and his soul is tormented by a hideous apparition till the Last Day.

On the Day of Judgment the earth will be leveled and the souls of all people will be summoned and gathered in a large plain. One will see the other souls in the form of human bodies and they will appear like men. All will be questioned by angels on the command of God, "Why did you do that?" Someone with evil deeds will try to deny them. But something like a film will be shown to him and he will recognize that every detail has been recorded. On the scales, good and evil deeds will be balanced. If the good side is heavier, he will go to paradise. If the bad side weighs down, he will be taken to hell for a length of time proportional to his sins.

This is what the religion says—we do not know, but we believe it.

But when will come the intercession of the Imām Husayn and the forgiving of the sins?

On the Last Day.

So what is the difference between good men and evil men if the sins of the latter will be forgiven anyway?

Well, the evil ones are tormented all the while from after death up to the Last Day. Only then, maybe, God will forgive their sins.

But can God forgive all sins?

No, murder will not be forgiven. Grave sins will not be forgiven. In principle, no sins that violate the rights of men will be forgiven. But sins violating God's own rights can be forgiven and perhaps will be so.

But are not these sins forgiven already by simply repenting them?

Well, no. . . . Repentance can only be made for sins that were committed out of ignorance—then one can say, "Oh God, I did not know. . . . " But when a person did something wrong with the intention to redeem it afterwards by repentance . . . in this case, no, repentance would not be approved of . . . so they say . . . well. . . . A curious science they have fabricated! By God, most of it surely is a lie!

Take what you just said, that man existed already a million years ago: that means nobody knows where we came from and where we are heading—it is impossible to know. They say "the soul"! But imagine all the people since then! Where did they go? And the soul, does it really exist? We don't know.

How come that some people say the prayers but steal nevertheless?

Because of greed. If you are passing by an orchard, you will not feel a desire to take some fruits, but we crave to do so. No, I myself did not eat others' property, but only because I restrained myself. Don't you know that all this is due to a child's upbringing, that this takes its beginnings already in childhood? If a child steals a watermelon and his father says, "Wow, how nice, what a fine watermelon you've got!" then the child surely will steal two pieces the next day. If, however, the father rebukes the child, he won't do it again. In this way good and evil behavior is bred.

And yet, we don't know what will happen on the Day of Judgment. Hafiz of Shiraz said, "At times I come to think that I, who always sought to do good, and the other, who did not so, at the end shall find ourselves in the same row." But at least in this life, in this world, the effects of good and evil deeds are evident. If somebody fashions a good life for himself just by stealing and lying, his descendants will certainly see bad days.

But why do they fulfill the other religious obligations?

Some say the prayers and observe the fasting and make the pilgrimage and so on just to appear virtuous in the eyes of the public. Still, despite all this, we know very well who is good and who is bad. We know who is a thief, a deceiver, a dishonest man, or what not, like those who are mixing vegetable shortening into the butterfat to make more money. To such people one must go and say, "Look, the world is nothing, the money of this world is nothing, you cannot take it with you. Why are you stealing the property

of other people? Why are you making yourself hapless for a few toman?"
But their thoughts would be all caught up, revolving around this and that.
They would say, "I am busy with my work. Where is the Last Day? Who
has ever come from that world to say that it exists?"

Or, there are those who betray other villagers and talk badly about
them. In earlier times, for example, a successful hunter had to give one hind
leg of each killed animal to the Landlord. A man would not say, "I have not
shot anything," because the neighbors would notice anyhow, but he could
mention only one instead of two animals and distribute to the neighbors
and the Landlord accordingly. But there are malicious people who would go
to the Landlord and betray the man for a mere welcome—"Sit down, have
some tea!"—or a small gift. The chief would then send for the man and
assign him to carry a letter to some distant place. This would put him on
the road perhaps for ten days and by the time he would return, "chaff has
gone to chaff and grain to grain" as we say. He is behind in his work. Or
alternatively, the Landlord could send to him for a chicken to entertain a
guest.

The religion regards slander and betrayal as very bad. Such a person
will be known in the village for his deeds. Little respect will be paid to him
and rarely will he be given any help in his work. Also, God will punish him.
But people did it and still do it.

Why so?

Because of greed. Any doubts would be just waived. He would throw
them behind his back, saying, "Whatever exists, exists; what do I have to
do with it?" The fact that a person might be poor is no excuse. It would still
be greed. He could go to the Mullah and tell him about his plight. The
Mullah would advertise the case anonymously—so as not to injure the
needy's honor—collect the alms, and give them to him. Greed and seeking
pleasure are the two main causes for evil behavior. If there is much of it in a
village, earthquakes, floods, and diseases might come as God's punishment. Somebody's dream would tell the people that it was a punishment,
not just an accident.

So what influence does religion have on behavior?

For example, I did not go plundering although I could have done so. I
did not go because the religion prohibits it. Likewise, about half of the
villagers did not plunder because of the religion and the fear derived from
it. Among the other tribes everybody went. Even one who was a *Hajji*
went.

Also, the fact that help is given to poor families, that people refrain
from adultery, that by and large they avoid raiding another's property—all

this is due to the religion. The effect of the religion is that people are held responsible and punished. When a person is stricken with God's wrath, we say, "His deeds have become his own puttees," which means he has been caught up in his evil deeds, he is held responsible for them, and he is incurring God's wrath.

Does this account for the animals you lost this spring?

No, the size of the herd goes up and down. From my father I got fifteen animals. They became sixty or seventy, then disease came and so on—now there are much fewer again. No, animal husbandry we consider to be a matter of good fortune. Any gain, like more animals, butter, wheat, grapes, is due to good fortune. Fortune is a permanent companion. We say, "It is God's wish," when we see a calamity like the one that happened this spring with the grass and the animals. Only very few people would angrily argue with God over that. Rather, it is considered a trial, and if somebody shows patience, then it is good and it earns merit.

Can one protect oneself at all from hardships?

Sometimes a misfortune is announced in a dream and one can ward it off by alms. This is done. And against the evil eye hitting our house and against harm from the jinn my wife burns wild rue regularly . . . eh! They also say that the damband is efficacious against a wolf's attack on one's animals, but I don't use it. I have never tried it out. These are things . . . well, some work, some don't.

We have been told so many things! Take the fossils we found today. You say they are millions of years old. And what are we told? Incredible things they have fabricated! Didn't they tell us that from the beginning of the world till the Day of Judgment there will be 50,000 years? And now it is found that things existed already millions of years ago!

Who fabricated these things?

The 'ulamā'. Nothing about this is written in the Qur'ān. The 'ulamā' fabricated such things to keep the people ignorant and under their thumb—so that they can say, "People, you shall do this, but not that for the Day of Judgment will come and everybody will be questioned and will have to pay for his transgressions."

Also, they do it to reap a profit. Once I was in another village and imagine, it was the ninth day of Muharram and they held a wedding feast there with dancing and oboe and drum and all the rest. I asked the mullah, who was even attending the feast, how he could have possibly approved of that. He said, "They wanted me to permit it, so what can I do? If I had not agreed, I would be finished here."

What else did they fabricate? The veiling of women?

No, the veiling is in the Qur'ān. A woman should not have her legs and arms and body uncovered. That's obscene. A young man who sees a graceful girl with firm, fresh breasts and all the rest gets into such a state that he will go after her. If a woman were at liberty to give privileges, then the family would certainly not prosper. The sons would give no regard to the family and would desert it. We Iranians have a sense of piety and attachment to the family. That is why we are afraid in warfare. We think of our wives and children. The Russians, it is said, can fight so fearlessly because they have no family.

Now that the veil falls into disuse, clearly the religion is decaying. Maybe this deterioration will go on. When it will become very bad, the Imām of All Time will come and re-establish order.

Is the Day of Judgment fabricated, too?

No, this is one of the five roots of the religion, as there are: (1) that God is only One, (2) that God is just and merciful, (3) that the prophets have been sent, (4) that there are twelve Imāms, and (5) that the Day of Judgment will come.

What do you wish from God?

First, good health; then faith, that is, that I may always lead a virtuous life, so that God is pleased and won't torment me on the Day of Judgment—one is always fearful of the Last Day. Finally, I wish that I may always have enough for a livelihood.

15

The Calm: Grassroot Morality and Cosmic Harmony

The Calm, an illiterate man in his early thirties, is from a large lineage and has a wife and three young children. His economic condition is slightly above average, due mainly to his good-size flock. He has a shepherd of his own and can support his younger brother in high school in a small town outside the tribal area.

In his enterprises he largely relies upon himself and his wife. Although the brother of his recently deceased father helps him out occasionally and cooperates in the irrigation activity, he has no brother, son, son-in-law or other regular partner with whom to share the labor of the dual economy of agriculture and animal husbandry. Nevertheless, he keeps the animals in outposts all year round, which forces him to shuttle constantly between them and the village. Like others in similar situations, in winter he spends alternately three to five days in the outpost, taking care of the shepherd, the goats and the buildings, and one or two days in the village with his family and the sheep. To cover the three miles between the village and the outpost sometimes takes him half a day of struggling through knee-deep snow over a steep pass while goading the pack animals loaded with food and fodder for the outpost, or firewood for the village. In spring and summer he has to make the trip even more often, as the family and flocks in the outposts and the fields near the village require increased attention.

Thus, he moves in persistent, calm, steady dedication to meet the needs of men, animals, and fields, working from eleven to fifteen hours day after day and season after season. The only breaks are one or two religious festivals over the year and a few days spent on a shopping trip to a town in fall. (1971).

What is your life like?

Our life is great toil. But toil is not the constant moving around and hard work. Toil is hard work that is for nothing, hard work that leads nowhere. Toil is the trouble you take to fasten the load and on the next steep descent it will slip forward again and unbalance the animal and you will have to take it down and pack it up all over again, sling the rope and tighten it with fingers stiff with cold. Toil is when you labor all summer to secure the winter fodder, and you give the animals all the care, even run an outpost, and then, in late winter, just when they should lamb, they die in an epidemic—as it happened this year. This is the toil I mean. It makes us weary. For example, it would be possible to grow poplar trees here in the outpost and use them for our houses here, but we fear that someone may come and burn the house down when we aren't here, and then the whole trouble of growing the poplar trees would have been for nothing.

To take pains simply must be. Unless one is tired, one ought not to rest. I am taking pains so the animals will do well: keeping them in an outpost all year round, building a special stable for the kids that is warmer, getting additional fodder like the beet pulp from the sugar factory. Some people don't do this. They say, "Whatever dies may die, the rest for me." I take these pains not for religious reasons. I do it for my own good. If I didn't clean out the stable now, the animals would get sick and die, and the fields would not be fertilized; in the end I would have nothing to eat. But the religion, too, says one should work so that one can provide for the children and give to the poor. If I did not have bread for them, I would have to be ashamed of myself. The Prophet worked and we must work. The Imāms worked and so must we. Even if it is hard work, I do not worry about it. I am content to have my daily bread. When we die, we take only three meters of cloth. The rest we leave behind, so that God may give it to the children.

This is our life: eh . . . fields, animals, these houses, rocks, hard work, toil, scarcity, some bread, a little buttermilk. That's just the way it is. We happened to come into this existence and now we are bound to do things in its way. What else can we do? We have no other choice but to do it this way. Our life is this way.

Do you see any change?

In former times it was bad. About twenty-five years ago, for example, this outpost here was surrounded by tribes who drove away all our animals. This was in reprisal to the harm our chiefs had done them earlier. My father didn't get along with the chiefs, either. He had won a rifle from one of them in a bet that he would hit a partridge with one bullet. Later, the chief requested him to do something bad and my father refused. So the chief reminded him of the rifle. My father simply took the rifle and gave it back to him.

The insecurity was very bad. When I was eighteen, I went to work in Bushire. I saved 400 toman. On the way back—at that time we had to travel on foot and it took us ten days—on the way back with my companion, just when passing the village of another tribe, we were attacked by three robbers. They ripped off everything we had: money, shoes, even our shirts. Because it came to nothing the first time, I never went again to work in a town. The gendarmerie was powerless. They just said, "Show us the thief and we will get your property back." When we went after such thieves, men got killed on both sides.

This sort of brigandage has disappeared now. This is because of the gendarmerie stations all over the area and because many jobs are available in the harbor towns like Bushire. Now people can work and won't have to steal. But besides these facilities, the attitudes of the people themselves have improved.

The character of a child is formed by example and by advice and instruction. True, with some it does not work and beating them would not help either—they just turn out badly. Also, if his father or mother ate something forbidden, something that has been stolen, it makes the character of the child bad. But above all, it is the evil behavior of the parents. It creates miserable conditions for the children and it corrupts their character. In former times this was worse. Now the character of people changes through literacy and education and what we learn from the towns.

For instance, my brother, who is in high school and has read things himself, will tell me what to do and what not to do, although he is younger than I am. He says that the conditions in the towns are better than those in the village. The town is clean, the village is dirty. I do not even let him do any work here. I want him to study and so to free himself from our way of life. If I had some money I would run a shop in the village, to have an easy and comfortable life, but if I had a lot of money I would of course live in the city myself.

My brother also meets people in the city, good ones and bad ones. Once he got sick. The principal of the school inquired into his circumstances and gave him 150 toman to pay for his hospital expenses. I travelled to town to look after him and to return the money to the principal, but he would not accept it. He said, "I gave it in the way of God, I gave it to God, not to your brother." To help another person who is alone like this earns special merit.

Isn't your shepherd alone, too?

Yes, he is an orphan. He has nobody in this world, only a half brother—by another mother—who, until recently, used to take all his wages and still claims part of it although I think the shepherd should keep it all for himself. He has a crippled hand—it was not treated properly when he broke it as a child; his brother didn't care—and so he needs some savings.

Formerly he was the shepherd of a Sayyid in a nearby village. There, they did not even give him his daily bread, let alone his wage—there are only a few Sayyids who are not dishonest. Seven years ago we brought him here. Now he is eighteen and owns six animals and three kids in my herd. As a year's wage I give him five or six kids or lambs which, I think, is rather little. Sure, the custom is to give ten for each hundred animals herded and I have only thirty-five, but I don't wish to skimp on anything that is due to him. He should not tell others that he is dissatisfied and give me a bad reputation.

Sure, this is also a religious obligation. He is an orphan and I have to take care of him. So, for example, in winter when we are alone here in the outpost, I always sleep with him under one quilt so that he won't feel alone and have thoughts that worry him—the same way as we visit and talk with sick people to prevent them from having distressing thoughts. He is a plain, simple boy. Alone at night he would feel deserted and very low and without anybody in this world.

We shall see what will happen. If he wants to leave, I will give him even more than his accumulated wages. If he wants to stay, I will have to provide him with a wife and possibly also an inheritance. But then he would no longer do the herding—we will get a boy for that—rather, he would take up a share in all activities.

Are there also people who care for you?

Yes, there are. Our family group is one of the largest in the village. Especially the brothers of my late father give me a lot of help. They would, for example, water my fields, even if I could not manage to join them when it is our turn to draw water from the canal and irrigate our fields. Or they would sweep the roof of my house after a snowfall in winter if I happened not to be in the village at the time. Also, they settled the inheritance with me very fairly, without greed or oppression. They do this for religious reasons. They are very good men.

Outside our family there are other good people, such as the Representative, who defends our rights against the landlords, or the elder who supported my claim to settle here in the outpost. I am even better with him than with my wife's father; he, too, is a very righteous man, never unjust.

There are also bad ones, like some of the old-timers here in this outpost, who wanted to drive me out. One and one-half years ago when I came here and began building my house, they resented my coming. They feared that their own animals might get less grass. So one day they attacked me. Actually, the night before, I had dreamed that three black dogs charged at me. This means that a quarrel will happen. To avoid it, I left the village and came here to the outpost. I found the others working on the site I had selected for my own house. Quite apparently they had planned to challenge me. I claimed the site for myself, at which they started to beat me up with fists and sticks and even a hoe. Another old-timer separated us finally. I was so badly knocked about that I lay in my house for seven days.

I took the complaint to the court in town. Once it became clear, however, that I was in the right, I withdrew my charges. If I had persisted, they even might have been sentenced and in that way become destitute. That would have been very bad behavior on my part. Also, they are relatives of my wife. And they came to me and said they felt sorry about it. So eventually, I made peace with them.

They have no proper understanding of things. They live all the time in the mountains and do not sit with people of intellect. They did not want to recognize that every villager may come and settle in our outposts. The pastures around them are common property. Sure enough, in a quarrel each party feels to be in the right. But one must consult an arbitrator and abide by his decision. If one continues to quarrel, he is evil and has no moral excuse for it. In my case the whole village was against them. But now it is all right. They felt sorry about it and it is all settled and we sit together again.

Will they be punished on the Day of Judgment?

Well, for the religion it is evil to beat someone up who is alone and without guilt. They say—I am not literate so that I could read it myself—they say, that an evil-doer will be punished in the next world. But because I have waived it, quite probably nothing will happen to them from the side of the religion, either. Sure, they say their prayers meticulously, but some say the prayers only to be well-regarded in the village. Of course, we recognize the real character of those anyway, at least some of us do.

Certainly, the good deeds I do and the evil deeds I avoid—that is for fear of the Day of Judgment. Impious people probably tell themselves that the talk about the Day of Judgment is a lie. Then they will not be able to answer there, just as someone who has committed a crime cannot answer here. God gives mercy to those who have no sins, but not to the evil ones.

But whoever has an evil character will see the consequences also right here. If one has bad thoughts and an immoral behavior, his efforts will result in nothing. Recently, in a nearby village a wolf got into a stable through a tiny hole and killed or injured twenty animals. The owner of the animals was a habitual gambler. The others had for some time told him how wrong and evil this was, but to no avail. Now misfortune struck him. Anyone whose deeds are bad will see bad days. God wants it this way.

Look at the colors of this kid. Its head is red while its body is black. It's the wish of God that it is this way. And look at these two. One has a white spot on its forehead, the other one is all black, but both are from the same mother. God has done this so that we may know Him and have no doubts. Who can have doubts at that? This is not made by the hands of man. We cannot do things like that.

What will happen on the Day of Judgment?

On the Day of Judgment the human bodies will get up. Men emerge as far as to their waist, women only to their neck, so that their breasts won't be visible. Then they will be questioned. "Did you believe in God? Were you loyal to the Shah?" and so on. Then the good ones will be brought to a pleasant place, which they call paradise. There are gardens, fruits, a pleasant climate—all good things. The evil ones will be brought to an unpleasant place, which they call hell. There the conditions are perhaps like those of our life here.

And what happens right after death?

The body becomes dust. That we know for sure. The soul is carried off. First they question you in the grave, then the souls of good people are taken to a good place—they say—and of bad people to a bad place. There they will stay until the Day of Judgment. These places are paradise and hell. In hell they weep over every newcomer; in paradise they rejoice. Paradise and hell exist already now, but I don't know how this fact is related to the Day of Judgment. I don't know why the questioning takes place twice.

So when you give to others, you do it for the Day of Judgment?

Well, we feel pity when we see others in need. For example, when a poor woman comes and asks for some butterfat, our heart burns for her and we give it to her. For the same reason it is sinful to throw bread into the fire or to step on it. Is it better to burn it or to give it to the chickens or the dog?

Also, we have the custom to give part of an animal we slaughter to our neighbors. Three weeks ago when one of my animals fell off a cliff and I could cut its throat before it died, I sent meat to every house around here. This is our custom.

Aren't you troubled when you lose an animal like that?

No, it was not my fault. It was not its lot to live longer. Besides, all animals must die—just as man has to die. We cannot escape death. Therefore, I am not worrying about my own dying either. I am, however, fearful of the Day of Judgment.

Even if you have no sins?

That's hardly possible. You see, it may happen that a chicken is hit by a stone and I shall have to kill it. Then I shall have taken a life. God has arranged it this way, but, well. . . . Or I throw a stone at an animal to prevent it from invading a field and it gets hurt. Or I get angry at somebody, get into a quarrel and strike him with my fist. Or I walk over a clover field and squash the plants under my feet. Or I put a load on the mule that is too heavy. Or I do not give enough chaff to the animals. All that may be sinful, but hardly anybody can avoid it: so we have to be afraid of the Day of Judgment.

Did you make a pilgrimage?

Not a long one like to Mashhad, not yet. But when we travel into towns, we visit the shrines there. They are our Imāms—so we must go to their shrines. If, however, one helps the poor and commits no sins, then this is better than a pilgrimage. Helping the poor is very highly regarded by the religion.

What is the meaning of the prayers?

Those who are not literate do not understand their meaning very well, although most do say them. I have learned them from my father. I think they mean that God shall have mercy on all and make things available. With religious matters it is simply this: we do whatever we can get done; we do it if we can. But our conditions do not permit us to do everything completely the way it should be.

About written prayers, sure, one can protect the animals from wolves by a damband, but I don't do it.

Why not?

The costs are certainly trifling—several men around here can make it and they take only very little for it—but it should be renewed every week and we can not get to that. Whatever God may give me is all right. Whatever the wolf's share is, may he get it. The wolf must live on something, too. Likewise, when we are sowing, we say, "May first the birds and other animals have their fill"—and together they eat quite a lot—"and then, oh God, give me my daily bread, too."

The Qur'ān says that we should take good care of our possessions, but . . . eh, what shall we do? We don't get to it. The damband sure is effective to protect the animals, but misfortune just must hit them and—may it not be decreed—the wolf just has to eat them. Some misfortune or another just must hit them: if it is not this, then it is that.

Whenever a misfortune comes, we say it shall hit, for example, a chicken instead of perhaps a child. Thus, when a cow gets sick, we thank God that the misfortune has hit the cow rather than a child. If a child is very ill, we make a vow and we shed the blood of an animal and distribute it to the poor. For the sake of the blood the illness will be spared. Likewise, if, for example, a stone happens to fly toward a child but misses it or only injures it, then we would also kill an animal and distribute the meat, thanking God that the child has not been killed.

And why the killing of an animal when there is a twist in a wheat field?

A twist in a wheat field develops when the wheat turns out well and weighs down heavily. Then the people will start talking, "Look, how well his wheat has turned out!" and similar things. This is liable to bring about some damage, and to prevent it we shed the blood of an animal. If we did not do so, a loss would hit us.

If everything prospers especially well—plenty of wheat and milk and so on—then we are likely to suffer a great loss; for example, someone of the family may die. One year we harvested thirty man of wheat for every man sown, and from the eight man of barley that we sowed we reaped 300 man, and we had an abundance of butterfat and the like. That was in summer. In fall my mother died. In later years, the yield was never more than ten times of what we had sowed. Sure, after that rich harvest we gave to the poor, saying, "This we offer in dedication to God, so that no misfortune will come," but . . . well. . . .

Is the dedication you make to the mosque in Muḥarram also made for the prevention of some misfortune?

No, the dedication of the Imām Husayn and Imām Hasan is something else. That is not given to prevent misfortune. Rather, they are our Imāms and they have been martyred and therefore we make these expenses. From everything we have we must give. We cannot eat it all ourselves. Something must be given to God: for our welfare, health, and safety in this world, and so that He may have mercy and come to our rescue on the Last Day. So I and my wife decided last year that the Imāms should get one kid as their share of our animals. It did not find a buyer though, so I castrated it and it shall be sold this year. We won't shed its blood but sell it and use the proceeds to share in the expenses of the mosque during the mourning ceremonies. After all, there must be something available for the chest beaters and the singers and the rest. It is like the mourning for any dead person: the house that lost a member is taken care of by neighbors for that period. Sure, the house will also offer hospitality to visitors on its own, but the house itself is provided for by neighbors. In the same way, we contribute to the expenses of the mosque in Muharram.

Certainly, however, sometimes, if God chooses to improve the conditions of a house and wants it to be well off, He may also give plenty without a damage or loss later.

And how about this year? You lost many animals. . . .

I lost about half of them. Should I weep about it? One year is this way, the other year that way. One time things are good, another time things are bad. Of course, it is the wish of God: can we perhaps do something about it?

So God destroys in a few days the hardships of a whole year?

Yes, but in its place something else will do well—for example, the fields. Such misfortunes just must happen. We do not know what other misfortunes would have happened if the ones that did happen had not occurred.

Things we don't want must come. Animals must perish, men must die. This is destiny. One year many of my animals might die, but then the wheat might grow well. In exchange for losses something else will do better.

It is not known how the next year will be, better or maybe worse? One year is like this, the other like that—that's the way it is.

16

The Pragmatist: Immanent Ritualism

The Pragmatist, who is a member of a very large local lineage, has some literacy and is around 40, cares for a household of nine people, two young sons among them. He is fairly well-to-do, with enough animals to make maintenance of a herding outpost profitable. Yet, like all men in a similar economic position and with no sons to help carry the work load, he is hard put to manage both fields and outpost, and is on the go from dawn to dusk all year round. Somewhat less sociable than most others and very methodical and orderly, he likes to keep to himself and to spend his spare time on various small craft projects around the house rather than in the company of others. (1976).

What do you say about the way you live?

We are in need of some daily food, and, well, more or less we are getting it. The Lord is bound to give it to us. It is my belief that it must come to us. Of course, we have also to work hard and can't sit down expecting our neighbor to take care of us, but God provides. We'll always find a piece of bread. The livelihood we have to have we are going to have. But we are not making any progress. All we are able to do is make a living. And we are pleased with it. We have some tea and sugar, a shirt, these pants which are now four years old. In fact, we have got everything in this mountain waste: tomatoes, onions, potatoes, butterfat, honey. Any kind of food I would like to have now—God be praised—I could prepare. But we are not making any progress; that is, things are not getting better.

The reason for this is our lack of discipline and order, our failure to be good to each other. We do not pay the khums and zakāt. We do not respect the rights of our brothers, the rights of our neighbors. We are selfish. We are lying a lot; I myself say a lot of lies—that's the plain truth. It has become our habit to lie. It is because of this fault that we make no progress, that we are caught in trouble and hard work.

So it is not because God wanted it this way?

No, it is me who wanted this troublesome work, not God; I myself have chosen it. My brother and others went to school and then could become teachers. But I quit school after second grade and was not eligible for the Teacher Training Institute. So I myself wanted this sort of life rather than the other. But even here we could do things to improve our condition. We know how to do it. We could also manage to get to it. But we do not do it. So we ourselves cause us this trouble.

God—what kind is He? What sort is He? Praise be to Him—He gave us everything: eyes, hands, feet, everything. This body of mine is hale and well and healthy. I could make, for instance, a better door here, but I don't do it. In my view we could do everything, but we do not do it. This is the pure truth. I am talking of myself now, I am not referring to others.

I am guilty before God. This daughter of mine here is fourteen years old and she is illiterate. I have sinned by not sending her to school. True, household work is good. But today we want more than just a living; today we are thinking of social status. Now I am concerned she will feel grief about it. The other girls her age are literate and she is not. All my acts are like a mirror of my inner self. As a mirror shows my outward forms, so are my actions, at least to a certain degree, revealing my inner self.

No, our condition is not a matter of good fortune (*shāns*). It depends on us. You have to lift your feet yourself to get somewhere. We are envious and miserly towards each other, we do not like each other, we do not care for each other. If we were good to our neighbors, to brothers, sons, father, if the members of a family were of one heart, God would set things right, too. Then progress would come, too. It is this brotherly love that brings about good.

In this world or the next?

In this world as well as the next. But I believe in this world. It is all here in this world. All good and bad is in this world.

And not in the next?

Well, has anybody ever been taken to that world and then come back? No, nobody has ever come back from there. Only a Qur'ān was sent from the side of God. It says that the other world is so and so and so. But until now no person has died and come back from that world after two years or six months or one year to tell us what he has seen.

Do you think there is no other world?

Perhaps there is, perhaps there isn't. As I am saying, from that world nobody has come back, only a Qur'ān was sent. Not that I am not believing. I am not without faith. Of course there exists some being that has created us, some power, some essence. We are in need of everything, and everything is being provided. Sure, some account, some condition, some foundation, some truth, some God, something of that sort does exist.

But you regularly say the prayers. Don't you do this in view of the next world?

No, saying the prayers has no rewards. It is a way to mark time. It gives us a bit of discipline. When we get up early in the morning to say the prayers . . . well, it's good. And to perform the ablutions three times a day is good, too. Again, I am not denying the religion: I hold it in all respect. But what is important are the other acts, the service to the people: that has to be good. What I want to say, out of my own understanding, is this: we are in this world and we have to do good so that good will come into this world.

What did our prophets and Imāms do to become so great? Did they have an additional hand or foot or eye? No, they had the same bodies we have, didn't they? What they did to become prophets was good deeds and good actions. That's what I believe.

But evil acts result in evil. And the gravest offense is to harm other people. The Qur'ān says, "Drink wine and burn pulpits, but do not harm others."[11] Our Former Landlord badly oppressed us, taking from us by force whatever he could. How wealthy he was at that time! One day I saw how seventy loads of winter fodder were delivered to him. Now he has nothing. Now he lives in hell, in hell itself. He saw paradise, now he is in hell.

We also witnessed the case of another man, one just like us, neither good nor bad. But when he died and we wanted to put him in his grave—and it was a wide, spacious grave—the sides drew together, it narrowed in, it narrowed in so much that no matter what we did, the body would not fit in.

Does this mean he has to suffer in the next world?

Possibly he has to. They say there is a paradise in the next world, right? And that there is a hell where men are punished. I don't know. That's said according to the Qur'ān and the prophets. All I can say is that this happened. It is impossible to say for sure that he was an evil-doer—after all he was our kind, a creature of God; he died and we shall die too—but, well, to a certain extent his conduct was apparently not approved of.

Did that blind man in the village do something wrong, too?

No, he didn't. He was born blind. But it is possible that if he had not been born blind, he might have committed a grave offense, so to speak. We can't say that for sure, but it's possible. His blindness is the decree of God (*taqdīr Allahī*). The same God who has created us decreed that he should be blind when he was in his mother's womb. It has not been his share or destiny (*nasīb, qismat*) to see.

Recently, a landslide flooded one of your fields. Was this destiny, too?

No, again it's our own fault. We should have never started taking pains in this mountain waste. But still, I am hanging on to it instead of doing something better. The main irrigation channel has been destroyed, but here I am already digging a new ditch to save the small field of alfalfa over there. Also, it is our own fault when our animals get sick and die. It is because of our negligence. We do not attend to them in time and consequently they perish. Not that we wouldn't know what to do about it. We do know it, but we don't do it. But when, for instance, an animal falls off a cliff or is killed by a wolf, that is a misfortune sent by God (qazā').

Is there a way to prevent such things from happening?

Against the wolves we have the damband to spell-bind jaws. I have seen the effect of this perfectly well myself when once a wolf got into my flock for which I had made a damband, and could not kill a single animal. For this reason I always have a damband made for my herd. There is one hanging on the wall right now. In fact, I have never lost an animal to a wolf. But whether this really is the result of the damband we do not know. If it is, it may even not be good to make a damband because misfortunes simply have to come, and they should hit the animals rather than one of the family.

To ward off misfortunes from the family we get prayers written by the Prayer-Writer, we make vows, and we give alms to the poor on various occasions, for instance, on the first day of the month, or when we see in a dream that a misfortune is about to come. I have here this book in which the dreams and their meanings are written down. If it was a bad dream, we have to give alms to a poor family so that the evil will be warded off. This book contains also a portion of the Book of Luqmān, the Wise, who wrote down all diseases and their remedies. As you have noticed, I keep it around always and I consult it whenever one of us falls ill. Of course we see the doctor, too. But the wisdom of this book is very great: often it is of more use than the pills and injections of the doctor.

Do you also make pilgrimages?

Once every year we make the pilgrimage to the shrine of Imāmzādah Mahamad, a good day's travel from here. We do this first of all because he is an Imāmzādah and we have to pay him our respect—my father and forefathers have done it and I have to do it, too. And also, because we have vows to fulfill. For instance, when my youngest brother came up for military service, we vowed to give ten man of wheat every year if he were exempted. This is one vow we have to fulfill, and every year there are others. Also, one of my daughters is now promised to this Imāmzādah.

What does it mean, that your daughter is promised to the Imāmzādah?

When our oldest son was ill some years ago, we made the vow that if he recovered, we would give this daughter as an offering to the Imāmzādah, that is, give her in marriage to the guardian of the shrine—or whomever he may indicate in his stead—without taking any bride price. When this guardian came to our village, as he does every year, we told him that we had dedicated our daughter and asked him what we should do with her. He gave her to one of his cousins, saying he did not want her for himself. So when she comes of age, she shall be married to his cousin, and we won't take any bride price. That belongs to the Imāmzādah. Now we have given her and we can't turn back.

In the same way, my wife's sister had been promised to that Imāmzādah and upon marriage was given to a descendant of the Imāmzādah living in our village.

This Imāmzādah has worked many miracles, more than the other Imāmzādahs in our area. His shrine is now about a hundred years old and it has been rebuilt twice. The man who strikes the first blow with his pickaxe to demolish the old structure has to die within ten days. I remember when a Sayyid started the repairs last time. It did not take ten days before he fell ill and died. Of course he knew that in advance, but he was willing to perform this service.

Why haven't you been to Mashhad yet?

Because I cannot properly fulfill the rules and regulations of the religion. If I were to go there and people then called me "Mashhadi," would this be enough? No, I mustn't lie, I must live truthfully. But I can't. I believe that doing good to one's brother or neighbor is as if one went to Mashhad. Going to Mashhad is for this world, not the next. Everything is here in this world.

17

The Mashhadi: Ritualism without Certainty

The owner of a fair amount of land and animals and with only a small household to provide for, the Mashhadi, who is in his late fifties and illiterate, belongs to the better situated men in the village. He can finance his older son's university studies, can afford a relatively high standard of living at home, and has made the pilgrimage to Mashhad with his wife twice. His younger son worked with him for several years until he found a government job and left the village. Alone now, the Mashhadi and his wife continue to farm, still operating both the outposts for the herd and the fields.

A deliberate, solid and strong man, who comes from a well-respected lineage, the Mashhadi is one of the weightier men in the village and both he and his wife are highly regarded. (1971/76).

Recently you said that heaven and hell are in this world. How do you mean this?

If one lives in leisure and comfort, has a lot of money, and does not have to work—that's heaven. But one who has to toil and has nothing to eat is in hell. Someone who can simply take his car whenever he wants to visit someone, who lives in a city house, who is far from all discomforts and troubles, he is in heaven. But someone like the old man we have just passed, who in his old age still has to take pains in the fields, he is in hell. And so am I. You are in heaven and we are in hell. Everyone has a certain destiny. I have two sons, one a student, the other an employee, and neither is working with me here. I have to do it all myself. That's hell.

Does God take this hard work into account as merit?

According to our religion, hard work is a part of worship. Ali worked his own fields the same way as we do. He worked so hard, I can't tell you how. Once some people came to him when he was just planting melons, greeted him, and said, "Oh Hazrat, you are working yourself?" Ali, sweat covering his back, said, "Yes, our religion, our God tells us that work is a part of worship. Man ought to work for his daily bread." This is what is said.

Do you then expect to be rewarded for it?

In a way, we do. When, on a summer day, hungry and thirsty, we take pains and do our work, we say, "There must be something in this work." We'll see what will come of it. We are not without hope, but neither do we trust to be definitely going the right way. We can neither say we'll be given mercy, nor can we say we won't. We'll see what will happen. Do you know whether or not we will be rewarded? No! I don't know either. They say we will. They say on the Last Day we will be given the reward. What shall I say? Shall I say it will be given, or it won't be given, or what? Do we know it will be given? Ha?

If it is unknown, why do you observe the fasting, the prayers, and so on?

This is requested of us. Maybe someone will give us credit for it, maybe not. But these things we have to do. Our religion has ordered us to do them, and we have to obey. We'll see what will come of it. In any case I am observing everything and then—then shall God do with me whatever He likes to.

The people of any religion, be they Muslims, Sunni, Jews, or whatever, all say that their own religion is the best. But, as one of our former chiefs once said, "Everyone carries his religion in his heart." Things you do not like yourself, you must not do to others. As you do not want to be abused, do not abuse others. As you feel bad when things are stolen from you, don't steal. As you are offended by others looking at your wife, don't look at someone else's wife. In this sense the religion is in everyone's heart. If your eyes are not coveting my possessions and my eyes not yours, isn't that good?

If we want to belong to the religion of Islam, we have to follow its rules: not to covet others' possessions, not to look at others' womenfolk, to observe the fasting, to say the prayers. Whatever our Prophet, who has propagated this religion, has said, we have to do. Saying the prayers is good. Once a person who didn't say the prayers developed a large tumor. No matter what they did, it grew larger and the disease got worse. Finally a man came who said he would cure it. He washed it with water several times a day, and that cured it. He told the person, "To say the prayers and do the ablutions is good; it gives man well-being." Saying the prayers is really good.

But our religion regards especially stealing and lying and adultery as serious offenses. Like what our Landlord did in the past. We were taking pains and cultivating the fields, and then at harvest time he came and carried it all off, clean to the last straw. But I am guilty myself. I was one of his retainers. I knew it was evil to lend a hand to his oppressions, but I acted out of necessity. I had to protect my family. I tried to keep him from his wrong-doings, oppression, plunderings, adulteries, but to no avail. I quit as soon as I could and I repented my behavior before God.

Now this land reform came about. This land reform is like straight from the *Nahj al-balāghah,* the book of Hazrat-i Amīr. It says—I can't read myself, but I have heard it read at gatherings we used to have—it says, when Umar, 'Uthmān, and those came and wanted the Hazrat to oppress the people, he said, "I cannot do this. I cannot suppress the righteous. All land belongs to God and we are all equally the creatures of God. Everyone ought to work his land himself and so earn his daily bread."

The Former Landlord did not heed these words. Now he is impoverished and has a bad time, a thousand times worse than all the sins he committed. This is God's punishment. To us this is an evidence that God exists: that a person who committed such evil as our Landlord is punished for it.

What about punishment in the next world, after death?

After death the soul leaves the body and the body decomposes. Beyond this we don't know. Once a lumber trader was here, a Jew. He said that after death the soul goes nowhere. We'll see what will happen.

But there is what we call "summons of the soul." In the past, it is told—I was a child then—there was a rebel living in these mountains. He used to cut the knee tendons of any soldier who fell into his hands and abandon him in the wilderness. So they say. I have heard it from the Mullah and several others. They say that after his death his soul was summoned. Some men know how to do that. They have a prayer and do certain things and then call on the dead to appear. When this rebel was summoned, he said, "I have still not paid off the punishment for a single knee I've cut. I am being tortured and tormented and it will be for another hundred thousand years that I have to atone for my sins." So they say. Whatever! Only God knows.

Do you then believe in the next world?

If I said there is no paradise, and one exists, then there wouldn't be any for me on the Last Day. So I say paradise exists, hell exists, the Last Day exists, God exists. If I doubted that, then there just wouldn't be anything for me on the Last Day. So I have no other choice but to say, "Yes, all this exists." But listen: now it is eleven o'clock; who makes it twelve o'clock? Who turns night into day and day into night? Man has to have a bit of faith. Whatever religion it may be, it's good.

What is the reason why some are rich and others are poor?

This is the wish of God. It pleases Him to give to the one but not the other. It is not known on what grounds He is doing so. One is working day and night and has nothing, whereas another sits there in leisure and everything works out fine for him. One who has been doing evil throughout his life may be very rich now, whereas one who is pious and virtuous may live in need and want. Take the younger brother of the Former Landlord. He doesn't believe in anything. Sure, he says the prayers and he is also fasting a bit, but that's worthless. He was a thief and plunderer, and yet everything goes well with him.

The *ākhūnd* and *mujtahid* even say that one who worships more and whose conduct is more pleasing to God will be less prosperous. They say, "Lowliness to the faithful, glory to the unbelievers." This means the faithful have to be poor. But, take the trader of that small neighboring village. A man of such piety and integrity is not found again in the whole province. His eyes are blind to the property of others; his eyes are blind to the wives of others; he doesn't oppress and harm others. And yet he has plenty, in fact he is so wealthy that he will have to make the pilgrimage to Mecca soon.

Thus, nobody knows these things except God. We say rise and fall comes from the One above, from God. To the one He wants to give, He gives; to the one He doesn't want to give, He doesn't give.

Mustn't then a poor man disapprove of God?

A poor man has no other choice but to give thanks to God and to praise Him: to give thanks for the fact that his body gives him no trouble, thanks for his children, thanks for whatever he has. He has no other choice than to do that because cursing God would not help him in anything. The blasphemies of the whole world wouldn't even be a mere speck of dust for Him, just as the worship of all the world is not doing anything for Him. Thus, a poor man who shows patience, endurance, and gratitude is very good and he earns merit for it. When I will come home now and eat

contentedly my bread and buttermilk without upbraiding my wife for not
having cooked rice and killed a rooster—then this is very good and it earns
merit.

The Amīr al-Mu'minīn himself ate only barley bread, but at night he
used to go to the poor people and give them food and jewels. And God
made him very great. He was even present when the Prophet was taken near
the throne of God in the night of his ascent to heaven (mi'rāj); and the next
morning, when, as evidence of his presence, he gave the Prophet the lion-
shaped ring he had taken from him on the road and the other half of the
apple he had picked up at the meal, the Prophet recognized his greatness,
saying, "It is impossible to say that Ali is God, but neither is it possible to
say that Ali is separate from God."

What about blindness, accidents, and so on?

The blind man and the cripple we have in our village were born like
this. They were made like this by the One who created them, either God or
whoever. Can you ask God why He did it this way? No. Well, only He
himself knows. In the case of the blind man though, it may be that his
grandfather committed sins. He was a notorious hunter and shot a lot of
game animals, which is sinful.

As to the young man who was recently killed in an automobile accident, that is what is called destiny (qismat), the work of God. If it hadn't
been the work of God, he wouldn't have taken on that particular day that
particular bus which was to turn over on the road. And why should out of
fifteen people just this one get killed? As I have told you, rise and fall comes
from the hand of the Omnipotent. And only He knows why He is doing it,
and the Imāms knew, nobody else. Anyone else who were to say he knows
the hidden would say a lie.

If such things are destiny, why are you giving alms to ward off evil?

Well, these alms we give with the intention that God may turn away
His wrath. For instance, we use to give five or ten toman to a poor person
when setting out on a journey so that we may go and come back safely. We
give such alms especially when I or my wife have a dream foreboding some
evil. Besides, every year we pledge one kid or lamb as an offering, then sell
it and give the money to the poor—so as to ward off evil. And we make
vows to Shāh Charāgh and Sayyid Mahamad and Bībī Hakīmah, and then
travel to their shrines and bring them whatever we promised. Also, we
figure out what our zakāt is every year and give it to the poor. And we give
a bit of wheat or rice to the poor every Thursday night for the benefit of my
late father and grandmother. They have worked for us and we have to care
for them now. Finally, we have the written prayers to ward off the evil eye,

diseases, and other afflictions; and the damband and other spell-bindings to prevent wolves, boars, and other wild animals from ravaging our herds and fields. Certainly I believe in all this; if I didn't, I would be really in a different row.

The pilgrimage to Mashhad I have made twice already, each time together with my wife. Fifteen or twenty years ago, when we went for the first time, it was still a lot of trouble: jammed up in a bus, no facilities, and very expensive. But now it has become quite comfortable. Last time we remained there for some eight days. Every day we visited the shrine of the Imām Rezā several times. The glory of the Imām is boundless. He has six hundred servants at the sanctuary alone, and thousands of men find employment on his lands: an amount of wealth no king in this world can match. The pilgrimage to Mashhad is only a desirable act (mustahabb), but, they say, it is more obligatory (vājib) than the one to Mecca because the Imām Rezā was a stranger in this country when he was martyred. If we can afford it, we will travel again this fall. One should go there every year. Why? Because it is our religion; because the Imām was martyred there, and we feel compassion for him; and because they say it earns merit . . .

. . . which will be given on the Last Day?

IF it will be given—IF! They say so. . . . We'll see if it is true.

18

The Lower Peasant I: Low-Key Religiosity

In his mid-thirties, this peasant, who is from a marginal branch of a large lineage and has no formal education, struggles hard to care for his wife and five young children. Despite diligent, hard work, his meagre resources in land and animals allow him only a very modest life under the best of circumstances. Expenses for his oldest son's medical treatments of a birth defect and the recent severe illness and death of a brother taxed his resources even further. Constantly on the move and working under considerable pressure, he tries to make ends meet for his family as well as to help out his brother's widow and children. Like other men of similar background and standing, he is rather taciturn and generally neither given nor accustomed to express himself. Nor does he participate much in the sociopolitical life of the village. (1971/76).

What do you say about your brother's sudden death in the middle of his life?

We say it was his destiny to die. His life was just so long and not longer. It was written on his forehead at the very hour he was born. One person dies as an old man, another one dies young, like my brother. It is the destiny of the Lord. We say, "Oh God, thanks." We say, "God gave it and He has taken it."

His death is causing us great distress. Especially when I am out in the fields and alone, I am grieved and start thinking. I tell myself we ought to have taken him to the city sooner: maybe, if we had done so, he would have been cured. God knows. But it was his destiny. Otherwise, if the Lord had not wanted to kill him, He would not have made him ill. But I am turning these things over in my mind, troubled that we didn't take him there sooner. Or I am thinking that the fault was that the local doctor did not recognize the disease. We don't know. But well, it was his destiny. His measure was full. He just had to live that long and not more.

Did you make vows when your brother was ill?

Yes, we made vows and killed two sheep, asking God to save him. We took him to the doctors here and in the next town and, finally, in the city. Of course, we had to pay. We even gave money to the local doctor although he is from the Health Corps. Otherwise he wouldn't have come to our house. Altogether we spent 5000 toman. As long as someone is living, there is hope, and you have to try hard, spend money, fight for his life, take him to the doctor, to other doctors, do everything, and see whether it will have an effect or not. In our case it didn't have an effect. If one knew that an ill person would inevitably die, one wouldn't spend money on a doctor. But nobody knows, except God Himself. Some diseases get cured and others don't. But you have to make all efforts.

Is this also why you made the pilgrimages with your son?

Yes. One of his feet was crippled. He couldn't walk. First we took him to the doctor who couldn't make him well. Then, when he was five, we took him to the shrine of Bībī Hakīmah and to the shrine of Sayyid Mahamad. After that he started to walk. He started to walk because we took him to these shrines and implored the Imāmzādahs, saying, "Oh, Bībī Hakīmah may this child get well; may he be able to walk!" And, of course, Bībī Hakīmah is one who heals and so is Sayyid Mahamad. We also made an offering. We sold two kids and gave the money to the guardians of the shrines. Now the boy is ten. His foot has a small defect, but it's all right. He can walk.

But one of his hands is still crippled. The English doctor in the city said that it is paralyzed, that it was paralyzed in the womb of his mother. He said it is incurable. We implored him and said we'd give him any amount of money he wants. But he said, "It's not a matter of money. Don't spend your money—it's of no use." Now, in the fall, if we are alive, we will take him and his mother to Bībī Hakīmah again. His mother has made this vow and the boy himself asked me to take him there. So I'll take them. Maybe God will give him healing again.

Why did God do this to him in the first place?

Well, it was his destiny. This illness has to be. The works of God are there to show. They show man the things that can happen to him. The boy's destiny was that his hand be crippled; another one's destiny is to be well. It is impossible that all people be well or that all be sick. To one person God gives an illness, to another He doesn't, so that the one who is well may see the one who is crippled and do no harm to others and remember God.

But still, we have to go to the shrine. We think this way: let's take him to Bībī Hakīmah or the Imām Rezā or another shrine, and see if the Lord gives him health. It was his destiny to be this way. But if it is the wish of the Lord to heal him, should He be unable to do it? So it is possible to implore Him to have mercy on the boy.

Did you also get written prayers for him?

Yes. A Sayyid passed by the camp where my wife and children tended the flock, and they got a written prayer from him. But written prayers are useless for this disease. For some things there are written prayers and they are good, but for this disease there aren't any. Such a disease is up to God. If He wants to make him well, He will do it. If He doesn't want, He won't do it. But with written prayers it's impossible. That's how we think.

So it didn't happen because you or your wife committed a sin?

No, no. Neither was it the evil eye or the jinn. We say it was destiny to be this way. When his mother was pregnant with this daughter here and travelled to town once, the car came off the road on a pass and crashed down, turning over four or five times. One of the passengers was killed, but nothing happened to her and the child. All the doctors we took her to, here and there, were filled with astonishment that the car had crashed and she wasn't hurt. Well, the Lord didn't intend to kill her. It was that man's destiny to be killed in that hour, but not hers.

Or take the accident in which this young man was killed recently. He was already seated in the minibus leaving for town when he saw that a woman had no proper place in the pick-up that was to leave, too. He was troubled by that, got off the bus, and went over to her, saying, "Woman, come and take my seat." So she got into the minibus and he took her place in the pick-up. Just down the road from the village the pick-up turned over, as you know, and of all the ten people in it this one man was killed. It was destiny that that one person was to die in the group. He was in the minibus first so that we may see that what happened to him was his destiny. No, it wasn't because of sins he may have committed. His measure was full then. He just had that much to live and not more.

In your opinion, does God ever send punishment in this world?

Maybe He does. . . . Well, it does certainly happen. Sometimes one suffers some pain or has an accident and gets injured. This may be a misfortune sent by God as a retribution. We say, "For sure this person did something wrong that he is now afflicted by this evil." So we say. Yet only God Himself knows. We don't know. But we think if we suffer retribution here in this world, it is better than in the next.

Do you think it was God's punishment that this poor and crippled man lost so much in a flood recently?

No, it was his destiny. It was his destiny that the water would carry off his possessions. His hut stood in the path of the torrent, he is lame, he couldn't do anything about it. So his household was carried away. But certainly, if the Lord took this now away from him, maybe He will give him more somewhere else—one of his fields may yield more, or his animals may give him more butterfat. That's what we say. When, for example, a sheep dies or a crop fails, we say, "God will give something somewhere else instead." So we say—we don't know whether it is so or not. . . . But yes, it is so. We say, when one door is closed, God will open two others. That's how we think.

What is this poor man then supposed to say?

Nothing. He cannot make a complaint. He cannot complain about the hand of God. He has to say, "Thanks, oh God; it was Your wish."

When we suffer a damage or loss, we cannot say what it means. Maybe it happened because I am guilty of something, maybe I did something wrong. But maybe it was good so. For example, when an animal dies, we think maybe a misfortune was about to come and hit the family, but hit this animal instead. And we say, "May it be a sacrifice for the children. May it have died so that the children won't die." Even if I lost all my animals and possessions, as long as the children are well it would not matter. I can always go and do some wage labor to earn some bread for them.

However, in the case of our Former Landlord, who had so much in the past and is now living in misery, it is God's punishment. He committed oppression and now suffers the retribution for it.

Can you say that poverty is a form of retribution?

No. Poverty has to be, too. Some people have to be poor. Not all can be merchants; not all can have a car; not all can be rich. If all were rich, nobody would work for anyone else. Or would he? Would he perhaps follow someone's order? As long as he is not in need of work, one won't get him as a worker. So it's not possible that all be rich. Somebody has to be poor and another has to be rich so that the one carries out the orders of the other.

No, that's not injustice. When one is poor it is his destiny, as it is my child's destiny that his hand is crippled. That has to be so, too. People will help him, they will collect money for him, they will give him alms; so he will survive. The one with a lot of money gets by, and the one without any gets by, too. Somehow he will find a piece of bread to eat. But it may happen that this poor man, or his children, become rich, and the rich man becomes poor. That's also possible. That's how the Lord has made it.

What about the hard work you have to do: is this a punishment?

No, it isn't either. It is destiny that we have to do this hard work. This means that for the time we are living we earn a piece of bread so that we have something to eat and these children have something to eat; that we get a can of butterfat which we can sell to buy some sugar, some tea, and some clothes to put on; that we cut some grass and store it so that these animals won't die in winter, and we get butterfat and cheese next year. If we do not produce that, it won't come. By God, if one does not apply oneself but just sits there, it won't do.

What relationship does this have with the religion?

Well, the Lord has created us to do hard work. It's not only us: everybody has to work. A teacher has to give lessons and teach the children to get a salary. Certainly, his work is less tiring, but, well, he got an education and I didn't. He went to town and spent money and studied and now has an easy life. We say, the eyes of God have rested on him. Whomever the Lord wants to raise, He will raise; whomever He doesn't want to raise, He won't.

So God liked him more?

No, God likes everybody, but, well, it was his destiny to become a teacher. If everybody was a teacher, nobody would follow anybody's orders. If everybody was a merchant, nobody would carry anybody's load or do menial labor or work for those companies. Would he do it? No.

Will God take this hard work into account and give you something in return?

Sure, this wheat I am now harvesting I sowed in fall and now He is giving it to me.

I mean in the next world?

The next world—nobody has come back from there yet. Nobody knows what it is like. This body, which is of earth, rots away and the soul is taken to the next world. We'll see what the Lord will do to it. Nobody has come from there that we would know whether one will be given a merit badge or pains and trouble. They say that the good ones will be rewarded and the evil-doers will be punished. But we don't know whether it is true or not. They say that it is so, and we say, "We have heard it; it is so."

What's your own view about it?

My own view? Well, it is said one should do good in this world so as to fare well in the next world. If one is doing bad things, maybe he will be also bad off in the next world. That's how it is said. Yet I don't know how it is. We have a saying: "A sheep is hung by its own legs, and a goat is hung by its own legs." This means, everyone will fare according to his own deeds: a good one will be all right there and a bad one won't be. But—God alone knows. Nobody has come back from there so that we would know.

Nobody has come. . . ?

Well, the Lord has told us in the Qur'ān to do good. When one doesn't do good and turns onto the road of evil, the Lord will write down . . . well, He will know that evil; and He will know the good. On the Last Day the good ones will be saved. But evil and depravity are not good on the Last Day. According to the Qur'ān it is so. Because it is said by our Prophet, we faithfully say that it is so, yes, that it is so. For sure it is so. But what I am saying is that nobody has returned from there. Nobody came alive again so that we would know whether it is true or not. But we believe it.

Are you now giving the Thursday-night alms for your deceased brother?

His wife is. When we divided the family possessions among us four brothers, he took a special piece of land for the purpose of giving the Thursday-night alms for our mother and father. Now that he has died, we asked the Mullah what to do, and he said that because his wife now has this field, she ought to give the alms for her husband, too. She gives them to one of our neighbors, who will then say the prayer for the dead, the fāti-hah, for our brother. It is this fātihah, not the alms itself, that will reach him, and he certainly has a benefit from it.

Do you say the prayers regularly?

No, one day we say them, the other day we don't. That's worse than not saying them at all. This is, however, one of the aims of the religion: the religion tells us to say the prayers so that the Lord may give us a livelihood, or grant salvation on the Last Day—of course, nobody has as yet returned from his Last Day. It tells us to observe the fasting; to sacrifice a sheep; to say, when a child is sick, "Oh Amīr al-Mu'minīn, make him well again"; to give alms when we are in some difficulty; and so on—just so that we get by, that we get by for the time we are living. We shall see what will happen then.

19

The Lower Peasant II: Trustful Surrender to God

Although from a large, well-established lineage with large landholdings, this illiterate peasant has only little land, due to inheritance divisions in successive generations of large sets of brothers. One of the smallholders in the village, he can provide only a very modest livelihood for his large family of nine children despite hard work and long workdays. In his thirties now, he does not have much help from his sons because those old enough to work prefer wage labor in towns over agricultural work at home. Therefore, he has to do most chores himself. In the winter he tries to augment his scarce income by weaving and selling baskets locally. Busy, quiet and inarticulate, he does not feel at ease talking about transcendental matters, but is well-regarded among his people as a staid, reliable kinsman, and neighbor. (1976).

From the point of view of the religion, is agriculture better or wage labor?

Agriculture is better. That's because the crops we are growing we grow on our own. There is no stealing in it. It's clean and lawful. But with wage labor there is stealing. Yes, by God, there is. You see, if I am working with a company, I can lift this and that. And that's something that matters. It's wrong. But here I sow my own field, with my own seed, my own oxen, everything of my own—and I put my trust in God. Then it is a matter of what blessing He will give.

The boars, the worms, the birds, they will all eat from it, too. That's their share. We get our share, too. This year the boars ate a lot of the wheat in one of my fields. A few days ago we harvested it and it turned out that there were still three loads. The boars ate their share and we have our share, too.

So I sow a bag of dry seed in the field. The blessing that makes it prosper is then up to God. Sometimes we find that a field yields much, sometimes very little. Whatever God may give! We say, it was our lot (qismat) to turn out this way. We consider everything, good and bad, to come from God. Good comes from Him and bad, too. Yes, bad too, of course. When my finger got hurt today, well, of course, it was God's wish that it should happen this way.

Why should He send bad things?

What shall I say? God knows. We reckon this way: A person has to go the right road; he must not go round harming anyone, or stealing from anyone, or deceiving anyone. If he does so and God chooses to send him some grief, he still has to say to himself, "It doesn't matter." But if—what God shall not want—a thievery or some such thing slips his hand and then, sometime, someplace, he gets into trouble, that's of course because of that thievery he committed earlier and for which now he has to pay. But why has someone been born blind? That too is His wish. Or why has this poor man lost all his possessions in the landslide? Only God Himself knows. Sometimes, you see, God retaliates upon the wrong-doer himself and sometimes upon his offspring. So maybe the father or grandfather of this man has caused trouble to someone and today his offspring is paying it back. God knows.

Will he have to pay it back in the next world, too?

Again, only God knows. Nobody has come back from that world so that we would know what it is like. They say that some of those who have stolen or done other bad things have to suffer the retribution (mukāfāt) for their deeds right here in this world, while others must suffer for it in the next world. But this world man can see, while that world nobody has any information on—except God Himself.

As to my own belief . . . well, God knows. They say that heaven exists, they say that hell exists. Of course, in the Qur'ān, the book of God, it is pointed out by the Prophet that an evil-doer goes to hell, while a good person, one who goes the right way, is said to go to heaven. But that only God knows. A human-born has no information, no knowledge about what it is like. Of course, if one can avoid doing wrong throughout his life, that's very good for him.

But retribution here in this world we have seen in our own village. Most recently, there was a young man who had worked in Kuwait for several years. When he returned from there, he took his mother and all his family on a pilgrimage to Mashhad. Nobody ever believed that he would steal from his neighbors. But first he stole three cows. When people found out, they did not say anything. Then he lifted some money from a store. Finally, to make the measure full, he broke into another store one night and carried off goods which later were discovered in his house. Now he has been in prison for one or two years and he doesn't see his wife, nor his children. That's what we call retribution. This one has to pay it back right now. But there are others, God has pointed out in the Qur'ān, who must pay the retribution for their bad deeds in the next world.

Yes, I believe in this. It is pointed out in the Qur'ān, the book of God. In it the prophets have taught us what bad is and what good is. These things are known, that is, they are pointed out in this book. But this world man can see, that world nobody can see—no, nobody can see it.

But all these questions are very much beyond our reach. What we've got to do is to behave according to the words of God and the Prophet. Whatever He has said we have to do. So that things go well for me, I must not steal from others, harm others, or do anything bad against others, but rather mind my own business. When day breaks, I say, "Oh God, I put my trust in you. I want to go after my work, after my own lawful work, my own wheat field. I sowed it and now I want to harvest it." But I must not go and cut my neighbor's wheat and take it home. Our religion ordered us to do good as well as we can and to avoid evil. Whoever is able not to steal but to go the right road—that's of course the better for him.

And as to the prayers?

It's the same thing. If one can do it, saying the prayers is very good for a person's welfare. But there are people who are saying the prayers and stealing at the same time. Like that young man who embraced the shrine of the Imām and then came here to steal. That, we say, is bad. Others do not say the prayers and are not bothering anyone either. I, for instance, do not steal nor do I bother anyone, but I don't say the prayers. How this will be judged—that again only God Himself knows. Of course, regarding my own benefit, if I said the prayers regularly it would be good for me. I say them in fall and winter, at least at times, but now we are busy with our work. Saying the prayers has its rules. It needs to be done well and clean and with devotion. One ought not to say them in haste and, having hardly finished, run out of the room to work, or say them one day and skip them the next day. In this case, I think, it's better not to say them at all.

Also the fasting is up to a person. If someone, in his own good interest, observes it, it's very good for him. If someone cannot do so but doesn't bother anyone, again, we don't know whether God will forgive it. I am not observing the fasting, but give something away as alms to the poor. That's for not observing the fasting. Also, the fasting has its rules and trouble: you have to get up in time, say the prayers in time, and during summer it's very hard.

What if animals perish suddenly?

This is a misfortune (qazā'), and we must not be distressed about it. Maybe an illness—God forbid—was to come to this child and God cast it onto these animals instead. Only God knows where the illness came from, maybe from heaven, but He cast it onto those animals. Therefore we must not be upset about it; it's in the hand of God.

To ward off such evil from the family, we give some alms on the first day of every month, alms for a blessed month, as we say. We give some tea and sugar or some bread to the poor. These invoke God, saying, "Oh God, if some trouble were to come to so-and-so's child, You waive it."

There are also vows. One, you see, may pledge ten man of rice and cook it and invite people for a rawzah. Or one may offer an animal to an Imām and then sell it and give the money to the poor. Many here in the village dedicate a row or two of their vineyards to the Martyred Imām or the Amīr al-Mu'minīn and then give the grapes from these rows to the poor. No, I am not doing this. We haven't got that much. We are—God be praised—six brothers and each has only a few rows of grapes. We pledge something else instead. These vows are made for the good of the family, not the flocks. If the animals get sick, we treat them with medicines.

It is said that the people's talk may cause damage.

They say that if a person passes by a field with a good crop, looks at it, and says, "Hei, look what good a crop he has," without saying "*māshā'llah,*" it is like a scourge: some sort of damage or harm, it is said, will happen to the owner of the field. Sure, this does happen, especially with people from a certain lineage of this village. Last year one of them came up to a tractor in a wheat field and didn't say, "*Māshā'llah,* it is working well," but only said, "This tractor is working well." By God, it broke down instantly. Yes, when somebody's wealth becomes talked about by the people, it is harmful. But for us it is not important. By God, we have neither a car nor a large flock. At least at present the people's talk is not a danger for us. And for the future we shall see what God wills.

What did God create you for?

What shall I say? By God, that's not known. We must do this hard work because we haven't learned a job. From our first day we are dependent on this land. This was my father's occupation and now it's ours. We have no other choice. If some other work with a greater income became available here, I could give this up, but, as it is, I can't. We haven't got much, but . . . eh, God helping, we'll make it. We get up in the morning and go after our own work, the wheat, the irrigating, and such, and as we set out we say, "Oh God, I am doing this hard work trusting in You. May things be as You wish!" Then we lay everything in the hands of the One who has created us.

There are people who say, "To so-and-so the Lord has given that much wealth and to me He gave nothing." But what do I gain from such thought? Nothing. If my brother has and I don't, I am still content with the will of God. Of course, that's His wish. High and low and everything is made by Him—it is God's hand. Why should I rouse bitter feelings in me by saying my brother has and I haven't? Rather, I say, "God, everything as you wish. I am doing a bit of hard work, a bit of bread I am asking of you. Everything is in your hands."

20

The Wealthy: Legitimization of Good Fortune

A wiry, agile, literate, and smart man of about forty-five, the Wealthy is one of the most successful farmers in the village. He comes from a well-established, prominent lineage and has relatively large landholdings and herds. As all seven children living with him are in school, he cannot rely on his sons for much help, but this does not curtail his herding and agricultural activities because he has the means to rely on hired labor and seems to be able to find competent workers for his jobs. Recently, he even invested in trucking and, as in all other enterprises, is doing very well. Although one of the wealthiest people in the village, he does not spend much on consumer goods. His house and the living standard of his household of ten people are modest, and he and his wife are working very hard, spending little time on leisurely socializing in the village. Nevertheless, his industriousness, economic success, and personal conduct make him a highly respected man. (1976).

What do you think is the source of your success?

To plan before acting, to think in advance. If you want to move into the mountains tomorrow, you have first to go up and see what the grass is like and where it is best, and make sure that the campsite is safe from a flood in case it should rain, and think of all the other things that may happen while you are not up there yourself, because your wife and children cannot help themselves. So you have to think first. And you have to take preventions against certain things. For example, we have a disease called anthrax. If you do nothing to prevent it and it suddenly attacks your animals, it will kill them. You have to give them shots in advance. This spring we lost about fifty lambs and kids. This happened only because I was not in the herding outpost myself. Otherwise I could have prevented it. I was here in the village because of my injured arm, and there was nobody up there to properly take care of the animals. So they died. This has never happened when I was in the camp, because I have injections and other means. Also, I take care that the stables and other conditions of the animals all are the way they should be. After all, whatever it is, you have to take care of it and attend to it properly.

So one has to use foresight, and take preventions, and the animals need proper management. You have to take care of them, attend to them, provide fodder for them, pasture them, and take trouble. But not like a hired shepherd who doesn't care and only wants the day to end so as to get his pay. No, you really have to apply yourself.

Aren't all people working hard?

They are, but, well, some of them aren't working as hard as they could. Some could, for example, go to the far away pastures I use, but they don't. They think of the trouble, but I don't. I think of the animals. Sometimes I can't help thinking, "All the people are here in the village and I am going away to this outpost. Why am I doing this?" But an animal cannot talk. When a man is hungry, he can go into a house and say, "I am hungry, give me a piece of bread." But an animal cannot talk. When its belly is empty and it is hungry, I will be held responsible for it on the Last Day. For I am its master and it is my obligation to provide for it. I have to see to it that it won't go hungry. It would be sinful if I didn't.

People say you have received a gift from the jinn and that's why you prosper.

A gift from the jinn? That's laughable! No, that's nonsense. You see, that's the talk of the people. They say God—or whoever—gave him a truck and this and that and what not. They do not think how I have gotten these things. I have worked hard and taken pains. They, too, should work hard and produce!

Yes, people talk more about us. They say he bought a truck, he has herds, he is well-off, he has this and that and I don't know what. This talk of the people is worse than anything else. It's more dangerous even than a gun. Indeed, misfortunes are brought about by it. As you know, recently my son fell off the roof and broke his leg. That, I think, happened because of the talk of the people.

What can you do as protection against it?

God has to protect. Man only needs to keep God in mind in all he is doing. As to myself, I never wish anybody, not even an enemy, to suffer harm. I wish everybody would become wealthy. I do not look enviously at a person who has a car or a large herd. Even if he had 10,000 animals, I would honestly say, "Māshā'llah, may God make it more!" I will always help out a poor person by giving alms or giving him a loan over five, ten years, to pay it back whenever he can. And if he can't, I won't press him and demand immediate payment. So God will help us, too. The amulet against the evil eye (*nazarband*) protects against the talk of people, too, for the evil eye and the talk of people are of the same kind.

Do you use such means also to ward off evil and prevent harm and misfortune?

Certainly, to make vows and offerings and give them away is good. To give alms to the poor and destitute is good. One may have a bad dream and give alms and so ward off the evil. Also, to make sacrifices is good, that is, to slaughter an animal and give the meat away to poor families. Sacrifices are good for the herds, for men, for everything. It is possible that a sudden misfortune that is about to hit a person will be driven away by such a sacrifice. But sometimes it happens that somebody's sheep or goat or mule or cow dies. Then it is possible that the Lord had intended to send a misfortune onto this person or his family, but cast it onto that animal instead. So this person mustn't be distressed and complain of having suffered such a loss. Besides, we believe that in any case God will provide one with a livelihood if his faith is good. So if he should suffer a loss in his herd, his livelihood will come from somewhere else, unfailingly.

Yes, I am also using the damband to spell-bind the jaws of predators. I know how to make this myself. But sometimes I make one and then again I don't. We haven't had one for a while, and a few days ago—our shepherd must have walked away or, I don't know, been asleep or what—a wolf attacked our herd and killed three or four animals. If we had had a damband this wouldn't have happened.

Against the evil eye we do this: Let's say, somebody casts the evil eye onto a sheep and you know who it was. If you immediately burn a piece of his clothes or some of his hair under the feet of the animal, that will help. But it has to be done at once, so that the evil eye won't take effect. Once it settles, it's too late. There are people whose evil eye strikes instantly.

What about pilgrimages?

These are good, too. This spring I made the pilgrimage to Bībī Hakīmah because of my injured arm. It surely got better, but it's not yet completely well. However, the pilgrimage to Mashhad I haven't made yet. We have here a proverb, saying, "The grace of Mashhad is in front of your door." This means, helping the poor man in front of your door is as good. Once two men set out on the pilgrimage to Mecca. As they left town, there was a poor man sitting beside the road. At the sight of him, one of the two stopped, gave him all his money, and went back home. The other one travelled on to Mecca, but wherever he went on his pilgrimage, he always saw that other man walking in front of him. Thus, more important than anything else is to keep God in mind and to give help to the poor and destitute.

Does such behavior also bring blessing?

Yes. God says, "From you the action, from Me the blessing." That means, of course, good action, such as not to slander, not to steal, not to commit adultery, not to lie, not to covet one's neighbor's possessions or his wife or his daughter, and to do good things, to help others, and to say, "Oh God, I trust in you. All I ask of you is a lawful piece of bread." Then the Lord will, of course, give blessing.

Indeed, the Lord is not a miser. The moment a person's germ drops into the womb of his mother, the Lord allots him a livelihood. Even to a person who busies himself with thievery He gives one. He gives him his livelihood by the very means of this thievery. But this person will only have in this world, not in the next. On the Last Day he won't have anything. On the Last Day he will have to suffer torments I have no words for.

In general, what will happen on the Last Day?

This is the day of reckoning. Everybody's record of deeds will be brought forward, and he will be asked, "Why did you steal that person's property? The Lord allotted you a livelihood. Why didn't you pursue that?" Nobody will be asked, "Who was your father?" Rather, he will be asked, "What were your deeds? How did you earn your daily bread? And in what ways did you spend your wealth? Did you clothe the orphan? Did you feed him? Did you give bread to the hungry? Did you give help to the destitute? Did you say the prayers, observe the fasting? Did you avoid slander and adultery?" These are the questions they will ask on the Last Day. Somebody who followed the orders of the Lord will be dear to Him and he will be carried to paradise. But somebody who committed thievery, adultery, and those things will be thrown into the fire of hell. For in the Qur'ān the Lord says, He has opened the road for us and He has opened the pit. If one leaves the road, he will fall into the pit.

But the Lord is forgiving, very forgiving. For example, I am saying the prayers; but if I didn't say them, God would forgive it if I am doing good.

Also, if one repents his wrong-doing, saying, "Oh God, all the time up until now I have been a thief. I was ignorant, I was weak-minded, I lacked understanding, and so I did these things. Yet now I am repenting, I am turning towards you, and I ask you for a lawful piece of bread. Oh God, give me a lawful livelihood; no longer will I make my living by stealing,"—if one repents this way, the Lord will forgive it.

How come then that hell and punishment exist at all?

Well, making repentance is good only on the condition that one doesn't do these things anymore. No, God certainly exacts retribution. There is retribution in this world and retribution in the next world.

What is the kind of retribution given in this world?

If, let's say, a person does some harm to another one, the Lord will in turn inflict some calamity on that person; inevitably He will. He may go someplace and a mishap may happen to him: he may fall off a cliff or something. Sure, such retribution exists. In some instances the Lord afflicts immediately, but, well, He doesn't say it. Nevertheless, it is known. Yes, there are such cases in this village, but they cannot be told. That would be slanderous. After all, only the eyes of God see the true inside of a person. Of course, in the case of our Former Landlord who is now living in misery, it is an obvious thing. When somebody hasn't done any good and only acted to the detriment and harm of the people, his wrong-doing is evident to the eyes of everybody.

No, the flood that came down recently and carried goods and animals away, that was not a retribution: that was simply an act of God. Nor was the injury of my arm: that happened because of the ignorance and carelessness of the doctor.

What about poverty?

Well, with some people it is brought about by themselves. They are lazy, they do not work, they work laxly. With these it's their own fault—in fact, with most people it's their own fault. With the others, well, first of all God allots everyone a certain amount—one is wealthy and another one is not. Not all people can be equal. If all were equal, the affairs of this world wouldn't get done. Nobody would submit to anybody else, nobody would work for anybody else. One has to have and another one not, so that this one will work for that one and earn a living. But only God knows why it is that one has and the other one hasn't. For example, we have this blind man in our village. He was born so. That's the work of God. We cannot understand the works of God. Well, God knows, it's possible that this may be because his father or his mother had done something wrong. But it's impossible to think that way.

But well, man has to take pains in this life—he has to work hard to gain a piece of bread. Most of the people here are ashamed to work for somebody and earn a wage. Or when they work for themselves, they do not apply themselves with zeal so that their work gets done well and right. When you cultivate a field, you have to water it. If you don't do it, will you get anything? You have to water the field regularly so that it won't dry up. Then, at the time of harvest, the Lord will, of course, give you a livelihood in proportion to your work. Thus, we have to work hard. Working hard is the aim and meaning of this life. You have to work hard so as to develop your livelihood. A proverb says, "Drop by drop the water gathers to become the sea." Little by little, we keep on working, bit by bit we are advancing, moving up.

21

The Poor: Suppressed Revolt

With little land and a large family to care for, the Poor, who is around forty and illiterate, belongs to the 15% of villagers who are considered poor by local standards. The one-room house in which he lives with his wife and eight children has barely any floor covering, no pressurized kerosene lamp, few household goods. Dress is poor, food meager. He has no help in his work because his two only sons go to school. Realizing, however, that he will not be able to provide a livelihood for them on his small landholding, he insists that they get an education to be better able to fend for themselves later, rather than work for him or be hired out as shepherds. (1971/76).

It's a hard life for you and your family, isn't it?

Since the beginning of winter we've lost nine sheep and goats. Now there are six left. What is it all good for? Now we think these six are plenty. But only half our children have buttermilk to eat with their bread. There is not enough to go round for all of them. I ate plain bread for dinner and for lunch I had the same. We are not the only ones like that. There are many families in the village living this way: toiling, nothing but toiling, only rarely getting a rest.

Still, I can't say we have no blessing. When a large family like ours manages to feed all its children, it has more blessings than one that works equally hard, but has only few children and yet remains hungry. After all, I am only one person working and all eight children and my wife need to be provided for. I simply can't make ends meet. No matter how hard I work, I cannot make ends meet. They are nine and I am only one. Also, if these children were boys, it would be easier. A boy may run about half naked and it does not matter much. But six are girls. If a girl's clothes are torn or too short and her body shows someplace, it is sinful. People will feel pity for her. A girl's body must be covered well. But with a boy, no—anything is all right.

If there were some other kind of work, it would be good. But even so we are all right. Eh, we are working hard and we have something to eat. We have no savings, but be there none! It's only bad if one has debts. Well, we have debts, too. Nevertheless, God is great and He provides.

Why is it like this?

It is because I have no good fortune (shāns). Suppose I and you were brothers; you have a cow, you have sheep and goats, you have money, you have everything, and I have nothing: that's because of good fortune; God has given to you, to me He did not give. To one God gives plenty, to another nothing at all. The one can eat everything he likes, the other has to eat plain bread and go to bed hungry. To one person God gives no children at all—but look at us: māshā'llah, all these God has given to us. And in the cities one is a rich merchant, another a beggar. If He wanted to give to the beggar, He could, but He doesn't. Nobody can understand why God is doing it this way. You have studied a lot and still you don't know why God is doing it. Nobody knows, only God Himself. Not that God is hostile towards me. God isn't hostile to anybody. If He gives to someone, and not to me, it is His wish.

They say, God mustn't give to all equally much. If He made all equal, nobody would submit to anybody else. The work of one unable to do it himself would not get done. So one has to be poor and another has to be rich. But what is the result? The one who is rich has a comfortable life all to himself, and I have to go and work for him so that he may give me five toman and my children get something to eat. No, God ought to give to all. Why shouldn't all have something? Why should one live in want and the other in plenty? Nobody grasps for what reason things are this way.

Giving and not-giving, it's all in His hands. Possessions do not come from cleverness and such. It's not so that I can acquire possessions if I am clever—God has to give His blessings. Neither is our daily provision determined by our work. Rather, God gives whatever He wants to. Of course, we have to work—God says, "From you the effort, from Me the blessing"—but even if I killed myself working, He would not give me more than what is my daily provision. If it was five toman a day and I wanted to work hard so as to make it ten toman, it would be impossible to do.

Is it because of a person's morality or because of his prayers and fasting?

If I am saying the prayers day and night and observe the fasting, but my inner nature (*batin*) is not good, what is it good for? Observing the prayers and fasting is good, but, in my opinion, if your faith (*'aqidah*) is good, if no enmity and malevolence is in your heart, if you do not steal, speak ill of others, or have your eyes on their daughters and wives, it is better than saying the prayers and observing the fasting. The Prophet has ordered that if you want to fast, everything has to fast: eyes, tongue, stomach, and all.

But whether or not the Lord gives is not because of such faith and integrity and good and bad behavior. Certainly, if a person's deeds are good, God is more pleased with him. Which of your children do you like better, the one who carries out what you say or the one who doesn't? Or take Hazrat-i Muhammad: for what reason did God make him the Prophet? Because he was pure, he was truthful, he did no wrong. But the giving of wealth and possessions is something different. It is not on these grounds.

Take my neighbor. He has a quarrel with his son. If his son ate plain bread beside him, he wouldn't give him a cup of buttermilk. He would rather throw the buttermilk away than give it to his son—and yet he owns a lot. If God went by such behavior, He would not give as much to this man. On the other hand, there may be someone who is entirely content with a piece of bread, never harms anybody, and prays very much—and God does not give him anything. They even say that the Lord gives more to those who are very avaricious and do not believe. So they say.

So poverty is not God's punishment?

No, that's not God's punishment. God does not punish here in this world. At least, if He does, nobody knows about it. Well, there are some whom God has made destitute in this world for their evil deeds and oppression. But there are very few of this sort. Rather, they say, it is on the Last Day that God will punish.

Will then, on the Last Day, a poor man be rewarded for all his troubles and hard work?

What do we know about the Last Day? Will He give, will He not give? Only God knows. If one has a good life in this world, may the next world come in the end. But now we are in this world. If I am hungry now, shall I go to sleep telling myself that on the Last Day things will be good for me? No. But if I am not hungry, if God gives me enough so that I don't have to sleep hungry, let then the Last Day come in time.

You do not even know what will happen tomorrow or in an hour. And the Last Day you would know? All expect it, but who knows? They say that the good are carried to heaven and the evil-doers to hell. But it is not known whether this is true or not. Maybe they are lying when they say that heaven and hell exist. Nobody has come to life again to tell us how things are there. When somebody dies, he is put under the earth. After that nobody knows what will be done to him. What do we know as to where the soul will go, where God will take it to? Nobody knows these things. The mullahs don't know either. They say they have studied, and that it is written in the Qur'ān—perhaps it is, but nobody knows, except God Himself.

Do you believe in it?

Yes, I believe in it. Just as now it is night, and a new day will come, there is hell and heaven. How come it is now night, and day will come? How come you plant wheat, and it greens and grows, and you can harvest it? I have no doubt that all this is made by God. Yes, I believe. If I didn't, I would not be a Muslim.

What is then the correct behavior for the poor?

If a poor man's inner quality (bātin) is good, it is all right. But if his faith ('aqīdah) is bad, it is very serious. For example, if he were displeased that his neighbor has something to eat, or if he were to say, "That one has and I haven't"—that would be sinful. For God's eyes have seen both men: to the one He has given, to the other He hasn't. The poor has to put up with his poverty contently and say, "Oh God, thanks."

If he is doing so, does it earn merit?

God knows. Nobody has ever come back from the Last Day. But I shall say this: you, who are wealthy, are better able to give help to someone or satisfy someone's hunger; so you earn more merit. But I, who have nothing, from where do I get the means to give one a piece of clothing, so as to earn merit? Evidently you are the better one: you give away, you help, you make vows, you give alms; that's good.

But they say that on the Last Day God will give more to the poor, that He loves them better. What loving is this supposed to be? One who is wealthy lives in leisure and comfort; and I am getting up early in the morning, have to eat a piece of plain bread, go after my work, toil until noon, then eat another piece of bread, and get back to work again until evening. Shall I then tell myself that on the Last Day God will love me more? What loving is that? If He wants to love me on the Last Day, He has to help me also here, so that I won't be in debt, that my children won't run about in clothes I have to be ashamed of, that I can buy some meat or new clothes for my wife when she wants it, that my daughter won't have to walk barefoot and be without a veil, that my brother's wife or any other woman won't say my daughter has no skirt, she is barefoot, she has nothing to eat.

When they say that on the Last Day God will give more to the poor, it is a lie. They say this so that I, who have nothing, won't suddenly get a heart attack and die. They want me to say to myself, "Only now it's bad like this. On the Last Day it will be better." But just think: you are wealthy, I am hungry; you give me a piece of bread, and I become satisfied: this has merit. Or I have some debts and you help me out: this has merit, it pleases God. It will be good for your Last Day. But I, having nothing I could give away to anybody, what merit do I have?

Do you think this is an injustice of God?

God can do anything He wants to. Certainly, if a father gives only to some of his children and not to the others, we say it is an injustice. But in regard to God we don't say that. That would be blasphemy. Rather, we say it is His wish. God's eyes have seen the other and they have seen me. To the other one He has given, to me He hasn't. If I said He oppresses me, what would I gain from it?

Nobody can get angry with God. Even if he got angry, what could he do? Do we perhaps have any power? So whatever He may be doing, we say, "Thanks, it is Your wish." Because we cannot match His power. If we were able to, we could challenge Him and say, "Why aren't You giving to me, too?" But since we have no power, we tell Him flatteries, and say, "Thanks."

Now this daughter here pesters me, saying, "I want a shirt," and that daughter cries and says, "I want a veil." Well, shall I say, God hasn't given me the money to buy it for you, and leave it at that? That would be sinful. When a girl is not properly dressed, it is sinful. It's the fault of God. Everything is God's own fault. But if we wanted not to consent to Him, what could we do against Him? Since we can't do anything against Him, we have no other choice but to consent.

When your animals die, is it due to a lack of good fortune?

No. Sometimes a misfortune is to hit a person and make him sick or die, but it is cast onto a sheep or cow instead. That's the way we think. We say a misfortune came and was cast onto these animals. It is said that once the Prophet stayed overnight in the house of an old woman. In the morning the woman saw that her chicken had died. She lamented and said, "That's your fault. You killed my chicken." He said, "No, if this chicken had not been here, I would have died." So it is said that as long as there are animals in a house, a misfortune rarely reaches people. God sends it onto the animals and these will die instead.

Do you say the prayers?

If we get to it, yes. Saying the prayers is difficult for us: you have to make the ablutions, there must be water, you have to do the ritual bathings.

It is only for our health. God doesn't need our prayers. Nor our fasting. I used to observe the fasting, but for the last three or four years I have had a stomach ache and can't. Yes, we make use of the written prayers (du'ā'). Last year we had two made for this child when she was sick. They are good. God has made them. But, of course, a written prayer is effective only if it is exactly the one for that disease; otherwise it has no effect. We also make vows—if we have something to give. We make an offering to an Imām, but never to obtain possessions. If God wants to give, He gives also without offerings; and if He doesn't want to give, He won't give—no matter how much you are vowing or crying or lamenting.

THE EFFECT OF THE
REVOLUTION

I returned to the village for a year in 1980–1981 and another two months in 1983. By then the nature of religion and religious practice had profoundly changed. At the time when these cases were recorded they were variants of the generally prevailing religious tradition, and the individuals representing these cases, no matter how skeptical or critical they may have been of that tradition, nevertheless felt part of it; in fact they were its carriers. Now, a new blend of fundamentalism and liberation theology had assumed dominant, official position, and its carrier was the regime-supporting youth. The individuals of this book, with two exceptions, had no part in it.

Religion, hardly audible and visible in the past, had become a loud and pervasive affair. It literally was screaming off the walls. Religio-political slogans profusely covered the house walls along the main street, and the walls and roofs of public buildings. A flood of posters emblazoned the walls inside mosques, schools, offices, banks, and shops. Banners spread across the streets, gates, and door fronts. Powerful loudspeakers on top of the mosques summoned people to religious services and rallies, and blasted prayer calls and hour-long sermons over the village. Young mullahs and seminarians from outside the village propagated the new Islam in sermons, slogan chantings, and special study classes. Revolutionary Guards gave instructions in Islamic ideology and weapon skills in schools. Heavily veiled women teachers from Qom taught special Qur'ān classes to school girls, rewarding the best pupils with free study trips to the capital. Specially trained teachers operated a new department for religious education. In schools, religious instruction fully occupied four subjects and pervaded all others. During vacations there were obligatory religious seminars for teach-

225

ers, and summer camps with video-taped religion courses for students. At home, radio and television presented more sermons and religious instruction on all levels of sophistication. Rituals and processions were conducted in the spirit of the new Islam. Also, lifecycle rituals provided mediums for the new messages. Funerals of village martyrs were turned into propaganda rallies, and at weddings girls chanted slogans like, "Death to the opponents of *vilāyat-i faqīh*", or "Salute to the martyrs" instead of their traditional wedding songs. Last but not least, the new type of religion transpired from the new Islamic dress code, hair style, and body language.

A full exposition of this new form of Islam as well as the other new ideologies of the youth must be reserved for another volume. Here it remains to be shown how the individuals of this book, who quite well represent the older generation of the village at large, responded to the new situation.

As will be seen from the following edited transcripts, the world views of these individuals have remained virtually unaffected. These men say they cannot find anything new in the new Islam, including its emphasis on fighting oppression; they had practiced it all along when they fought the Landlord; it was the mullahs who had condoned his oppression and even profited from it. Nor can they find much Islam in the Islamic government. Such a government, they believe, should provide for the well-being of its subjects. Instead, there are warfare, bloodshed, refugees, economic decline, inflation, unemployment, inequality, injustice, repression, decline of education, and a general lack of care for the people's condition. Furthermore, they see no good in the regime's hostility toward other nations and no sense in an isolationist policy of "Neither West nor East." They find the ratio ale for the war as a defense of Islam implausible and the martyr ideology suspect. They condemn the regime's vengefulness against officials of the former government, the harsh punishment of moral offenders, and the enforcement of Islamic rules by violent means. They reject the clergy's dominant role in the affairs of the state, because they feel it causes the government's blatant failure. They disapprove of a policy of economic self-sufficiency which works to their, the peasants' detriment. And finally, they see the infusion of current political issues into the public religious rituals as a corruption of their original spirit, and deeply resent it. In an amazingly uniform, though in no way organized reaction, they express this resentment as well as their resentment against the regime in general by boycotting all regime-led rituals.

With this categorical rejection of the new religious form these individuals have set their spiritual lives apart from what has become the officially sanctioned state religion and its cult, thereby foregoing clerical approval as well as public ritual expression of their beliefs. Thus, their world views, which hitherto had been part of the overall religious tradition, have now become, together with that overall tradition of the past, the schismatic sideline to a dominant state religion. In the past, the Doubtful, though acridly critical of the clergy's fabrications, had nevertheless walked side by side with the Mullah in the Muharram processions. Now, neither the Doubtful nor the Mullah participate in these rituals any longer. The people themselves are perfectly aware of the emergence of this schism. As one peasant, certainly not a sympathizer of the Mullah, said, "In the past we and the Mullah were all one. But now, the views and intentions of those mullahs coming here are different from ours."

Of the individuals in this book only two became followers of the new regime and its ideology, the Young Trader and the Fundamentalist. The former, because of his attitude, occupied by 1983 a position in the village council, as I had expected him to do, and the latter represents the rare, if not only peasant of the older generation to favor the regime. The fact that from all the individuals precisely those became regime supporters whose epithets—given them years earlier—suggest the strongest affinities to the new regime constitutes strong confirmation of the correctness of my assessment of their world views.

The only other individual whom I surely expected to be in the regime's camp was, of course, the Mullah. In fact, upon my return I expected him to play a very important role in the new administration of the village, possibly the whole region. Here an unknown factor upset the prediction. As it turned out, the Mullah had been an agent of SAVAK, the Shah's secret police. After the revolution he had been unmasked, defrocked, suspended from his status, and put in jail for some months. Not surprisingly therefore, his mood toward the regime was resentful. When I asked him bluntly, however, whether, if he were still a mullah, he would preach the regime line, he flatly conceded that he would do so. Thus again, history provided strong evidence for the accuracy of the epithet I had given his world view years before, viz. uncommitted formalism.

The following thirteen sections are, with the exception of the Landlord's, edited transcripts of the here-relevant parts of conversations I conducted with these individuals during my post-revolutionary visits. The remaining eight cases were either omitted because of replication of ideas or had to be disregarded because of death or senility of the individual. Although it would be interesting to the reader to trace post-revolutionary developments of attitudes case by case, the nature of the commentaries necessitates their anonymous presentation.

The Former Landlord

Immediately after the revolution, remembering Khomeini's condemnation
of the land reform, he had, like other landlords and tribal chiefs in the area,
expected some sort of reversal of the land reform and reinstatement of his
former possessions. Soon, however, he realized that in this case the enemy
of his enemy, the Shah, was his friend neither. In the spring of 1980 he was
suspected of connections with the coup d'état allegedly attempted at the
time. He was arrested and spent some three months in jail for interroga-
tions. This treatment, as well as the fact that other landlords of the general
area, who had managed to hold on to larger possessions despite the land
reform, were now stripped of all but average landholdings showed him
definitely that the times of grandeur had passed for good. He continued in
his righteous attitude, but withheld any comment on the regime.

The Young Trader

He is one of the two individuals in this sample who approve of the new
regime. This attitude seems to be well in accordance with his bigoted lower-
bazaar type of belief system. But it was not until three years after the
revolution that he converted to this view. Until then he shared the critical
attitude typical of the village at large. "I disapproved of them from the
beginning," he said in 1981, and when I asked him why, he gave these
reasons.

It's because they only talk about Islam, but do not put it into practice.
For example, when Khomeini was in Paris, he said that in an Islamic government there should be no army; the whole society, everybody must be a
soldier of Islam. From the point of view of the religion this is correct. But
the religion says also, if one hits you, you have to hit back; you must not
submit to oppression. In the Nahj al-balāghah Ali says, "One who submits
to oppression is worse than the oppressor." We have to defend ourselves.
And if all our neighbors have an army, we have to have one, too. Thus,
when this regime came to power, they should have prepared themselves to
properly protect the country, and therefore keep the army in good order—
every revolution has a lot of enemies. Instead, they said there must be no
army, and set about to weaken it. Then, when the war broke out, they were

stuck. Now, young men with no proper training go to the front and are senselessly killed. I don't believe they are martyrs going to paradise. Who knows how many young men have been killed. If there had been a strong army, as there was under the Shah, this would not have happened. Also, when this reverend sir came to power, he immediately started to attack the whole world, made everybody his enemy. He should first have set the affairs of the country right, and then, like the Prophet, worked to gradually establish Islam and to create an example of true Islamic life. Then the world would have said, "Look, how truly human that society is," and come toward Islam all by itself.

I don't argue against the revolution. The majority of the people wanted the Shah, who certainly was an oppressor, out. So it was all right with me. But when this regime declared it would install an Islamic government, they would have to do so socially also. To practice Islam means that public property (*baitu'l māl*), like the oil money, must be equally distributed to all. It also means that people must pay the religious taxes (khums and zakāt) for the poor. Thus there are no poor in Islam. But now we see people who earn ten times as much as others, and a villager over there cannot afford a half kilogram of meat a year. That's oppression. That does not exist in Islam. In an Islamic society my income must be equal to that of others, and what I am eating must be available to others as well. True, also under the Shah this was not so. But the Shah never claimed to have an Islamic government, so he cannot be blamed. But this reverend sir who claims to establish Islam would have to put it into practice.

When I see what this regime is doing I am getting upset. Some people even gave up praying and worshipping as a consequence. As to me, I still do say the prayers, but with the regime now running the mosque I no longer go there.

By 1983 the Young Trader had completely adopted the regime's viewpoint and had demonstrated the sincerity of his conversion by shaving his head and joining for some time a volunteer corps on the front. Obviously, he had become persuaded that the regime does live up to his zealous Islamic standards. He now says he realized that he had been mistaken in his belief that the regime did not put Islam into practice. It does. Thus, it fights America, which had kept Iran in subjugation, exploited it, destroyed its economy, and corrupted the morals of the people by spreading its own immorality—as best seen in the millionaire who spends a fortune on his

dog and has sex with it. The revolution has ended this oppression, and the
defeat of Sadam Husayn will be another defeat of America's oppression.
Islam orders to hit back and take revenge. Therefore it is obligatory to
continue the war. The Qur'ānic injunction to make peace when the oppo-
nent offers it does not apply in this case because Sadam is an unbeliever and
also the Iraqi soldiers are not true Muslims; otherwise they would stand up
against their oppressors. The blood shed by the Iranian martyrs is like the
water of an irrigation canal which gives life to the crops. From it the religion will grow. If the Imām Husayn had not given his blood, the religion
would not have developed.

The Fundamentalist

From the day Ali died 1400 years ago until today nobody has succeeded in
putting Islam into practice the way God has said it in the Qur'ān. But we
have to try, in the same way as the Imām Husayn tried and became martyred. Today Imām Khomeini wants to establish the true Islam, but again
many oppose him and try to prevent it: America, which incited Iraq to
invade Iran, England, the Soviet Union, the Arab countries, which fear a
revolution by their own people, the capitalists, feudalists, Kurds, and other
groups inside Iran, and the people themselves. From among a hundred, not
one approves of the regime. They all want to oust this regime so that its
goal will not be realized. They know that if today Islamic law should be
established, they would no longer be able to reap their profits. These are
the people who tell you Khomeini has ruined Iran and destroyed the religion
and since his coming prayers and fasting have been discarded. These people
reject Islam. They are thieves and capitalists who say that only to give the
regime a bad reputation. But the masses of the people, the deprived and
destitute, the classes of the peasants, workers, and traders all approve of the
regime. This revolution has been predicted. Muhammad Bakr, our fifth
Imām, wrote over one thousand years ago that in the year 1400, which is
the current year, there would be an Islamic revolution in Iran, 80,000
people would be killed, and there would be unrest for six years until Iran
became victorious. He knew that from the Qur'ān.
      Islamic government means that everything must be done according to
the Qur'ān, where all the laws of government and society are laid down.
One of the most important rules is that there must be no capitalism. Our
Qur'ān orders that in any work one does, the fruits of one's labor are
entirely one's own; nobody has the right to oppress anybody. According to

Islam land is common property. A piece of land is at my disposal as long as I cultivate it. If I stop doing so, someone else can take it over. Everyone can have as much as he can cultivate. But if he hires someone to do the work for him so that he can sit at ease in his house, then it is capitalism. Hiring a shepherd is capitalism, too, because I will pay him only a small fraction of the flocks' yearly income so that my son can go to school and then have a good livelihood. Wherever wages are involved, it is capitalism. By the same token, owning a truck and having it operated by a driver is capitalism. Factories should be owned by all who work there, and whatever profit is made should be divided equally among them. Note that Islam does not forbid industry. Those who say that Islam forbids industry do so only to dupe people so as to be able to sell them their own factory products. Now that we have started to change, all the spare parts for our airplanes and helicopters are made by Iranian technicians themselves.

No, these ideas are not taken from communism. It's the other way 'round. Lenin took the part about workers and capitalism from Islam to attract the people. Then, when he wanted to subdue them, he told them there is no God, there is only nature. Religion tells people to fight oppression, and by telling people there is no God he deformed their minds so that they would be resigned to his ways. People don't see through these things. They are like the students at our universities. Some professors tell them, "We descended from the apes; everything is caused by nature," and after a while they believe it and become communists. That's why they had to shut down the universities.

It is not only work and property that is regulated by religion. All science and technology is taken from the religion, that is, from the five books sent from heaven to the five Great Prophets. Whatever research in the works of God scientists have done, they have not been able to recognize the tiniest bit beyond what God has said in these books. Of course, when someone learns something from, let's say, the gospels, he wouldn't say so, but pass it off as his own insight. But it is all from the heavenly religions. Beyond what God has said there is nothing scientists can understand. With all their science, can they prevent earthquakes? Do they understand what lightning is? How come that while you are asleep here your soul can be at a place far away, and when you wake up you are back here? Did they find anything on the moon? Even if they go there for another 100, 200, 500 years, they won't see a thing and they never will. Has anybody seen the jinn which are in this world? So how can they see the people on the moon? God has given us just these eyes and not any other ones. If they would give the money they are spending on all that to those unfortunates who are dying away in Africa and India, it would be much better.

Anonymous I–X

I.

The clergy should not be directly involved in politics. They should only give guidance. It is true that Muhammad and Ali held all political and spiritual powers. But in the case of Muhammad, there was nobody like him; he was the Enlightened Prophet. Therefore he was the leader, issued orders, directed everything, and everything was in his hand. Ali started out the same way, but as things developed he realized that it would be better for the progress of the religion if he stepped aside. So he did. Of course he and, later, the other Imāms were out-spokenly against any oppression. They exhorted people not to submit to oppression. But they themselves did not interfere in the affairs of the state. After all, if I say, "The world is evil, secular power means nothing, what good is it to rule people," and then come and assume power and govern people, my words will have little effect. But if I have no power and do not rule and say that, I will be better able to educate people, to make them truly human.

This regime wants to realize Islam in its complete and perfect sense. But this is impossible, at least for the time being—people won't go along yet. Also, it is doing it with force and pressure. This renders religious observance worthless and, moreover, it turns people off, it makes them dislike the religion altogether.

But the regime itself does things which are not right by religious standards. When they came to power they should have behaved like the Prophet: when he returned to Mecca he declared a general amnesty. They should have done the same. Instead they started to execute people without real guilt, in large numbers and without due process. That was wrong. Ali told his followers that they were allowed to strike his murderer only with a single blow of the sword because he too had struck only once. They were not allowed to torture him. Torture is wrong, and I completely disagree with the regime on this. The hostage taking was wrong, too; it is forbidden in the Qur'ān. As to the war, of course Iraq wanted to profit from the situation and invaded us. But then Iraq was ready to settle property claims by mediation, without killing. To continue fighting under these circumstances is wrong. After all, they are Muslims! This means the war is continued for political, not for religious reasons. Iraq does not want to destroy our religion, as this regime claims.

This regime has created a marvelous repression. The times of the Shah were much freer. Only in religious matters things were deficient, but this was the people's own mistake. Nobody was forbidden to say the prayers or forced to drink wine. No, what they do now is not Islam. In fact, for many things that would be Islamic the time has not yet come.

This man who says he will spread Islam is doing more harm and damage to the religion than all its enemies. Of course he has studied, he knows theology. But this is politics. Since old times they have said, "To become a learned man, how easy! To become a man, how difficult!"

II.

Now they say prayer-invocations for victory over Iraq, and military feats are presented as miracles of the Imām! What abomination! This bunch of mullahs and prayer-sayers from the mosques who now want to run the country keep heaping lies over lies to give the semblance of truth. There is a story of Mullah Nasr ad-Dīn. One night he heard some bustle out in the street. He wrapped his quilt around his shoulders as it was winter and cold, and went out to see what was going on. There a thief hit him, took his quilt, and made off with it. Back home his wife asked him what had happened. He said, "Nothing. They came for the quilt and took it." Now the regime supporters are agitating people by raising a big noise about the oil, the country, the Great Satan, the threat to the religion—just so that people will follow them. While our youths get senselessly killed in the belief of going to paradise, they themselves drive around in bullet-proof cars, live in the best of circumstances, and make off with the wealth of the nation. It's all to their own benefit, for their own profit. What is happening now is just the opposite of all I had hoped for. There is no hope in this situation, absolutely none, except if this regime gets changed again.

III.

When Khomeini said in Paris he wanted to come and restore Islam, which the Shah had destroyed by means of women's liberation, wine drinking, and so on, and that, in fact, he wanted to establish Islam in its perfect form, I really liked it. Not that the Shah was all that bad. He certainly desired progress for this country from the core of his heart, and he certainly liberated the local peasants from the landlord's oppression. But there were two big mistakes in his country. One was the liberation of women—I think that was too soon for Iran: people are still too traditional to understand and handle it—and the other was the corruption of government officials. Anyway, when Khomeini announced he wanted to establish Islam, I was all for it.

But when he came back to Iran and I saw what he and those around him really did, I became of two minds. These people did things which were not Islamic at all. From the beginning it turned out they were lying. In Paris Khomeini had said that the clergy cannot govern the country, and that he would stay in a mosque and have nothing to do with the government. But then, when he came, he seized command over all affairs of the state and called himself Imām—although we have always been told that there are only twelve Imāms. So that was one lie.

Also, in Paris he had said that they would divide up the oil revenues among the whole nation and send each family its share. Not that I took this serious, but it turned out to be another lie. And so it goes on.

Again and again it becomes known that mullahs and others in the government are stashing public money away for themselves. It now looks as if they have ousted their predecessors so that they themselves can steal. At the same time they have ordered the confiscation of the money workers bring back from Kuwait (because it may be payments from outside agents for opposition groups in Iran), and pay it out to them in monthly installments. That is, they take away the savings of workers whom I know had gone there because of the hunger and the distress in the eyes of their wives and children, and who had worked themselves dead to earn it.

But worst of all is the war. Sure, the Imām Husayn has said we should not surrender to oppression. But does that mean we should without reason set out and get into a fight with Iraq so that the Iraqis come and rape our wives and daughters? Should we say the Imām Husayn has said we should do that? It rather appears that because they cannot provide for the nation they pick a fight with everybody—and then call this Islamic!

Until now this regime has simply not demonstrated that it really has put Islam into practice as it had said it would. Sure, it stopped the wine drinking, which is very good; it stopped the liberation of women—that is, that they can behave as they please, in unlawful ways—which is also very good. But that's not enough. The religion also requires that the affairs of the state be properly taken care of, and this the regime cannot provide. These men can be religious leaders but not leaders of the nation. They have made such a mess of it that it will take decades to recuperate. What else can you expect when a mullah who calls himself Imām gets on top of you?

IV.

From all I know about the religion I knew that Khomeini's claims were unwarranted. He claimed he would spread Islam over the whole world. Has

the Prophet been able to do that? Has Hazrat-i Ali been able to do it? And
who is greater, those people or this sir? And he should be able to do it? But
why couldn't Ali do it? Because God has created man with a free will.
Therefore He cannot interfere. If He were to interfere, He would be responsible for man's acts and He could neither punish men in hell nor reward
them in heaven. Prophets were killed; the Imām Husayn was cut to pieces;
Jesus was crucified. But did the sky cave in or the earth burst open? Of
course, God could have maimed and blinded their enemies, but that's not
the order of things the way God has set it up. Therefore, when Khomeini
made all those claims of what he was going to do, it was evident they were
lies. Of course he knows these things a thousand times better than I do. But
he cannot act on it. His desire to rule, his self-complacency, his hatred of
the Shah did not allow him to do so. He has become blind, drunk with
himself.

He also claims to be the representative of the Last Imām, that is, that
he came to prepare the way for the coming of the Last Imām. I know this
cannot be true because the Last Imām himself does not know when God
will order him to come. Besides, the prophets and Imāms did not display
themselves. They did not desire status, worldly recognition, domination.
They did not make a show of their powers. But this sir allows people to
venerate him in a big way. He does not object when television puts him into
such close relationship with the Prophet that it appears there was nobody
but him and the Prophet, and keeps exalting him so much that the very
patch of rug he is sitting on appears to have been sent down from heaven
for him. Nor does he object to constant suggestions that he has the gift of
prophecy and miraculous powers. In fact, he pretends in the most ostenta-
tious fashion to have such powers by laying his hands on the heads of
children whom he permits to be raised up to him. Obviously, he is pleased
by all this. He seeks the adulation of the masses. He desires status, reverence, and authority. This is haughtiness, the gravest of all sins. Even if you
only desire to be greeted by someone, it is already bad. The devil was
condemned for only one act of haughtiness, not bowing before Adam, and
this sir, who day in and day out acts with that amount of arrogance, self-
seeking, vanity, and ostentation should be the representative of the Last
Imām? Moreover, the prophets and Imāms had miraculous powers. The
Last Imām would have the power to instantly strike down his opponents.
Khomeini quite obviously cannot do that. Furthermore, the great ones were
forgiving. But Khomeini is vengeful. He was exiled by the Shah and now he
wants to take revenge by having all those people executed. Finally, the
prophets and Imāms were kind and compassionate. Before his final battle
the Imām Husayn exempted his followers from the obligation of jihād so
that they might save their lives. Khomeini, however, pitilessly incites people

to go to their deaths. All these things showed and show that his claims are unjustified. He is not what he pretends to be.

In the meantime, this has become even more evident by the destruction he has brought over this country. Either he knew this or he did not know. If he knew—that our cities would be ravished, that our wives and daughters would be raped, that our youths would be killed in masses, that our children would become orphans, that our possessions would be carried away as plunder—if he knew that such disaster would happen and that he had no power to prevent it, then why did he do the things that brought all this about? But if he did not know, why should we kiss his hand? Ali said, the basis on which leaders should be judged is how well they provide for their people. Also, it is written that a king who had excellently taken care of his subjects was punished for two years in the other world because in one bridge of his realm there was a hole which made a sheep break a leg. And this sir here who has caused so much destruction: I wonder if there is any commensurate punishment for him.

I keep thinking of the time of the Khan. One evening I saw him standing on top of a small hill, putting on great airs and showing off in his fancy dress, gun slung over his shoulder, and I thought, "Will there once come a day when he won't be but I will?" The day did come. Now when I see this sir on television in full glory, I ask myself the same question.

V.

Paradise has become full with all the martyrs. There is no more room for us ordinary people in paradise. That's the way things are nowadays. In the past, the Pahlavis ended the raiding, established security, rooted out the landlords, and gave me the means to improve my conditions. Now it is the era of breast beating. Formerly one month was reserved for that, now it is to be done all year 'round. For good reasons. There is no life left in this country. People are vengefully executed and in hordes driven to their deaths. Nobody dares to speak freely. The government is too weak to provide anything. So they go around begging for money while they let the oil flow into the sea. All this came about because they follow this sir who has said, "In an Islamic country everything must be Islamic"—what wisdom! It's all a fraud. They tell our sons, "Go and drink the sweet cup of martyrdom!" If this were of any benefit, would they say it? They would not even allow us to sip from it. But since it is death that's the issue, they tell us to go. I say, "Let's go together lest it's you who get all the profit and we who give all the lives."

Reza Shah knew them. He kept them in check. He warned them not to do any mischief. Indeed, we have been told, "Woe to the day when the mullahs should come to power." I knew there would be disaster if this sir should come back and the country become a playground of the mullahs.

VI.

My son now is telling me about the true Islam; they have to fight a holy war and if necessary get killed. I tell him there is no holy war in the absence of the Last Imām. He shouts at me saying I do not understand a thing. These young ones are like unfledged birds. When they try to fly, they fall from the tree and a cat eats them. They cannot discern the right road. I tell him to stay out of everything, to mind his own business, and do his studies; it's not the right time. But he won't listen. He will get hurt. Before things started, my wife had a dream. She dreamed that from all over the water reservoir of the village there emerged people, blood gushing from their bodies. My spiritual teacher, who happened to pass by, said she was right; that that was exactly what was going to happen, but not in our region. Then Khomeini came and started to destroy everything. With big ostentation he says we don't want anything from the West, nor from the East, nor from anyplace. They themselves cannot provide things either. Also, they pick a fight with every country. What else shall come from this but destruction? It has to come that way. That's what Khomeini had to come for. When we cultivate a field we plow it one way, then across, until everything is entirely dug up: only then a crop can grow. In exactly the same way things must become totally destroyed. It will get extremely difficult. You think it is bad now? Oh no, nothing has happened yet! Only then fortune will turn over another card. It will happen all in one burst, like when a match is set to a can of kerosene—not in the fumbling way of some of the youths who are trying to change things now.

Once, someone in Isfahan claimed to be a prophet. When he told people to moo like a cow, they mooed; when he told them to bray like a donkey, they brayed. Then one day a person with mystical powers took him up to the balcony of Ali Qapu. There he struck him with the illusion of a great flood, the water rising rapidly up to them, and a boat coming to their rescue. In utter panic the impostor stepped out from the balcony to where he saw the boat, and fell to his death. In the same way, God will send someone like that who will wipe them out all at once. Inshā 'llāh, it will happen soon. Know now that what I have told you is right.

VII.

The present plight may be God's retribution for the people's unthankfulness. They had received God's bounty and become prosperous, but—in the cities much more than here—they did not thank God, they wanted more, they abused the Shah who had provided for them. Now they have lost even what they possessed before. From the beginning I saw that no good would come from the revolution. I did so because I knew that Khomeini had opposed the land reform—that's why he was exiled—and I decided that someone who had opposed the land reform, which liberated us from the landlord's oppression, was not going to bring us any well-being. And that is what happened. Certainly, they say the important thing is that they have established an Islamic government. But we were not unbelievers who needed to be converted. However much I listen to them, I have not heard the least I wouldn't have known before. They have not added a thing.

Over the years, faith and practice of religion have indeed declined. My son does not observe prayer and fasting in the strict way I used to do at his age. That's due to education. The more the level of education goes up, the laxer become faith and the practice of religion.

But this Islamic government hasn't been able to change that either. Whoever said the prayers before will do so now, and whoever didn't say the prayers won't do it now either. All they have done is put a piece of cloth on some city women who now wear it out of fear, not belief. But at the same time our women are carried off and raped in the war. What is better: that the veil be taken away from a woman or that she be taken altogether?

In fact, since they took over, ritual practice has even declined. You have seen yourself how much better our Muharram celebrations were in the past. And we don't go to the mosque any longer. When we go to the mosque, we do so for the sake of the Prophet and the Imāms. What business do we have there with America, Iraq, or Khomeini?

Sure, they say the essential thing they have changed in religious practice is that they actually fight oppression. But it was the Shah, not the mullahs, who took off the yoke of the landlords' oppression from our shoulders. While we fought the landlords, the mullahs supported them and profited from them. Now they have put the word freedom in the mouths of the people, but the repression by their secret police is worse than that by SAVAK. And at no time under the Shah was there the oppression of bloodshed, destruction, and misery of refugees brought about by the war.

They say the Shah wanted to destroy the religion. If this was his intention, why didn't he do it? He had the power to do it. Whom did he forbid to say the prayers? Which girl did he force to go without a veil? They even say he wanted to introduce communism although, in fact, he was a fierce enemy of the communists. Obviously they accuse him of communism, which says there is no God, so that we may say their government is surely Islamic, surely of God, surely a good government. It is because of such lies—lies I have heard with my own ears—that I have little confidence in this regime.

And there is one more thing I dislike. Khomeini does not object to being called Imām. He is even pleased by it. Our Qur'ān says there are twelve Imāms and no more. But this sir has firmly taken hold of that title. This is great arrogance.

No, I have no trust that they can run this country well. They have done us no good. From the day they came to power it kept getting worse hour by hour. Neither have they benefited our religion nor our country. Both are coming to grief. So on what basis should we have trust?

Their work is just to talk. They want me, for example, to plant wheat rather than fruit trees. They say the religion orders us to seek independence. But all this has nothing to do with religion. Rather, because they are the enemies of the previous regime, they have to say the opposite of what the former one said. Thus, because the former regime imported wheat, they have to say we must not import wheat and tell me to plant it. They don't figure out that on the same plot of land an orchard would earn me ten times as much as growing wheat. If the former regime had stayed on, our condition would be five times more advanced by now.

I am not saying that religion should be separated from the state. The Shah upheld the religion and gave our children the same Qur'ān they are getting now. Rather, it is a matter of ability. I wouldn't mind if this or that Ayatullah would run the affairs of the state as long as he is able to do so. But with this clergy, religion has got lost in politics. They push all the able ones aside and put their own kind—uneducated as they are in governmental matters—in their place. Therefore, although I approve of their religion— which is, as I have said, not more than what we always have had—I disapprove of their government. That's another reason why we don't go to the mosque. If we were to stand behind that ākhund, it would mean we follow him. But if we don't go, he will understand that the people are dissatisfied.

VIII.

For centuries, the clergy have kept the people preoccupied with religious talk, talk that was never put into practice. Whatever there was of the true Islam they misused to make themselves a good life. They spread fabricated and distorted things and in this way deadened the minds of the people. They did it because of ignobleness, love of the world, craving for status.

Some of the clergy wore their garb to gather people around themselves and make them devoted to themselves. But they did not pursue the essence of religion, that is, freedom and humanity.

The Imām Husayn whom they are flaunting so much now—again only outwardly, not in truth—fought for that freedom and humanity and in this struggle sacrificed himself and his family. The Muharram celebration should be a remembrance of this and a reminder for us to follow his order to do the same, that is, not to submit to oppression but to fight it. But the mullahs never taught us that. On the contrary, to put some money into their pockets they condoned oppression and ordered people to celebrate Muharram with crying and lamentation, promising after-worldly merits to everyone who wept for the Imām. So they kept people busy with religious talk. And now that all authority is in their hands this is more so than ever. They were right when they called for a revolution against the Shah because he was an oppressor. But I don't think that this was a real revolution. The clergy do not allow it that those basic principles, freedom and humanity, become established. Nor do they allow our sons to learn western technology so that they will themselves be able to build industry in Iran. The religion tells us, "Pursue science from the cradle to the grave."[12] They proclaim this very much now, but they don't practice it. In developing this country we should hurry up, we should go by car as it were. But they say no, we should go on foot, that has religious merit. In this way the clergy is crippling the whole country. The Shah killed and imprisoned students and crippled their minds. But now the clergy say that if the students were at liberty, they would leave the road of Islam, and they, the clergy, would become weak and disappear. So again they have suppressed the students and shut the universities and thus again have closed the road to progress in Iran. Again it is oppression. In the past it was the repression by the Shah, now it is the repression by the clergy.

They refuse to stop this war in which our young men are being killed for no reason. They simply tell them that if they get killed, they will go to paradise. This is a very cheap thing to say. Is there a proof for it? Of course we believe in the afterworld. But in a matter of such gravity, when thousands and thousands of young men are sent to their deaths in this belief, one should have especially strong evidence. We are seeing what is really going on and we know they are telling lies, but we cannot say it. If we open our mouths they shut them by force. Like our former landlords, they have gathered a bunch of illiterate youngsters around themselves by giving them much more money than they could otherwise earn and tell them to suppress us.

IX.

For our class of people who cultivate an acre of land it was neither good in the past nor is it good today. Certainly, conditions had improved under the previous regime—the landlords were ousted, security was established, our sheep and goats were no longer stolen, I even built this simple new house—but I am caught in this job without income, and neither that regime nor this regime has changed that.

Now we say, "Khomeini, our leader!" All right. I approve of our religion and whatever this sir may say. But there is one thing: those up there have to go around the country and the villages, and ask and see what income I, a peasant, have—a peasant who harvests a thousand kilogram of wheat and with his family eats twice as much. In winter we are so much afraid of running out of feed for our few animals that when ten days of winter have passed we are very happy and say, "Thank God, ten days have gone." We are taking the days off our own lives! Because there is not enough feed! So we are running around our few possessions and keep wasting our lives.

The inflation makes things even worse. This regime is only good for the businessmen. Everything has become so expensive! A piece of cloth that was five toman is now thirty. My son, who earns us some cash as a laborer, gets eighty toman for the day; eighty toman! That's one kilogram of meat. Just that.

It's also good for the class of employees, despite all they are saying. I can see it myself. Their children have better shoes and clothes and money enough to buy whatever they want from the stores. But I, maybe once in twenty days or a month can I afford to buy meat. This is our life.

The peasant class is providing the bread for the country. But until now the government has given us not one sack of fertilizer for free and it never will. It does not help us. It does not care about us. Nobody ever came around to our class to inquire about our conditions. For us it would already be a reward if an official came and asked and looked at our hardship—even if he gave us no money or help, but just encouraged us saying, "Praise to you. Well done!" Where is he? Recently a mullah came to our village. All he did was tell people to come to the mosque at night, say the prayers, and listen to his sermons. If I had seen him, I would have told him, "Sir, I agree to share the evenings with you in the mosque, but when you get your salary at the end of the month, we should split that too between the two of us." When this sir gives his sermon in the evening, he does not know what I have been up to during the day.

Now it is said the country has become Islamic. But it takes many, many things for Islam to become realized. Many, many things are needed. Suppose the center would allot us some help. Then there will be a wolf here and a wolf there and they will stop things from ever reaching us. Is this Islam? Unless God wishes to do justice in the next world, I don't know. In this world anyway I see no justice. Where is justice? Is it justice when a teacher, who is guaranteed his 10,000 toman every month, goes up to the irrigation canal and, to water his garden, cuts into my share, taking the water away from me whose livelihood depends on it? When the fertilizer shipment arrives, anyone who has the money and gets there quick enough can take what he wants. By the time I have scratched together some money and reach the place, there is nothing left, and I am forced to buy the fertilizer from someone at a higher price. Is this justice? Only hardship is our lot.

It's not known whether we shall be rewarded for this hardship in the next world. Nobody knows about that world except God. Maybe that sir who is at ease here will be so in the next world as well; and maybe a person who in this world is hard pressed and destitute will be so in that world, too.

God has told us to go the straight path: not to steal, to hurt, to harm others—this is Islam. I am going that road as well as I can. I do not observe the fasting because my job does not allow it. I am saying the prayers only very rarely because I do not get to it. I have not gone to Mashhad or Mecca, nor will I ever do so. I am just doing this hard work. I do not covet other people's property. I am not hurting anyone. This is the way I am living. As to the other world, God Himself has to know. Nobody knows about that world, nobody. This Imām Khomeini does not know either.

X.

Over the past ten years everyone's condition got better. Mine did, too. But now it is again going towards the bad. This regime has ruined all people. Formerly, at this time of the year, more than two hundred men from this village went to work in the cities and after three or four months came back with 2,000 or 3,000 or 5,000 toman. During the last two winters nobody has gone. The companies have been shut down and there is no more work. The two rental rooms I had added to this new house are standing empty. If it were as before, the rooms would be rented to some employee or shop-keeper, and I would have some income. Last year the government gave me a loan of 5,000 toman. But despite taking great pains I could only pay back 2,000 toman so far. So this year they refused to give me a new loan. My wife scolds me for not taking her to a doctor in the city. But we can hardly afford to travel to the small town an hour away, let alone a major city. We just don't have the money.

If everything were in the hands of Khomeini, it would be all right. But who listens to him? He says, "We shall come to the aid of the deprived." But who is coming? Where do they help destitute people? He is sitting in his house and has no idea of what is going on in Iran. He doesn't know that I am going without work.

Now they say the country has become Islamic. But what is it that has been added to our Islam? In the past we said there is a God, so we do now; we believed in Hazrat-i Muhammad, so we do now; we said the prayers, so we do now. Nothing has been added. Sure, they say that now they are fighting oppression. But the oppression is now greater than before. Is this perhaps no oppression when a worker who provides the bread for his family finds no work?

Before things were "Islamic," people had greater affection for the religion. More people said the prayers and observed the fasting. Now they are worried about the war, the bloodshed, the progress of their work; and they are distressed because their sons might be killed. You have seen our Muharram celebrations in the past: how many people there were, what devotion they had, what solemn performance they gave. This year there was nothing of the sort. These celebrations are meant to be for the Imām Husayn. But now they bring the war and other things into it. If you want to mourn for somebody and one tells you to mourn for somebody else instead, will you be pleased? They tell us to beat our breasts but to say Imām Khomeini instead of Imām Husayn. They are putting Khomeini in place of the Imām Husayn. That's not right. However good he may be, he won't be the Imām Husayn.

Why has all this happened? Because it was the wish of God. It was the wish of God that Khomeini would come to Iran, that the Shah would leave, that Iraq would start a war. If it had not been His wish, it would not have happened. Maybe He wished to punish people for their unthankfulness in the past. Indeed, Iranians did not appreciate the things they had. They were very unthankful. Now, perhaps they are seeing God's retribution for that. It was the people in the cities who behaved that way, not these villagers here who are hard-working. But it makes no difference. When a wheat field catches fire, the wheat burns down as well as the weeds. In any case, whether it was because of this unthankfulness or for other reasons, it was God's wish that things happened this way. Why did the war break out last year and not five years ago? Because it was God's wish that it would happen last year. Whatever happens is the wish of God.

The time of the Shah was very good. But you cannot say, "Why hasn't the Shah stayed forever?" Why hasn't Hazrat-i Ali stayed forever? They have to come and go. If we say the Shah should stay forever, it may not be God's wish that he stay forever. If it had been God's wish, the Shah would still be here. Not that God was on Khomeini's side. God is on no one's side. Why haven't the prophets stayed forever? They had to come and go. The Shah stayed for fifty years. Before him there was someone else; before that one someone else again, and so on. They came and went. Every shah developed the country in some way. What will come from this regime is not yet known. With this regime it is still like waiting for a meal, not knowing whether the rice that is being cooked will be enough for all. So it is not yet known whether this regime will be able to develop the country like the previous one.

THEORETICAL COMMENTARY

The Question of Religiosity

The cases presented show that in the thought of these people religious conceptions are taken as absolute realities which pose demands, threats, and promises each person feels bound to deal with, and provide the intellectual idiom in terms of which a large segment of each person's life is conceived, understood, evaluated, and filled with meaning. Besides these, there are other idea systems, notably the conceptions which inform the pragmatics of agriculture, animal husbandry, technology, and folk medicine; the indigenous, vanishing realm of manly heroism centering around hunting, bravery, conquest, raiding, and romantic love expressed in folk poetry; and the body of folk notions pertaining to property, status, politics, and marriage. These systems are based on their own logic, premises, and values, which sometimes are even contradictory to religious norms, but, although they are part of the people's picture of the world, none has the pervasive and comprehensive quality we commonly associate with a world view. Rather, for the people of this book—with the possible exception of the Old Teacher—the world view is provided by the religious idiom. It is the intellectual medium in which and out of which these people live. This realization may serve to deconstruct the myth of the "irreligious" Basseri of South Iran. In his study, Barth (1961: 135, 146) described the Basseri as "uninterested in religion as preached by Persian mullahs, and indifferent to metaphysical problems," and revealing "a ritual life of unusual poverty." On the basis of this description, the Basseri have later been elevated to exemplars of "an irreligious tribe" (Douglas 1973: 37), and "godlessness among nomads" (Spooner 1973: 39). From the present material it is obvious that there is

245

much more to a religious world view than mullah-religion, metaphysical problems, and ritual (narrowly defined at that [Peters 1984]). The notion of irreligiosity must be therefore dismissed as baseless. It serves as a good example of the kind of yarn theoreticians sometimes are moved to spin out of thin ethnography.

The Problem of Diversity

The cases presented demonstrate an amazing variety of individual world views in a single, rather homogenous village. I say amazing variety because it appears in the framework of a religion which probably more than any other denies the laity personal discretion and insists on the unquestioning acceptance of what has been defined by an elite as orthodoxy.

In this village, Islam can take the form of a bland legalism or a consuming devotion to the good of others; an ideology legitimizing established status and power or a critical theology challenging this very status and power; a devotive quietism or fervent zealotism; a dynamic political activism or self-absorbed mysticism; a virtuoso religiosity or humble trust in God's compassion; a rigid fundamentalism or reformist modernism; a ritualism steeped in folklore and magic or a scriptural purism.

Similarly, Islamic morality can be taken as requiring total commitment, permanent remembrance, and absolute inner purity or simply avoidance of harming others and punctilious performance of ritual. It can be taken as a justification for exploitation or the foundation for Islamic socialism. It can be taken as an uncompromising call to fight oppression or the sedative injunction to accept one's lot contentedly and gratefully. It can be taken as a declaration that inequality among people is as natural as the inequality of the fingers of a hand or as the injunction that no man must be the servant of another. It can be taken as demanding the expulsion of one's son if he should violate the drinking taboo or as repudiation of this and similar taboos as fallacious graftings upon the true religion. It can be taken to justify the subjugation of women or to assert their equality. It can be taken as a work ethic or a formalism which classifies ritual as more obligatory than agricultural work. It can be taken as disapproval of secular education because of its threat to traditional mores or as a request for it as a means to better the human condition.

Confronted with such fundamental diversity, we have to discard any essentialist conception of Islam. Instead, Islam has to be understood as the totality of all symbolic forms considered Islamic by people regarding themselves as Muslims; i.e., as an essentially unbounded complex of symbols and principles which on most any issue offer a wide range of possible, even opposing conceptions, meanings, attitudes, and modes of thought, each formulated with sufficient fluidity to allow ever more spinoffs, elaborations, and interpretations.

But this material teaches us also not to overlook the subjectivity of the individual believer. As we try to do justice to all, we must not forget to do justice to each. For Muslims, theologian, scholar, or layman alike, God can speak with but one tongue. Consequently, there can be only one true Islam, and that is usually the believer's own version. What we perceive as diversity, for the believer is a matter of right and wrong. Thus, while we acknowledge the various Islamic forms—African, Arabian, Indonesian; traditionalist, modernist, fundamentalist—as equally authentic expressions of Islam, we have also to acknowledge that in this sea of diversity each believer upholds his form as the only really true one. No doubt there will be even those Muslims who will be scandalized by the fact that beliefs they condemn as fallacious, corrupt, and totally un-Islamic are presented in this book not only without criticism but as Islamic.

Diversity of individual belief systems—though recognized—has been a secondary concern in anthropology. The thrust in anthropological research always has been to find the general pattern, the norm, the shared culture. Geertz (1966: 39) has made it even a methodological postulate "to put aside at once the tone of the village atheist and that of the village preacher." Consequently, we have become used to thinking in terms of the world views of The Azande or The Balinese. On the other hand, the portrait-type studies of single individuals (Crapanzano 1980; Critchfield 1978), although extremely valuable in other regards, are not apt to address the problem of diversity either.

I think we have to face up to studying diversity for at least two reasons. (1) As our descriptions get thicker, our methods more refined, and basic religion-of-the-Nuer-type studies plentiful, we will want to know details such as what kinds of persons use which concepts for what purpose under which conditions, or such characteristics that have been called world view vectors (Jones 1972: 85), or the distribution within a society of variables Geertz (1966: 41f) suggested for comparison between societies.

(2) The full range of existing beliefs has to be known before we can attempt to formulate generalities. If, in the study of Shia religion, we were to put aside at once the tone of the late Shah and the tone of Khomeini, we would see this religion not "in a clear and neutral light" (Geertz 1966: 39), but in a narrow beam that leaves much of it in the dark.

Consequently, our methodological guideline will have to be in a sense the reversal of what Geertz suggested, i.e., to fashion descriptions of religious systems in which the voice of the atheist and that of the preacher are equally well heard. The problem is just how to accomplish this.

I think two approaches can be dismissed entirely for the purpose; namely, the construction of shared culture and that of composite pictures. It has been claimed that anthropologists study mostly what members of a society share (Dundes 1972). If in the present case we were to limit ourselves to this, we would have to omit not only most of the ideas of such individuals as the Representative and the Mystic, and all of folklore, but also such core Islamic concepts as ultimate justice. The resulting description not only would be very rudimentary but outrightly trivial. Stromberg (1986) arrived at the same conclusion in his study of a pietist church group in Sweden. I think the notion that anthropologists study shared culture must be dismissed as a myth. Rather, what anthropologists actually present in their descriptions are composite pictures, systems meticulously pieced together from the most explicit, elaborate, and plausible accounts available on any given subject. The problem with this approach is that it gives the impression that everything presented is common knowledge, whereas, in fact, virtuosi and anthropologist were collaborating as high priests in creating the authentic text. Individual views which won't fit this text are appendixed as deviant or variant. This approach appears requisite in cases where no previous summary presentation exists to provide the basis for later work. In literate societies like the present, however, a composite account would amount to not much more than a partial reconstitution of orthodox texts, popular religious literature, and folklore compendia, with the possible addition of some local accretions, specialties, and applications. Diversity would be lost.

I think there are essentially two acceptable strategies to deal with the problem. One is the format used here and by Stromberg (1986), namely, keeping world views separate and trying to weave the general patterns abstracted from these portraits into a theoretical discussion, as I will do in this and the following chapter. The advantage of this approach is that it retains the structure of individual systems, the specific context, tone, and quality of individual beliefs, and the irreducible identity, genius, dignity, and creativity of each particular individual. Also, it preserves primary information as resource data for subsequent novel ways of analysis. The drawback is, of course, the inevitable tediousness of repetition of general patterns. There is also the danger of exaggerating differences, especially when, as in Stromberg's work (1986), individual views are paraphrased and summarized by the anthropologist.

The alternative strategy would be to present each concept and issue in terms of the whole range of existent meanings and possible uses the way I have just presented Islamic morality. In the case of the concept of qismat, e.g., one would show what kinds of persons hold which meaning of qismat and use it for what purposes under which conditions. Or, in the case of eschatological beliefs, one would abstract the commonalities (in the present case hardly more than the beliefs in heaven and hell, the Last Day, and the intercession of the Imām Husayn, and even these are not held by all), and then describe, with reference to specified categories of individuals, the details surrounding these beliefs, the various modes in which they are held, the forms in which they are put to use, and the ways their inherent contradictions are being handled. Through this method, one can gain a systematic presentation of general patterns but at the cost of the advantages offered by the former approach. Obviously, there is no best solution.

But this is not all. While on one level the problem of diversity is apt to throw the monkey wrench into our attempt to write smooth ethnographies, on another level of abstraction it prevents us from making smooth comparisons. For it forces us more than is comfortable to acknowledge the fact that in our descriptions we are dealing not only with various kinds of social groups (Shia, Islam, rural Iran, etc.), but also with various kinds of religious types (activists, mystics, pilgrims, peasants, etc.). The Representative is not only a Shiite who believes in Husayn's intercession and so radically differs from a Moroccan Sunni, but he is also a religiously inspired social activist, and as such, much closer to the charismatic Moroccan saint Lyusi (Geertz 1968: 29ff) than to any person in his own village. By the same token, the Mystic meditating beside a stream is closer to the quietist Indonesian Sahid (Geertz 1968: 28) than to any of his co-villagers. And the second Lower Peasant's world view is much more akin to that of middle-level peasants in a North Indian village (Lewis 1965: 253) than to that of his own uncle, the Old Teacher, whose humanism finds its congenial counterparts, again, outside rather than inside the village.

Such variation of types cannot be ignored for the sake of studying shared culture. These persons find the substance and meaning of their lives not—or at least not primarily—in the fact that they are, unlike their counterparts in other regions, Shiites, but that they, much like their counterparts, fight social injustice, seek mystical insights, work hard to make ends meet, and strive for public enlightenment. Of course, I am not arguing that we ignore group particularities. We could not possibly understand Khomeini, the Islamic Revolution, and some Iranians' zest for martyrdom without knowing the specifically Shiite form of Islam. But if we ignore in-group variation, ignore the fact that there are also quietists in Morocco and zealots in Indonesia, as we tend to do when we want to work out the ethos of a group (Geertz 1968; 1974), we will exaggerate contrasts to the point of stereotyping, and paint a picture of reality in rather unsatisfactory black and white.

Thus, a belief system, like an illusionist drawing whose two images constantly alternate to the vision, at once represents a particular group and a universal type. In its first aspect it looks inside the group for similarities, in the second to the outside. This Janus nature of belief systems is what we must learn to work with, though it may make it more difficult to talk about the Nuer conception of God, the Javanese sense of self, or the Moroccan comprehension of social experience.

The Dialectics Between Individual World View and Religious System

On the basis of the presented material we can formulate a model of the genesis of world views. In so doing I am following Berger and Luckmann (1966: 159) in an attempt to take into account equally well the roles of the individual and the surrounding social structure (cf. also Ortner 1984; Kracke 1978: 245), thus avoiding the social structural bias of traditional anthropological schools on the one side and, on the other, the overrating of individual autonomy in interactionalist studies or, more recently, negotiation analysis (Rosen 1984).

An analysis of the cases shows that in the formation of individual world views at least seven factors are critically operative: (1) the individual's personality, including mode of perception, psychoanalytic constitution, intelligence, memories, needs, etc.; (2) his social and political interests; (3) his socialization and education; (4) the social milieu he is living in; (5) his existential situation; (6) the perceived empirical evidence for certain beliefs; and (7) the preexisting world view.

These factors should not be understood in isolation; rather, each is intrinsically shaped by all others in a network of permanent dialectical interplay and interdependence. Thus, for example, a person's interest will influence the effect socialization has on him and the choice of the milieu he wants to live in, whereas, vice versa, socialization and milieu will, among others, contribute to the specification of his interests.

It is in the field of forces constituted by these factors that the individual's world view is forged. Under its impact—constraints as well as opportunities—a person's subjectivity interacts with the symbols and systems of symbols lying "in that intersubjective world of common understandings . . . outside the boundaries of the individual organism" (Geertz 1966: 6). In this essentially life-long process the person consciously and unconsciously selects, weighs, defines, gives meaning to, combines, structures, and integrates the concepts of the public cultural system he is confronted with and so creates a system indelibly and unmistakably his own. Thus, religious symbols do not simply "establish powerful, pervasive, and long-lasting moods and motivations in man" (Geertz 1966: 4), as if they possessed an inherent force of their own. A forked branch in the forest of Zambia which carries a cloud of meanings for the Ndembu (Turner 1967) is not much more than a piece of wood for the naive traveller passing it. Symbols have to be processed by people to attain meanings, and it depends entirely on the way they are processed in the field of forces described which meanings, if any, they will be given and which moods and motivations, if any, they will establish. Thus, the eschatological notions an individual may come to learn about will in his world view take on quite different forms depending on whether, for example, in his disposition he is more or less metaphysically speculative, his interests call for more or less morally questionable actions, his socialization was more or less intensive or fear-instilling, his milieu favors or ridicules the notions, his existential situation provides more or less comfort, the perceived evidence for the notions is more or less convincing, and the overall system of his world view is more or less amenable to them.

The material shows also that in a given case one or the other of the factors tends to have special import. In the world view of the Representative, for example, the impulses from his personality (a political genius and natural leader with sharp intelligence, unblinking courage, and a deep sense of responsibility; energetic, eloquent, judicious, assertive yet sensitive, reflective yet forcefully active, unconcerned with creature comfort in his relentless pursuit of pressing issues) and psychoanalytic forces (as suggested by his traumatic episode in his youth when he was cured by a vow to resign from landlord service, and his deep emotional crisis at the experience of the Landlord's sexual license) are clearly noticeable. The force of interests is conspicuous in the case of the Landlord advancing notions intended to legitimize his status and claims over the peasantry, i.e., notions that have, to use Max Weber's expression, an elective affinity with his interests. Also, it shows in the case of the Wealthy demonstrating Weber's timeless phrase that "good fortune wants to be 'legitimate' fortune" (Gerth and Mills 1958: 271). Similarly, the world view of the Old Teacher appears to be decisively shaped by the factor of education, that of the two Traders by the milieu factor, and those of the Poor and the two Lower Peasants by their existential situation.

The predominance of one factor does not, however, mute the others. In fact, each factor operates in every world view. Thus, as to formal education, all those individuals who reflect some kind of traditional orthodoxy had a form of religious education obtained mostly in Qur'ānic school; all those who can be called purist-modernist had some form of secular education; those one might call ritualists had very little formal education; and the Lower Peasants had none at all.

Our material thus requires us to conceive of the genesis of individual world views, and implicitly of the ways a cultural system impacts on the individual, in more complex ways than to merely single out early childhood experiences (Spiro 1967: 75f), everyday practices (Bourdieu 1977: 93f) or, as is generally done, the socialization process and give them determining status. Also, it appears too simple to say that it is in ritual that "men attain their faith" (Geertz 1966: 29). Not that ritual has no effect in the process—I would include it as part of the socialization factor—but there is simply more to it. If in this village people had only the more elaborate and public rituals to go on—which, as I have said, are very scarce—they would hardly be able to attain their faith at all. Besides, this factor is, as I have pointed out, dependent on all others. Thus, for ritual to be effective in the formation of the world view, the synergistic force of the other factors has to be such that a person does in fact perceive the ritual as it is meant to be perceived (the very meaning anthropologists try to discover), and attend it in the first place—something which for different reasons did not happen in the cases of the two Teachers, the Craftsman, and the Prayer-Writer, and currently is happening with none but the two regime supporters in the sample.

Applying the proposed model to the other aspect of the dialectic between individual and structure, i.e., to the way in which individual practice comes to shape the cultural system, results in the following conception:

An individual's world view created in the field of forces described will, whenever it is expressed, become part of the intersubjective world of cultural patterns. Thus, what for the individual is part of his own subjectivity constitutes for others an objectivated cultural pattern, or, to say it shortly, one person's world view is another person's culture. This means that all patterns in the realm of culture are issues of individual world views. As man lives in a culturally mediated world, that culture is itself an individually mediated world. Concepts taken from the intersubjective realm and processed by the individual are projected back into that realm where they function as resource material in the formation of still other world views. This implies that the specific form an individual gives to the received notions—i.e., the way he at once reproduces and, however minutely, modifies them—becomes part of the array of cultural patterns and so affects its nature. Thus, as a person shapes his world view, he shapes the cultural system, and the modifications he thereby generates form, like mutations, the building blocks of cultural evolution.

The spread of these "mutations" is then more than anything else a matter of power, access to distribution networks, and the ability to present them with such persuasion that they come to be perceived as eminently true. In this way, an individual world view like that of Khomeini (or, to be precise, those aspects of it which he deems fit for public consumption) may be propagated and enforced by the full thrust of nationwide networks and government agencies and so come to dominate the cultural system, to inform a large population, and be adopted by wide segments of it. Even so, however, no matter how impressive the system may be and how much it may be seen as the embodiment of texts conveying the absolute truth, we have to recognize that it is ultimately but the projection of an individual world view, and that any adoption of it will again never be its exact copy— just as the Fundamentalist's world view is quite different from that of his maktab teacher, the Representative. Indeed, Khomeini, like many a reformer before him, may shudder at the realization of what his followers make of his ideas.

Meaning and Action

In his breakthrough article on religion, Geertz (1966: 24) said that the religious response to the Problem of Meaning "is a matter of affirming, or at least recognizing, the inescapability of ignorance, pain, and injustice on the human plane while simultaneously denying that these irrationalities are characteristic of the world as a whole." There is, of course, no doubt that in Islam religious symbols formulate just such conceptions, and many of the present cases make, in one form or another, use of them though there are also those individuals who castigate the religion in caustic, though flippant ways for promoting these ideas. But the present cases show also that this is not the whole story. It appears that religious conceptions serve not only to recognize the inescapability of pain and injustice on the human plane, but equally well to deny it. One recognizes the existence of these things but refuses to consider them, in principle at least, inescapable: they ought to be transformed, and one conceptualizes this transformation in religious terms. Symbols are used not only to reconcile man with these experiences, but to formulate the expectation that they will be changed, here and now, in a concrete and tangible way. In other words, the confrontation with suffering and injustice is a Problem of Meaning not only in the sense of affirming that suffering is endurable and injustice not ultimate, but to redress the suffering and injustice. The Problem of Meaning is not only a matter of intellectual comprehension of and affective orientation toward suffering and injustice (Geertz 1966: 14), but a matter of action upon them, and this action is conceived in terms of religious symbols.

I shall discuss three areas where this latter aspect is evident.

1. *This-worldly reward and punishment.* The cases show a strong tendency to connect moral conduct and earthly well-being. Some individuals

are adamant in their belief that misdeeds inevitably will be punished in this world. For others, the realization that immoral people enjoy a good life raises serious doubts about the validity of religious doctrine. Conversely, there is the pervasive tendency to expect that good people fare well in this world.

For the religious establishment this linkage always has been troublesome. Though it may in some cases be advantageously exploited, it nevertheless tends to put religion to an empirical test which it cannot but fail. And any failure may fundamentally challenge the validity of what theologians are propagating, and so jeopardize their position. Consequently, they have to play it safe and, like the Mullah, maintain uncommittingly that reward and punishment in this world may happen but must not happen. More eloquently the point is stated in the biblical story of Job. In it, the establishment makes it dramatically clear that the good may indeed come to suffer terribly, but that when this happens, it does not mean that God—and justice—do not exist, but that, quite to the contrary, it shows the wisdom of His doings. But this very effort betrays the fact that human beings thinking in religious terms expect justice to prevail in this world, and transcendental forces to bring it about. To see only the clergy's version as the religious perspective, as Geertz does, is thus not enough. The popular expectation to see God's hand in this world must be equally recognized as part of it.

2. *Injustice.* The case of the Poor illustrates another area of concrete this-worldly expectation. He faults God for allowing poverty, saying, God ought to give to all people. Also, like most peasants, he rejects all certainty of an after-worldly enactment of justice, adding that such promises are no good if one is hungry: if God loves, He ought to show it by improving his present condition. Thus, for the Poor religion means not the denial "that justice is a mirage" (Geertz 1966: 22) but, instead, the provision of concrete help here and now. As this fails to come, his attitude is one of resignation: because we have no power over God, we have no choice but to accept His wish and tell Him flatteries. Likewise, the Ba-Ila referred to by Geertz (1966: 18f) do not glorify suffering, as he claims, but simply resign themselves to it.

Of course, one could call the Poor irreligious or an unbeliever (Geertz 1966: 24, 43), and so avoid the challenge to theory. But this would not only necessitate the rather questionable step of adopting a particular form of religious system as a true standard, but completely fail to appreciate the particular nature of the Poor's religious conception, a conception as authentic as that of traditional orthodoxy. This conception, in essence, holds the same idea which moved saints, charismatics, and reformers, including Khomeini and, of course, the Representative, viz., the radical transformation of human conditions including the redress of poverty and removal of injustice.

Such persons translate the Poor's demand for divine action into a divine command for human action and, seeing themselves as instruments of God, take it upon themselves to realize this goal. In doing so, they do not affirm the inescapability of social ills on the human plane, but, in principle at least, deny it.

3. *Suffering.* Another area to make my point with is the whole realm of what we rather condescendingly call popular or folk religion—the realm of vows, shrines, saints, written prayers, invocations, offerings, almsgiving, magic, mysticism, spirits, and the maintenance of virtuous and charitable conduct by means of which people attempt to take action on the tangible realities of their existence. This realm is so intrinsically tied up with religious conceptions, so pervasive in the lives of these people, and so explicitly dedicated to the purpose of avoiding suffering, that one wonders what Geertz (1966: 19) had in mind when he said that "as a religious problem, the problem of suffering is, paradoxically, not how to avoid suffering, but . . . how to make [it] sufferable." Maybe he thought of a late Western religion which under the impact of science has withdrawn into religiously phrased psychological support.

Overall, given the massive evidence, the avoidance of suffering is as much a religious problem as is sufferability, in the same way as both are also medical, psychological, or for that matter, economic problems. Again then, this is an area where religious conceptions are dedicated not to affirm the inescapability of suffering on the human plane but to deny it, demanding action and proposing means to concretely transform realities here and now. It is only in the very end, when deed and hope have no more in store—and then only if the field of forces in which the individual operates permits it—that the Geertzian formulation will be employed. First, however—and this is what seems to form most of the stuff of religion—man will bring to bear the means a religion offers to concretely influence the shape of things. When the Mystic, after his ill-boding dream, gives alms, he does so to escape misfortune; and when this escape (in his mind at least) indeed happens, his world view, which asserts—not absolutely, of course, but nevertheless in principle—the escapability of suffering, is conspicuously confirmed.

I have drawn attention to a particular dynamic of religious systems which requires us to revise established notions. Once this dynamic caused by man's insistence on the transformation of this world by transcendent forces—either directly or through their human instruments—has been recognized, we can better understand the persistent appearance in the history of religions of phenomena anthropologists have rather tended to ignore, at least from the point of view of critical theory: religious wars, persecution, witchhunts, inquisition, condemnation of science, enslavement of societies, burning of heretics, stoning of adulteresses, and terrorism in the attempt or the name of establishing the Kingdom of God on earth; human sacrifice, cannibalism, and headhunting to guarantee survival and well-being of a society; the bondage of mind and emotions, obsession with guilt and fear, martyrdom, self-mutilation, and self-enslavement in the service of an ethic defined by an elite; or the rise of chaos in man's soul when the transcendent fails to appear, as in the desolation on the cross or the anger of the Poor.

Thus, while it is true that the threat of chaos may drive man toward religious belief (Geertz 1966: 25), the reverse appears to be as true, viz., that the religious conceptions themselves, in suggesting the manifestation of the transcendent in this world, drive man physically or mentally, in one form or another, into chaos. So far, the anthropology of religion, muted by relativism, has been largely confined to the study of the first aspect, i.e., the innocuous realm of cosmologies, rituals, and cosmic guarantees of meaning and order. Maybe it is time we come to terms with the fact that the "moods and motivations a religious orientation produces" cast not only "a derivative, lunar light over . . . a people's secular life" (Geertz 1966: 41), but also, at times, the scorching glow of a pyre.

Peasant Thought

The present cases demonstrate an authenticity, creativity, and agility in peasant thought which is being increasingly appreciated in the literature (Geertz 1974: 32; Herzfeld 1985: xiii; Scott 1985). These traits appear especially in the astounding sophistication of some individuals' theological arguments, and in the ingenuity of the peasants' construction of systems that bestow intrinsic meaning and dignity on their work, something the clerical establishment has largely failed to do. Also, they are revealed in the poesy of the Representative's reasoning about the true meaning of life, in the sensitivity of the Calm's concern for life, in the Pragmatist's unadorned self-critique of his exploitation of his daughter, and in such insights as the idea that in anxiously checking off the days of scarcity in winter one in fact takes them off one's own life.

Characteristic of this aspect of peasant thought appears to be a con-siderable independence of minds. The people of this book, probably like peasants everywhere, are not subjected to a particularly intense and elabo-rate religious socialization, but they are living in a social milieu which, phrasing its ethics in Islamic terms and inducing conformity to Islamic norms, has a considerable conditioning effect. Nevertheless, individuals as-sert their own autonomy of thought. The Poor rejects the theory of the inherent necessity of social inequality, the Craftsman caustically repudiates the efficacy of prayer-writing, and the Doubtful and others entertain the suspicion that perhaps the injustices of this world will extend into the next. Many proclaim an unambiguous anticlericalism, and others—usually the less educated—maintain, parallel to their belief in eschatological issues, the quasi-agnostic, for orthodox ears shocking notion that nobody knows about these things, that nobody has ever returned from there to tell what they are like.

With the same perspicacity and mental autonomy peasants penetrate religious mystification. Thus, the promise of after-worldly reward for the poor is exposed as an empty lie propagated for the sole purpose of reconciling them with their present misery, popular practices as humbug fabricated by the clergy for their own profit, the ideal of martyrdom as euphemism for a death that benefits the establishment, and Khomeini's image as the result of media stage management. One woman in the village, illiterate and obviously stating an idea of her own, even surmised that perhaps the whole religion was made by men to suppress women (Friedl 1980: 171).

The capacity to penetrate ideological mediations has also been described for peasants in other areas (Scott 1985; Thompson 1966). However, the claim that "the penetration of official platitudes by any subordinate class is to be expected" (Scott 1985: 319) has to be dismissed as an overgeneralization. There are obviously broad areas of commercial and political propaganda everywhere which are not being penetrated by subordinate classes. None of the ready-to-die-martyrs I talked with in Iran pierced the ideology which led them to the battlefield.

Structures and Uses

What I want to elaborate on here is the phenomenon, plainly evident in the present cases, that on any given issue a world view offers not a single conception to interpret it with, but a whole set of alternative concepts each of which is apt to convey a different definition and meaning of the situation. This structural multiplexity or redundancy, or, as one could also call it, poly-paradigmatic structure of world views appears to provide a critical structural basis for the inherent plasticity of idea systems, a characteristic generally operated with but only inadequately understood in its mechanics. Thus, Rosen (1984: 43) grounds it in "a certain degree of vagueness" or "uncertainty" accompanying the use of any given concept. As the following examples will show, however, there is a clear grammar in the use of concepts, and the actors are quite certain when and where to apply which one.

The mechanics do not work primarily on vagueness, but on structural multiplexity, on the fact that several differing, even contradictory concepts can be brought to bear on any situation simultaneously. This allows an individual actor choosing among these concepts for one, to cope with the contingency of a particular situation in ways to safeguard personal needs, meanings, interests, identity, reputation, etc., and for another, to immunize his world view against threats to its veridicality. I will discuss this latter process in the next chapter. Here I shall illustrate the former process with two examples from the texts.

1. *Retribution and Forgiveness*. Regarding the eschatological question, world views contain two patently contradictory concepts: on the one hand, the basic Qur'ānic principle declaring that on the Last Day even the most minute delicts will inexorably be punished; and on the other, the specifically Shiite soterology maintaining that on the Last Day the sins of the Shiites will be forgiven for the sake of the Martyred Imām, i.e., the Imām Husayn who, in self-sacrificing devotion, shed his blood for the true religion.

This contradiction, to be sure, does not exist for the Mullah who, at least theoretically, minimizes the salvation aspect of Husayn's death or for Islamic scholars (Asghar 1969; Nasr 1969; Shehabi 1958) who entirely ignore it, but, as some of the cases show, it is quite unmistakably present on the popular level. When individuals are confronted with it (cf. the Old Trader, the Representative, the Doubtful), they try to reconcile the two paradigms, but in the process entangle themselves in even more contradictions. When, for example, in an attempt to uphold the notion of justice, they argue that punishment in hell is being meted out from the time of death until the Last Day, it implies the absurd conclusions that (1) instead of a day of judgment followed by hell and heaven there will be a day of forgiveness followed by paradise only; that (2) they forsake the benefit of Husayn's intercession for their own persons because they would certainly expect to enter paradise (which must exist before the Last Day if hell does) much sooner than the Last Day; and that (3) Husayn's intercession on the Last Day is utterly meaningless because by then the good will have entered paradise long ago and the bad will have atoned for their sins anyway.

If, however, at this point we stopped the analysis and concluded that internal contradiction and incoherence are simply a natural feature of world views, we would surely miss the point. For what on the level of pure logic appears as irreconcilable contradiction turns out to make eminent sense on the pragmatic, or use level. Studying closely how these concepts are being used reveals an amazingly consistent grammar, viz., retribution is applied to the bad, forgiveness to the good. Throughout the texts, whenever a person in one way or another receives the cue "bad" (Landlord, Yazid, sins against other people, oppression, stealing, more sins than merits on the Last Day, etc.), he is inevitably expected to meet retribution, but never forgiveness. Thus, the infamous Yazīd, although repenting and although having been given the redemptive prayer by the Imām personally, cannot be saved; he must go to hell. Conversely, when the cues suggest an essentially good person (an innocent victim, a martyr, not harming others, more merits than sins, and, invariably, the speaker himself) the notion of forgiveness is evoked. This association is especially striking in the expectation of the Representative that if a good person should run out of merits, he would be given as many as he needs to pay off his debts. Clearly, if a person runs out of merits, he has in fact more sins (and, in this case, the unforgivable sins against other people on top of it) and therefore, by "regular" standards, would have to go to hell. But, since he is coded as "good person," he will be forgiven. By the same logic, the Landlord expects forgiveness for sins he himself declares as unforgivable, and—to use an outside example to show that this thought pattern is by no means unique to this village—the worshipper in Psalm 26/11 can say: "I am coming to you in my innocence, save me and have mercy on me." In each of these cases the self is coded as good or innocent and so deserves forgiveness.

This grammar for the application of the two concepts reveals the semantics of the use to which they are put. By appropriating the concept of forgiveness for oneself and assigning the concept of retribution to declared evil-doers, an individual can at once allay his fear of the Last Day and instill it in others, gain assurance of his own salvation and expect the damnation of others. Thus, the concepts are used as devices to achieve guarantees for the safety of oneself, for the prevalence of justice, and—because the religious system is perceived as a divinely instituted social control mechanism—for the existence of social order. In other words, one achieves guarantees for the security of existence and for the existence of security.

Thus, while appearing irreconcilable on one level, the concepts are in fact complementary means of achieving an existentially more comprehensive and complete framework of meaning than strictly orthodox doctrine allows. As this is so, i.e., as people operate with a double standard, it raises the question whether we should not have to qualify the prevailing wisdom that idea systems serve as mechanisms of control in human behavior.

2. *Fate and Responsibility.* There are three major systems of concepts which have a bearing on this issue.

a) The system of basic morality. This system is given purest form in the world view of the Calm, but in one form or another it shows up in most cases. I shall present it first in schematic form, then paraphrase it. For the sake of clarity it should be pointed out that the individual components and

relationships in the schema reflect factual statements made by the people
themselves, not deep structures or other constructs of my own; only the
compilation and labels are mine.

   i. Basic mode

Participation in the bounty of God	→	Obligation to share	→	Reward or punishment	→	Thanks- giving

  ii. Intensification

Special participation	→	Special obligation	→	Special reward or punishment

 iii. Reversal

Giving to others	→	Favor from God	→	Thanksgiving

Ad i. Man is a participant in the bounty of God. The yield of one's
fields and flocks is a share that one receives by the grace of God just as
all other creatures—birds, wolves, mice—receive theirs. It is in this
spirit that one asks God, "Give me my daily bread, too," and accepts
gratefully whatever He sends. In turn, as one shares in God's bounty,
so one has to share one's own with others. This means that one has to
have compassion with and care for relatives, neighbors, the needy,
afflicted, lonely, strangers, orphans, poor, weak, the domestic animals, and even the wild animals, saying, "May they have their share,
too." It also means never to hurt anybody in any way, be it by stealing
or making a donkey's load too heavy. Depending on how one fulfills
this obligation, one can expect reward or punishment in this world
and the next.

Ad ii. The obligation to share with others is especially pronounced
when some extraordinary favor has been received. Thus, when a child
has narrowly escaped deadly danger, or when the harvest is unusually
plentiful, a special offering is called for. Any failure to make an offering is expected to bring disaster.

Ad iii. A spontaneous act of sharing can be expected to win God's
favor in return. To this end, one gives offerings and alms, and makes
vows, sacrifices, and donations with the intention of securing God's
assistance.

The principles of this paradigm are, like all religious principles, mod-
eled in exalted and dramatic ways by the Prophet and the Imāms. These
shared in the bounty of God more than others, and, in turn, shared it
generously with others by teaching the truth, fighting for it, and being
martyred for it. As reward, they obtained an especially high place before
God, a status which they again share by interceding for the sick, the sad,
and the sinners.

b) The cosmic system. This system is based on the notion that things are perennially and unrelentingly fluctuating between extremes which, in this way, balance themselves out. Thus, plenty forbodes loss; loss raises the expectation of gain; one year is good, the other bad; the wheat crop fails, the vineyard bears plenty instead; the harvest is abundant, but a family member dies; animals in a flock—just like political regimes—simply must go, but others come in their stead. This thought model amounts of course—though people would never admit it—to a kind of autonomous, cosmic law functioning independently of God's will. This heretical implication may explain why—in contrast to China, for example—it has never been recognized, let alone elaborated in the Middle East although it is most probably found widely distributed beyond this village.

In dealing with this system man has essentially two options. He can either let things run their course on the assumption that since misfortune simply must hit, it may as well hit where it happens to hit, or—if too much is at stake, like a child's life—he may try to interfere in its course by means of magic, the help of God, or the provision of a less valuable substitute target. Consequently, since anything struck can be considered a substitute for something else, one can comfort oneself with the idea that whatever happens is the lesser of two evils.

c) The will of God (qismat). This notion conceives events as the outcome of God's inscrutable will. Senseless and unjust as they may appear to the human mind, they should nevertheless be accepted gratefully as signs of God's infinite wisdom and benevolence.

Each of these paradigms possesses an inherent logic and certain basic meanings. The grammar of their application by an individual actor to concrete situations is based on this logic and these meanings, and serves the purpose of rendering these situations meaningful in the framework of the individual's existence.

The first, moral paradigm spells out the cognitive code in terms of which peasants conceive of existence and morality. It is a world in which all good emanates from God in a constant stream of genesis. This outflow of benevolence sets in motion a system of cosmic interchange functioning on the two principles that (1) any receiver has to give in return, and (2) that the haves in any transaction give substance whereas the have-nots give tokens. Man gives part of what he receives from God to others. But because the other ultimately is God (cf., e.g. the Representative's ". . . to do something for someone else means to do it for God"), He as the receiver is expected to give in return, either in the form of rewards in this life or the next, or—in response to offerings—in the form of help in misfortune or danger. Thus God, although the fountainhead of the system, is nevertheless part of it and so, strictly speaking, not super-natural. In this system, then, sharing becomes the supreme good, and doing good becomes inseparably connected with man's well-being here and hereafter.

It is in terms of this paradigm that peasants understand their work and moral selves. Thereby, their hard, back-breaking work is translated into the conception that peasants produce the food for mankind and that, as they provide it in a constant stream of sharing to their families, the poor, and needy, they are—though not as ultimate cause—sustaining life itself, which is one of their highest values. This conception makes their work intrinsically good work and their selves intrinsically moral selves.

This paradigm thus provides peasants with a frame of reference for their existence. By orthodox Islamic standards, which put heavy emphasis on a performance of rituals which peasants feel unable to carry out, peasants would appear—in fact, do appear in the eyes of mullahs—as very deficient Muslims. By using this paradigm instead, they avail themselves of a moral standard which they feel they are fulfilling better than most other people, including the mullahs, and which declares them as good. And being good they can expect forgiveness, reward, and help. Thus, the use of this paradigm gives them a meaningful identity, moral status, a guarantee of well-being in this life and the next, a sense of existential security and control over their fate, and, because one can expect others to abide by it, too, a guarantee of social order and ultimate justice.

The second paradigm is an interpretation of events in terms of cosmic processes which are essentially impersonal, mechanical, and amoral in nature. This implies that none of the events can be due to human agency. The paradigm therefore allows to effectively dispel any suspicion of personal failure; it precludes human responsibility. This semantic code programs the use of this paradigm. It is typically applied to explain misfortunes that come as a sudden, offensive shock, like some types of accidents and losses, especially the loss of animals. If in such cases one were to operate with the first, or moral paradigm, a misfortune could be explained only in two ways: either one failed to take care and work hard enough, or it was a God-sent punishment for some moral delict. Both explanations are uncomfortable. They would rouse feelings of failure, guilt, and distressing self-blame.

By applying the second paradigm, however, one is able to forestall such feelings and effectively exempt oneself from responsibility. For, by its logic, a misfortune is unconnected with hard work or moral behavior; it is not due to human failure or divine punishment but follows principles all of its own. In addition, the use of this thought structure allows one to avoid the incongruent idea that a compassionate God may intend to hurt one. Also, it allows one to adopt a number of comforting, stress-reducing images, like expecting some counter-balancing good fortune in the future, or seeing the misfortune as the lesser of two evils.

But although coming in handy in such cases, the paradigm does not form a satisfactory system all on its own. For since it cannot guarantee reward and punishment, it cannot give meaning to a peasant's hard work, sharing, and moral behavior, all of which are, in his conception, inputs into the system that should be compensated. Pursuing these things without any prospect of compensation would be utterly absurd; stealing and raiding would make more sense, i.e., extraction, not input. Also, in the absence of enforced moral standards, there would be no guarantee of social order and ultimate justice. Finally, this paradigm cannot offer a sense of existential security: the world, though predictable within limits, would be subject to inane blind fate instead of lying in the hands of a personal, compassionate, and wise God.

Thus, only to have the first, moral paradigm would require one to accept full responsibility for any misfortune and so add more stress to an already stressful situation. On the other hand, only operating with the second, amoral paradigm would deliver one into a world of absurd morality, social chaos, and existential drift.

The third paradigm (qismat) allows, like the previous one, the suspension of the first, moral paradigm in contexts where the latter would suggest personal moral failure. In its terms, events and conditions reflect the inscrutable wish of God, entirely unrelated to one's own conduct. Consequently, one is exempt from responsibility for them. There are, however, essential differences between these two theories of extra-human causality. The cosmic paradigm offers some measure of predictability and some means of control, but no idiom to provide meaning. In contrast, the metaphor of the decree of God precludes any predictability and human control, but offers meaning in the sense that anything issuing from God must have meaning although its exact nature may not be known.

These differences determine the grammar of the uses of the two paradigms. Misfortune which is experienced as a sudden, singular event is typically processed in terms of the cosmic system. On the other hand, when a misfortune constitutes a lasting existential situation, like poverty or childlessness, it tends to be interpreted as the decree of God. Apparently, in the latter situations immediate control seems out of the question and what becomes of paramount importance is to give meaning to them. Turning for this purpose to the first, moral paradigm would make things even worse. It would mark one as an evil-doer incurring God's wrath and only heap blame onto a situation already miserable enough. The second, cosmic paradigm is inapplicable because obviously the situation is not fluctuating; but even if it were applied in some other form, it would give no meaning because it lacks intelligent purpose. This leaves the individual bricoleur with the third paradigm, offering meaning in the form of the notion that a wise, benevolent God knows best what is good for one. As the case of the Poor shows, this may not present a satisfactory solution either. But this is as far as the repertoire goes. It is here, when symbols fail at the edge of the conceptual universe, that mystification is penetrated.

In this section on fate and responsibility I tried to demonstrate how in critical questions of their existence peasants manipulate a combination of three mutually contradictory, yet complementary paradigms. In this way, they can create a sense of existential security and meaning, moral excellence, social order, prevailing justice, predictability, and control while at the same time steering clear of the stress of total personal responsibility on the one side, the absurdity of nihilism on the other, and the incoherence of determinism on the third.

My purpose in this demonstration was to outline the use of these three paradigms in relation to the issues involved. It should be mentioned, however, that issues are only one dimension in which this manipulative process takes place. Another dimension relates, as the careful reader will have observed, to the type of person associated with the issue. As it is, the application of the paradigms varies with the same distinction described in regard to retribution and forgiveness, i.e., the distinction between good and bad persons and, implicitly, between self and other. The misfortune of other persons, especially those one considers morally questionable, tends to be seen in terms of the first, moral paradigm, i.e., as God's retribution for moral failure. In contrast, adverse conditions that affect one's own life, one's family, or good people in general tend to be attributed to extraneous forces, i.e., cosmic processes or the decree of God. Thus, through the use of the three paradigms misfortune can be turned into evidence for God's justice in this world without jeopardizing one's self-image of essential goodness.

Finally, intersecting with the other two dimensions, there is, of course, the dimension of the individual actor. As concepts are shaped in a field of forces, their exact meaning and use varies from person to person. Thus, in some world views, like the Calm's, the cosmic paradigm occupies an important position while in others, like the Representative's, it hardly figures at all. By the same token, some individuals, influenced by self-serving biases, use invariably the double standards I have mentioned while others appear more ready to apply the morality paradigm also to themselves.

In conclusion, it should be obvious that the mechanics of symbol manipulation entail more than "a certain degree of vagueness" in concept use. Rather, as the foregoing examples demonstrate, in this process of reality construction the poly-paradigmatic structure of world views appears to play a critically important role.

TOWARD AN EPISTEMOLOGICAL THEORY OF RELIGION

Evolutionary epistemology describes evolution as a process of acquisition of knowledge. The heuristic method by which such knowledge is gained is, as Riedl (1981: 178) has shown, in principle the same on all evolutionary levels. It consists essentially in a spiral progression from expectation (mutants, conditioned reflexes, associations, hypotheses) to experience (success/failure, reenforcement/extinction, confirmation/refutation), and on to new expectation. It is by means of this heuristic strategy that man, like all organisms, has perpetually reached into the unknown and extracted what knowledge of the world he possesses. It is my argument here that religious beliefs form part of that process. They are hypotheses reaching into the unknown, formulating assumptions about first causes, ultimate origin, final destinies, last meanings, and the fundamental nature of the world, society, and man, their needs and fulfillments, their dynamics and control. Thus they arise from the same basic evolutionary mechanisms which drive all organisms continuously to the formulation of hypotheses about the unknown (Riedl 1981: 73). Whatever origins have been postulated for religious beliefs—psychological needs, awesome experiences, projected archetypes, social sentiments, attempts at control, search for meaning, defense against chaos—in this view appear to be only specific paraphrases of these mechanisms.

In view of the fact that religions often proclaim their tenets as absolute truth and individuals are often so deeply convinced of these truths that they even go to their deaths for them, it may appear strange to designate religious beliefs as hypotheses. Yet religious beliefs have always been revised, replaced, and discarded in the face of confirming and disconfirming evidence, in transmittance from group to group, generation to generation,

266

and within single individuals. Thus, the Craftsman, for example, in his youth held orthodox beliefs with fanatical tenacity, but in view of later experiences checked them, and finally came to revoke and ridicule them. The Mystic, who is so convinced of the validity of his beliefs that he feels he knows the inner essence of things, says also, "We'll see if I have been deceived," and so renders them hypothetical. Similarly, when the Mashhadi says he believes in eschatological matters for the sake of safety, he obviously takes the orthodox doctrines as hypotheses which possibly could turn out to be true. Thus, this hypothetical aspect of religious concepts underlies the creation of individual world views and so ultimately the evolution of religious systems. This shows that religious beliefs are not shielded from selection (Riedl 1981: 79), are not ultimate ideas without evolutionary history (Radin 1957: 373), nor tenets of unquestioned validity (Horton 1971: 154, 163), nor Freudian illusions detached from all reality, but propositions that are being checked against empirical evidence and therefore susceptible to a selective process. This is not to say of course that religious hypotheses will necessarily come to produce the answers to the questions they pose. In fact, as the history of ideas shows, most questions posed by religion, if answered at all, were answered by thought systems outside the realm of religion. But this fact does not dispute their hypothetical character. Also in a science like medicine many hypothetical issues are settled by discoveries outside its proper paradigm.

Evidently, the phenomenon we call religion spans two seemingly paradoxical aspects. On the one hand, to be functional at all, religious beliefs, like most ideas that flood our common sense, have to be maintained with a measure of subjective certainty and conviction. They are seen as supported by concrete evidence, and myth and ritual clothe them with an aura of factuality that render them "inviolable by the discordant revelation of secular experience" (Geertz 1966: 4, 28). But this is not final. At the same time, to be relevant to particular individuals and groups and to maintain the relevance in the face of changing intellectual and existential conditions, religious beliefs have to be checked and revised, dismissed and replaced.

Of these two aspects, only the first one, the maintenance aspect, has received adequate consideration by anthropologists. In fact, as Geertz' (1966: 4) conception indicates, the functional aspect has come to define religion in general. In the following, I try to balance this one-sided view by exploring some of the areas of the second, more dynamic aspect of beliefs as hypotheses, as suggested by the present material. Specifically, I shall elaborate on the nature of evidence for such hypotheses, their inherent limitations, the challenges they are confronted with, and the types of responses they elicit.

The Evidential Basis of Beliefs

Earlier, I have identified perceived evidence as one of the forces that shape individual belief systems. Here I shall argue that specifically the perception of concrete, positive evidence provides an indispensable, critical basis for beliefs to rest on. Without such evidence they would seem absurd. One believes because one sees or because someone taken as authority says so. That is, one believes on the basis of personal experience or the testimony of others. It is the conclusiveness with which this experience and this testimony are perceived which determines the strength of the belief. If the conviction that certain beliefs are true were primarily generated in acts of religious observance, as Geertz (196: 28) claims, then the Representative and the Deep Believer, with the paucity of ritual they engage in, would be only poor believers, indeed. As their cases show, their convictions emerge from much more basic and unequivocal evidence. In the following, I shall discuss these two bases of belief, personal experience and testimony, as forms of evidence.

1. Primary evidence refers to the immediate experience of a person. As the presented material shows, such evidence is seen in every aspect of the religious system. God's existence is inescapably suggested by the immensity of the world, by the wonder of seeds developing into wheat, or the mystery of varying color combinations in lambs. God's direct intervention in this-worldly affairs is seen confirmed by the misery of evil men and the good fortunes of virtuous ones. God's favoring of the Islamic world is seen in its wealth of oil. Without the existence of God, social order cannot be imagined. The correctness of Islamic morality is seen supported by the supposed moral corruption of Western women. The existence and intervention of saints and, by extension, the validity of the entire religious system, is seen evidenced by recurrent miracles. The effect of alms-giving is seen proven by subsequent escape from misfortune. The spell-binding of dangerous animals is seen confirmed whenever a lost sheep is found unharmed. Likewise, the validity of written prayers, vows, and sacrifices is demonstrated by their effectiveness. The belief in the evil eye is seen validated by strange mishaps. The theory of a cosmic balance is seen exemplified by the death of a relative after an unusually rich harvest. Also the question of the afterworld is approached empirically, as when peasants say, "Nobody has ever returned from there to tell us whether it is true or not."

Besides such tangible forms, primary evidence may also come in the form of incontestable mystical inner experience. Thus, the Old Hunter believes he has seen the Last Day and paradise in a dreamlike experience. The Mystic, like all mystical searchers from Buddha to flower children, went through years of experiential testing to find the path to fulfillment.

His vision of Ali, and the controls and insights he believes to have, provide him with direct proof that his system works.

In their reliance on direct evidence for their beliefs, these people are certainly not unique. The same behavior is documented for members of illiterate as well as scripturalist societies. For the former, Radin (1957: 375ff) gives ample examples, and as to the latter, note, for example, the pervasive insistence with which the disciples and people of the New Testament are depicted to have sought direct, conclusive evidence for Jesus' claims.

2. Secondary or mediated evidence refers to the testimony of religious authority as embodied in myth and scriptures. Thus, in this case, belief rests on authority or, better, on the testimony given by authority. But this authority is not accepted in an a priori manner (Geertz 1966: 24)—although religious establishments have always tried to achieve this—but rather it is accepted in proportion to its credibility and authenticity.

Religious systems build up such credibility in various ways. The testimony is presented as given by God Himself, or the son of God, or other supernatural beings, or very wise men, or presented as distilled wisdom, tested experience or general consensus of past generations. Those who report it are certified by miracles, extraordinary wisdom, the veneration of the masses, and the testimony of others. For example, Muhammad is predicted by Jesus and recognized by a Jewish monk, Husayn is treated with awe by Muhammad who foreknew his redemptive deed, and Ali sits nearer to God than Muhammad himself.

This material shows that the acceptance of such secondary evidence varies greatly with differences in personality and socialization. For people like the Deep Believer or the Representative the testimony of the sacred texts is straightforward fact. They refer to it as evidence with the same certainty as if they had witnessed the things with their own eyes. For others, like the Mashhadi and the Lower Peasants, however, the evidence is not conclusive. They say, "According to the Qur'ān it is so, but nobody really knows."

Underlying this emphasis on concrete evidence is an assumption which in my view has been generally ignored, i.e., that transcendental issues are very much considered matters of knowledge. In Islam the assumption is that the truth is literally communicated in the Qur'ān. Consequently, because the Qur'ān can be known, the truth, including transcendental matters, can be known (Grunebaum 1955: 111). Muhammad is clearly assumed to have known the truth and not merely believed it. And in the profession of his faith, a Muslim is called upon to "bear witness" and not merely say the Christian "I believe." Accordingly, the religiously educated are able to maintain the conviction that they know. People like the Representative do not merely believe or have faith. They know that Husayn's redemptive deed was ordained in primordial times; they know that the devil was punished for his haughtiness; they know that judgment will be held on the Last Day, and how it will be held. They know because it is in the scriptures and because for them the evidence that the scriptures are true is conclusive.

In the world view of the Lower Peasants and their like the same basic assumption shows up, though, given the different structure of their views, it takes entirely different modalities. When, as an expression of their dominant attitude, they say, "Nobody has ever returned from there to tell us whether it is true or not," it is evident that they consider eschatological questions matters of positive knowledge. And when they profess their belief as they, as Muslims, must, the term belief means to them not faith but simply that, lacking proper education in these matters, they trust those who know—in the same way as a layman believing in the existence of quasars takes the astrophysicists' word for it. Again, the issue is conceived in the paradigm of knowledge, not faith. In sum, the religious perspective is not so unequivocally the realm of faith (Geertz 1966: 27) as Westerners under the influence of Christian theology have come to assume. One should probably say that belief takes on the quality of knowledge, or, even better, that belief and knowledge are not strictly and abstractly separated. As Radin (1957: 246) said it: "Primitive man . . . is . . . living in a blaze of reality."

Impediments to Cognition

So far I have argued that concrete evidence, or what is taken as such, forms an integral part of the basis on which religious beliefs rest. Because such evidence is bound to change as knowledge, logic, methods, values, social patterns, etc. evolve, religious hypotheses are of necessity bound to evolve, too. This process is, however, hampered by conditions which impede an assessment of the validity of such hypotheses and so serve to maintain them. Such conditions are given in the fact that they frequently are stated in vague and non-falsifiable terms; in their linkage with activities that fulfill important artistic, emotional, and psychological needs; in the power of established opinion; in the inertia of paradigmatic thinking (Kuhn 1970); in the suggestive force of collective activities; in the interconnectedness and mutual interdependence of the system's components; and in the fact that religious conceptions may be used to explain empirically successful behavior, as in certain medical and economic activities, and so appear true even if, in fact, they may not be so. Evans-Pritchard (1937: 475) lists others. Here I shall concentrate on three such obstacles which arise from the structure and inner logic of religious hypotheses.

1. *The Threat of Disaster.* A series of religious hypotheses predict dire consequences if certain conditions are not met. To these belong the belief in the evil eye, in malevolent spirits, unlucky days, dangerous substances, witchcraft, forebodings of disaster, and, above all, in this-worldly punishment and afterworldly damnation. In their impact, such hypotheses are comparable to public bomb or poison threats. One is forced to act on them on the scantiest evidence or slightest suspicion, although they may in the end turn out to be entirely fictive. Strictly speaking, they can be dismissed only if they become unequivocally refuted, that is, if it can be verified that no spirit ever hurt anybody, nobody ever goes to hell, nobody has the evil eye, no black cat ever forebode bad luck, or, for that matter, that there is no bomb in the terrorist's bag. However, the existential threats implied in such hypotheses effectively preclude such refutation. For neither will one usually take the risk of testing them, nor will one simply wait to possibly come to grief. Rather, one will either avoid the situation altogether or take protective measures against the possible dangers. In either case the hypotheses will remain, initially at least, untested.

To avoid the dangers of a situation one resorts to taboos, purifications, and cyclic-return rituals. Also, one will avoid certain activities after an ominous dream, on an "unlucky" day, or at other forebodings of misfortune, like a poison threat at Halloween. Similarly, one may avoid new medical treatments, new crops, unknown people, food and social premises. The consequence of such avoidance behavior is, of course, that it precludes experiences which could potentially lead to a refutation of the hypothesis.

To protect oneself against dangers, one will use such rituals as giving alms to ward off evil, attaching amulets against the evil eye, propitiating an angered spirit or, for that matter, driving very carefully on a triple-low day in one's biorhythm. In these cases, disconfirmation of the hypothesis will not be obtained either. For if the misfortune does not occur, it will not be seen as a disconfirmation of one's expectation, but as the result of the efficacy of the ritual performed.

Thus, hypotheses entailing a threat tend to block the generation of disconfirming evidence. And because very little confirming evidence is needed to keep them alive, they are inherently resistant to change. This tenacity increases with the importance of the issue and it becomes exacerbated when a hypothesis is stated in essentially non-falsifiable terms, like the hypothesis of afterworldly damnation. In this case, neither logic nor accidents nor risks can bring about relevant evidence. Thus, from the caustic freethinkers of the Renaissance (Burckhardt 1960: 542, 588) through Pascal and Voltaire to the Mashhadi of this study even extreme sceptics have been exceedingly cautious when it came to facing the afterlife. In this case, one believes simply to be safe and freely admits this attitude. The Mashhadi

argues that if he did not believe and fulfill the rituals, and there existed a
Last Day after all, he would lose out, and Pascal reasons in the probabilistic
language he created that even if there was only a minute chance of eternal
damnation, the stakes in the wager would be too high to take.

Evidently, such tenacity constitutes a powerful maintenance force for
the whole religious system, a fact which has been widely exploited by religious elites. In innumerable stories such as the story of the Fall, they warn
harshly that the threats are real and that testing them may have dire consequences. But religious authorities are, of course, not the only ones to use
them. Threat hypotheses form convenient tools in the hands of anybody
whose interests depend on the compliance of others, be it a political dema-
gogue, a businessman or a medical practitioner.

Thus, hypotheses of threat essentially preserve the status quo rather
than change it. Although they appear as wise survival strategies, on the
cultural level they form stubborn impediments to the development of anything from medicine to economic, social, and political systems as well as
international concords.

2. *The Test by Success.* Probably more typical of religious systems in general than threat hypotheses are hypotheses which promise some kind of
benefit such as symbolic forms offering explanations of past and present,
predictions of the future, meanings in life's many stations, assistance in
need, expressions of deep emotions, guarantees of justice and order, a sense
of safety and security, and the experience of mystery and the sacred.

In contrast to threat hypotheses, which induce behavior that acts to
shield them from inspection, these hypotheses encourage their application
and thus create conditions which expose them to potential checks. In this
case, the epistemological process is, however, hampered by a thought process which I call the test by success.

When people assess the usefulness of such hypotheses, they are not
concerned with the objective chances of success, i.e., the distribution of
failures and successes as compared to random expectation. Rather, they ask
whether there is any chance for success at all. When the Lower Peasant I
took his crippled son, whom neither folk nor Western medicine had been
able to help, to a shrine with a record of miraculous cures, he was not
concerned with the hundreds of people who had failed to obtain help there,
although he was aware of them. Nor did he expect a cure with absolute
certainty. But he considered it possible that a cure might happen simply
because cures had happened there before. Likewise, in the treatment of a
particular disease one tends to go again and again through the same sequence of diagnosis and therapy which brought some success in the past
and therefore might possibly do so again. Even on the basis of many fail-

ures one cannot discard the procedure because the promise exists, and to disregard it would mean to risk life. Thus, one does not look at the probability but at the possibility of success. As long as any success comes, even if only at random and sporadically, the hypothesis is not dismissable. It always holds the promise of potential success, a promise which will be especially called on in situations of crisis, when all available means have to be mobilized. When it ever should be dismissed, it will usually not be on the grounds of refutation but because another hypothesis proves more successful.

This logic of the test by success explains why particular shrines, witch doctors or amulets may be discarded, while the paradigm as such, i.e., the belief in shrines, witch doctors or amulets persists. Obviously, some representations may be revealed as constant failures, but others show at least inconsistent success and so confirm the validity of the system as such. This appears to be a more parsimonious explanation for the tenacity of religious paradigms than the alleged lack of abstractive power among traditional people (Evans-Pritchard 1937: 475).

Testing hypotheses by their success count is not a particularity of religious thought. It is, of course, the strategy of evolution itself. But whereas on the biological level hypotheses based on very rare success will soon be discarded, on the cultural level, removed from direct selective forces, they can often persist unchallenged. It is troublesome and often impossible to unravel the complexity of causes behind apparent success. No wonder that people present, and, in fact, see themselves, their actions, their products, their social norms, economic styles, and religious conceptions as successes. Since the task of disconfirmation lies always on the other, and therefore stands a good chance of not being undertaken at all, there is a great likelihood that people get away with these images at least for some time.

3. *Explanation by Free Association.* In science, explanation is subject to inherent and strict controls. When an object does not fall to the ground, one can explain this only with the theory of centrifugal forces when it is demonstrated that these are indeed at the time acting on the object to a degree that neutralizes gravity. In the logic of religious thoughts such constraints do not apply. To explain an event, one selects a hypothesis not on the grounds that objective conditions permit or even dictate it, but simply on the basis that it serves the purpose in a plausible way. Thus, when one of our villagers gets into an accident on Saturday, it is because he travelled on a Saturday—an unlucky day for travelling—and the fact that he gave alms for protection before departure tends to be ignored. If, on the other hand, he returns home safely, it is because of the alms he gave, and the fact that it

was Saturday is ignored. This also shows that there is no requirement of predictability. Explanations depend entirely on hindsight. Conclusions can only be made from the event to the postulated causes, but never the other way round. It is impossible to predict with any certainty that under prevailing circumstances the forces of Saturday will prevail and an accident will occur, or that God's mercy will prevail and prevent such an accident. With reasoning so unhampered by outside controls, it is possible to maintain a system which, though it can predict nothing, can explain everything. If an evil person lives in misery, it is in punishment for his sins, but if he lives in affluence, God has patience or God lets him have the world he wants so badly and will punish him in the afterlife. If a person dies young, it is because God reaps early those He loves, but if he dies an old man, God blessed him with a long life. If there is goodness found in the world, it is because of God's grace, but if there is evil, it is because of man's free will and his weakness to succumb to passion. If God punishes, it is because He is just, but if He forgives, it is because He is merciful. If one withdraws from the world, it is because the world is fleeting, but if one seeks to change it, it is because devotion to the others is the highest goal. If Husayn is to be panegyrized, one says that by his intercession all sins will be forgiven on the Last Day, but if justice is thereby seen jeopardized, one argues that sinners will be punished before that Day.

This is, of course, not to say that the selection of a hypothesis is made without regard to objective conditions at all. When the Deep Believer sought an explanation for his snake bite, he selected from some half dozen alternatives exactly the one which under the circumstances (building a new, spacious house) was the most specific and pertinent (the envious talk of the people). But in no case is the use of an explanation restricted by the requirement to objectively demonstrate that the postulated forces and conditions were indeed present and indeed acting in such a way that the event was predictable to a high degree.

This way one is free to apply to a particular case only those hypotheses which promise to give a satisfactory explanation and avoid all those which do not. As a consequence, all the hypotheses applied appear always confirmed and as deep wisdom, whereas those that are not applied effectively escape potential disconfirmation and refutation. Thereby, any given hypothesis is likely to accumulate confirmations which, as pointed out earlier, will make it all the more resistant to being dismissed as it entails the promise of success. These conditions critically obstruct the epistemic process. In effect, they create a system in which one is always right and never wrong.

Besides allowing a choice among different hypotheses, uncontrolled association is also used in the defense of particular hypotheses. For one, it is inherent in religious reinterpretation. Thus, when the Mullah wants to prove his point that the Qur'ān incorporates scientific knowledge, he reinterprets a Qur'ānic verse in such a way that it appears to express the nature of the solar system. Such maneuvers allow the implantation into the texts of ideas considered desirable and, conversely, removal from the texts of undesirable ideas. Thereby two results are achieved at once: the new ideas are presented as legitimized by the seal of Revelation, and the texts themselves are presented as timeless pieces of unfathomable wisdom which can only have emanated from God. Obviously, these possibilities make the technique the stock-in-trade of all religious reformers.

Furthermore, uncontrolled association plays a role in the practice of discovering desired evidence for a hypothesis in order to confirm it. When the Representative wants to demonstrate that sinners, especially those who grossly violate the rights of others, will surely be punished in this world, he is, in fact, able to find in the lives of all such infamous men some sort of misfortune. Conversely, it is quite feasible to discover some evil deed in the pasts of those presumably punished by God with some misfortune. Likewise, there appears to be little difficulty in discovering evidence for the evil eye when this notion suggests itself as a plausible explanation for a child's disease.

Finally, uncontrolled association allows the flourishing in religious thought of secondary explanations or, as Evans-Pritchard has called them, "secondary elaborations" (Evans-Pritchard 1937). This is the practice of defending a hypothesis by explaining away disconfirming evidence. Usually, this takes the form of particularization. A written prayer did not work because the prayer-writer lacked efficacy of breath; a damband did not work because it was carried across an irrigation channel. Likewise, the ranking of saints by their miraculous powers implicitly accounts for failures of vows at lesser pilgrimage centers. Such symbol manipulation is thus a necessary adjunct to what I called the test by success. It provides explanations for the failures occurring between the successes.

Again, like other mechanisms described, uncontrolled association is not restricted to religious thought or "the primitive mind." It floods everyday argumentation and leaves its residue in folk wisdom. For example, when a person fails to change, one can say, "You cannot teach an old dog new tricks;" but if he does change, one can say, "Never too old to learn." It also appears to be endemic in the softer sciences like psychoanalysis, the social sciences, and economics. Its hallmark there is the same as in religion: to be able to explain everything but predict nothing. About pre-world war II economics, Galbraith (1978: 3) has said, ". . . the explanation of (the business cycle's) irregularities had become a modest profession in which reason, divination, and elements of witchcraft had been combined in a manner not elsewhere seen safe in the primitive religions."

Challenges to Religious Hypotheses

Although the described thought patterns tend to inhibit the refutation and questioning of religious hypotheses, they cannot totally prevent them. The presented cases—and, of course, the general history of religion—demonstrate that in fact individuals constantly check the validity of religious hypotheses in the light of fresh evidence and experiences. In the process, established beliefs inevitably come to be challenged despite the barriers mentioned. These challenges can be divided into internal and external ones.

1. I call internal challenges those that emerge within the religious system itself. They may result from new experiences, new mystical insights, new meanings discovered in texts. In the present material, such challenges seem to cluster in a few areas. One is the realm of observable events: written prayers are found to be of no use for certain diseases; shrines fall into disuse because expected benefits are not forthcoming; the belief in jinn and the evil eye is rejected because of lack of evidence.

A more critical area is the problem of justice. Despite the mentioned possibilities of accounting for seeming injustice, gross injustice strikes a vital sentiment. Thus, the Poor criticizes God for making man unequal because this creates injustice and misery. Another peasant once argued, "Tell me, is there a God? If there was one, He could not permit this misery and injustice to happen." And another, referring to his experiences in the city where he saw obviously irreligious people living in splendor and luxury, claimed, "If others had seen what I saw, they would have left the religion because one tends to think, 'If these immoral people are not punished, but quite to the contrary have a good life, there can be no God.'"

The problem of justice is a sensitive point in morality religions, one of the points where hypotheses about God have to face hard reality. Religious authorities attempt of course, as in the biblical Job story, to emphasize that it is unwarranted to take experiences of seeming injustice as disconfirmations of God's justice, but that does not appear to be the way common religious sense tends to perceive it. Evidently, the moral paradox, while possibly driving man toward belief in God, as Geertz (1966: 25) argues, also tends to drive man away from such belief. After all, Job believed not because but in spite of his misery. And in the face of the holocaust, a Rabbi even felt compelled to revoke the Jewish covenant with God, his sentiments being shared by many others of his faith. (Zborowski 1955: 361ff). Such reactions are, however, not limited to Middle Eastern morality religions, as Radin (1957: 378) has shown.

What appears even more striking in the present material is the pervasive challenge of afterworldly doctrine. One of the Lower Peasants strikes a common theme when he says, "We say, 'Sheep will be hung by their legs and goats will be hung by theirs' . . . but nobody has ever returned from there to tell us whether it is true." The Mashhadi ponders that perhaps after death the body simply decomposes and this would be it. And the Doubtful considers it possible that perhaps in the end the evil-doers and he will all be in the same row. Such notions are not exactly the kind of ideas we have come to associate with people in Islamic cultures. Yet these statements are not the expressions of a few marginal individuals. They echo the sentiments of a whole class of people, in fact, the class which in the present case comprises most of the society. This attitude is definitely not a result of the spread of modern ideologies, as it shows up already in a text recorded by Mann (1910: 28) at the turn of the century. Nor does it seem to be a particularity of this area. In a north Indian village, Lewis (1965: 254/4) found that 44% of his subjects expressed unbelief in the afterlife. Strikingly enough they stated their views in virtually identical terms as the comparable individuals discussed here. "Heaven and Hell are here in this world. . . . Nobody knows what happens after death. . . . They say that there are gardens in Heaven (and) in Hell there are pits. . . . But nobody has seen it." Lewis sees evidence that this "positivistic" attitude may be rather widespread in India. Also, in another reputedly arch-religious context, among peasants in medieval France, LeRoy Ladurie (1978: 319f) found similar viewpoints prevalent.

Such challenges to established beliefs are also documented in cultures outside the realm of high religions (cf. Radin 1957: 375f). They may in fact be even more common than the available material indicates because anthropological methods, designed to elicit general conceptions rather than actual beliefs, are bound to miss them. "The anthropological study of religious non-commitment," as Geertz (1966: 43) said, "is non-existent." All this plainly disproves Horton's (1971: 154) elitist claim that in traditional cultures "absence of any awareness of alternatives makes for an absolute acceptance of the established theoretical tenets, and removes any possibility of questioning them. . . . Any challenge to established tenets is a threat of chaos." Quite obviously, tenets are not absolutely accepted, people do question them and consider alternatives, and, in the absence of convincing evidence, they seem to be perfectly capable of leaving the question open without feelings of horrific threat. Thus, there seems to be much more continuity between them and the great historic challengers of their religions, like Buddha, Jesus, and Luther, than is usually admitted. Common people, too, not only great shakers, are able to question and reject the ideas they grew up with. And we would probably understand those historic figures better if we could see them as parts of the broad range of variations they grew out from, rather than as the unique and isolated personalities of the history books.

2. I call external challenges disconfirming evidence originating from formal thought systems outside a religion, such as philosophy, logic, science and related values. The case of the Craftsman shows the impact of such challenges. When he refused to see the motorcycle accident he witnessed as caused by the evil eye—although all the evidence seemed to point that way—he did so not because he had witnessed just too many disconfirmations in the past (i.e., on the basis of internal challenges), but because he had adopted from outside the religious paradigm the idea that there just is no evil eye. On the same basis he rejects the written prayers, the saints, the belief in jinn. Even more incisive, the new idiom is used to refute the claim to divine revelation. With that, the sacred texts are reduced to a mixture of history, ignorance and fraud, and their claims become as good as any other.

Such challenges appear also in the form of ideas and techniques which come to be seen as better and more effective than the established ones, and consequently may come to replace the latter. Thus, when the Doubtful learned about the age of fossils found in the mountains, he immediately declared the corresponding religious accounts a lie. Similarly, the Prayer-Writer acknowledges the greater efficacy of some of the modern medicines. Since modern medicine is, however, seen to fail in some areas, e.g., the treatment of mental disorders, while the traditional methods still promise some success, there appears the strange mixture of traditional and modern conceptions and techniques which baffles western researchers. In the same way, modern social and political values and meanings may be seen as superior and consequently may be substituted for the established patterns. This could be done in an explicit, intentional way, as when the Craftsman and the Old Teacher ascribe purely secular social meanings to religious rituals, or it may happen in an unconscious manner as when the Mullah defines the morality of various behaviors almost invariably in secular, rational, and social terms rather than in terms of revelation, as the Old Trader would do.

An analysis of the present material shows that the effect of these outside challenges on the various religious subsystems seems to increase along this sequence: basic social morality—religious fundamentals (God and the afterworld)—ritual (prayers and fasting)—prescriptions (veiling, food taboos, Islamic law)—folklore (jinn, evil eye, amulets). Thus, basic morality is least refuted and least replaced by new ideas, whereas folklore, clashing sharply with new ideas and often replaced by them, is affected most. Because the strength of the religious support system (spiritual threats, social and political enforcements, centrality of the belief) decreases generally in the same sequence, it is predictable that folklore will be the soonest and most widely discarded, while religious fundamentals and morality tend to hold out longest. This finding is borne out by the evidence. Even people who are only slightly affected by modernity tend to distance themselves from at least parts of the folkloric system. (In its entirety, it seems to survive only with the Old Trader.) On the other hand, in the world view of the Old Teacher, basic social morality survives the religious system, from which only remnants of the fundamentals remain, in the form of a secular philosophy.

Responses to Challenges of Religious Systems

1. *Exclusion of new evidence.* In this reaction to challenges, any new evidence and any methods potentially leading to new evidence, such as the critical study of the scriptures, mystical experience or contact with outside thought systems, are considered a potential threat and consequently taboo. Of the individuals presented, the Fundamentalist comes closest to this approach. For him, secular education, for example, is evil because it leads to moral decline. But in general, this strategy is most typical of the clerical establishment. In their attempts to defend the established forms of religion—and of course their vested interests in it—they devise social as well as spiritual controls. In the Middle Ages the Islamic clergy directly thwarted the emergence of natural science by killing or exiling its practitioners while at the same time in Europe the Inquisition persecuted nature observation and experimentation (Burckhardt 1960: 317), and burned the newly translated bibles as vehicles of threatening new evidence. Spiritual controls serve the purpose in more subtle ways. Adam is punished for trying to gain knowledge in an unauthorized way, and Job is praised for holding on to his belief despite overwhelming disconfirmations of the conventional understanding of God's justice. Testing the sayings of the scriptures is presented as temptation by the devil, and Jesus blesses those who believe without seeing, i.e., those who accept the testimony of the authorities and forsake independent inquiry. This mode of defense of a religious system is of course most effective when the clerical establishment also controls significant social and political power. In the long run of religious evolution it is, however, a losing strategy.

2. *Integration.* In this adjustment to new evidence, the fundamentals of the religion, and usually also the notion of the divine origin or at least the uniqueness and supremacy of the texts, are upheld, but certain specific

conceptions will be changed. New ideas which appear desirable will be integrated in the religious context and traditional ideas which appear undesirable will be ejected. Sacred texts will be reinterpreted in such a way that they will express exactly the intended changes: for the desirable ideas a textual foundation will be found, while such foundation will be withdrawn from ideas that have become undesirable. If the texts cannot be reinterpreted satisfactorily or if they show other obvious shortcomings, it will be argued that this in no way refutes their validity, but only shows the wise adjustment of the texts to specific historical circumstances: in the past, people had not been ready for the full truth.

The new interpretations will be presented as the pure original meanings of the respective passages, whereas the traditional ones will be declared popular corruptions, mistakes or outright fabrication by the clergy, or necessary adaptations to an uneducated, tradition-bound populace. As to these vestiges, it is necessary to expose them as "the remains of crude old culture which have passed into harmful superstition, and to mark these out for destruction," as E. Tylor (1889: II, 453) demanded for his religion under the impact of the new anthropological evidence. In this way the texts may come to embody seemingly modern ideas, and the fact that such ideas—unearthed only now—had been apparently expressed already ages ago is presented as another evidence for the timeless wisdom and unmatched spiritual supremacy of the texts. The fact that this wisdom actually is the wisdom of the interpreter is conveniently ignored.

In Islam as in other world religions, the scope of such innovations is very wide. At one end of the scale are the cautious, rather limited, almost cosmetic adjustments of interpreters like the Mullah. In his interpretations, the texts emphasize the pursuit of science, development, and education; they embody scientific notions like the solar system; they permit contraception, education of women, and the view of human evolution; and they reject the practice of full veiling and the beliefs in jinn, the evil eye, and written prayers. But they leave all the traditional eschatological, moral, social, and political structures perfectly intact. Towards the other end of the scale is radical reformist thought as advocated by thinkers inspired by liberal or Marxist ideas. Although still maintaining Islamic fundamentals, these approaches may challenge the entire social and political traditions, give totally new meanings to mythology, ritual, and even eschatological issues, and may deny scriptural foundations for even the most hallowed prescriptions.

Two types of reformist adaptations should be singled out because they entail basic alterations. One is the universalistic orientation represented by the Craftsman. While maintaining such fundamentals as the existence of God and the laws of social morality, he rejects the claim of divine origin of

Islam and, for that matter, any religion. Consequently, he finds the desirable ideas, especially the principles of a humanist morality, in all religions alike, and repudiates generally such undesirable ideas as the absolutist truth claims of particular religions.

Another basic potential adaptation is the strict separation of knowledge and belief. In this case, under the impact of a stricter conception of positive evidence, it is admitted that the evidence for the fundamental religious beliefs is, indeed, inconclusive. But this is taken as part of the very nature of religious tenets: they cannot be known, only believed. Evidence can only lead up to a certain point, then a leap into the realm beyond reason is necessary. This leap of faith is an absurdity, but it is exactly this absurdity which matters. Anyone can know, but the faith of a believer goes beyond knowledge. Thus, science and religion are declared as separate, distinct paradigms and so are able to coexist without contradiction. The former is built on empirical evidence, the latter rests ultimately on a leap of faith. By this strategy, religious ideas and experiences are relegated to a sheltered position where challenges from science, philosophy, textual and historical scrutiny cannot immediately assail them because they are outside the former's field of competence.

This option for dealing with new evidence is characteristically absent in the present data. I shall argue that it is absent from Islam in general, and that the lack of this option may have far-reaching consequences.

3. *Dismissal of Religion.* The final step in coming to terms with new evidence and especially with a stricter definition of positive evidence is to see no longer a compelling support even for the religious fundamentals, or to see them altogether refuted. Liberals of the older generation, like the Old Teacher, seem to have tended toward the former, agnostic form, whereas some of the younger, educated generation lean more toward the latter, atheistic form of dismissing the religion. As indicated earlier, however, the precepts of social morality and even of a sense of prevailing cosmic justice tend to survive the strictly religious context in secular philosophies.

Currently in Islamic countries these three reactive modes are taking on comprehensive and radical forms. The exclusion reaction by the clerical establishment appears to be today far more uncompromising than ever in the past two hundred years (Rahman 1966: 253). A scientific study of the Qur'ān and the Hadith is categorically refused out of fear that this could destroy their validity. Even when new ideas like democracy, science, or the equality of women are presented as originally Islamic, as in Iran today, they are de facto not implemented.

The reform reactions are becoming ever more comprehensive, proposing entire new social systems in which the true Islamic ideals should be realized. Fundamentalist plans, like those of Iran or Egypt (Ibrahim 1982: 5), advocate a return in every detail to an utopian past, while modernizing plans, like those of Ali Shariati and the Iranian Mujahedin, by integrating Marxist notions, advocate the capture of an utopian future. Finally, complete rejection of the system is becoming more frequent. Professed atheism spreads in the educated youth with the growth of Marxist political ideologies. In the middle class we observe an increasing agnosticism and secular humanism, like that of the Old Teacher, but also an increasing indifference, secularism, and materialism (Rahman 1966: 252).

On the basis of the foregoing analysis I think that these conditions are at least partly due to the basic epistemological preconception in Islam mentioned earlier, i.e., that knowledge and faith, unlike in most forms of Christianity after the Reformation, have never been strictly separated. Instead, there reigns the inviolable claim that the Qur'ān is the word of God. This implies that not only transcendental matters but also a moral code, political institutions, historical accounts, hygienic injunctions, and scientific ideas expressed in the Qur'ān are the truth revealed by God. Thus, the Mullah finds in the Qur'ān proof for biological and astronomical notions, and the Mystic and the Representative see in it the source of Western technology. The Young Trader exalts its superior medical wisdom, and the Old Trader knows from it the age and future duration of the world. The Prayer-Writer takes its curative powers for granted, and some of the educated youths consider it the blueprint for an utopian society. An essential difference between these various secular aspects and the strictly transcendental ones is not and cannot be made. They are all equally the word of God.

This characteristic makes the Islamic belief system vulnerable. Continuously, a wide range of conceptions has to be defended as ultimate truth, conceptions which in effect are responsive to challenges from growing empirical knowledge and emerging new value orientations. In contrast, a religion which is limited to transcendental matters and possibly some general moral directions, and considers other matters secular issues is not so easily affected by changes in the latter. Also, in a religion which encompasses transcendental matters as well as matters of empirical knowledge, the slightest suspicion cast on the validity of any one item constitutes an immediate challenge to the validity of the religion's very basis. If new insights question the Qur'ānic account of creation or the dignity of the veiling of women, then not only these particular issues but the very claim of the divine origin of the text and with it the whole religion are drawn into question. In contrast, in a religion ultimately based on faith, inconclusive factual evidence is an accepted property and not a threatening challenge.

Under these conditions the reaction to new ideas—especially when they emerge in great numbers—will necessarily be radical. Exclusion has to be total and rigid for changes in any single aspect—like the status of women—appear already as attacks on the system's basis, and any opening-up to new ideas—as democracy would inevitably bring with it—appears to entail uncontrollable risks. Analogously, reform efforts have to be all-encompassing. To safeguard the claim of divine origin they have to demonstrate that what is challenged by the new ideas is not the true Islam but only fallacious interpretations and practices of the past, and that the true Islam, as embodied in the new interpretations, is indeed superior to the new ideas. To allow the mere suspicion that one or the other aspect of the Qur'ān may reflect human ignorance would throw the whole system into doubt. Both strategies are, however, finite. In the end, because mounting evidence and a stricter conception of positive evidence will render them increasingly implausible and unconvincing, and because a leap of faith is not a culturally established, meaningful option to take, religious beliefs will tend to be dismissed. Given the inner logic of the system, this final solution must be expected to become more prevalent in the future. The current revitalization movements appear to be not a reversal but only a symptom of this decline.

It is, of course, possible that the rigidity of the described preconceptions will be broken. A sign to this effect is that despite orthodox dogma there exists among the liberal middle classes the tendency to separate transcendental issues from secular areas of life. While maintaining faith in the fundamental spiritual and moral message of Islam, they claim that the specific rituals, prescriptions, and "scientific" statements of the Qur'ān were meant for the past and by now have become obsolete. But whether this trend will ever be formulated in a theologically acceptable theory—and with it Geertz' (1968: 116) flight companion will, without inherent contradiction, be able to hold on to the Qur'ān and drink his scotch too—remains to be seen.

A SYNOPSIS OF THE CASES

The MULLAH's version represents an essentially formalistic, even bureaucratic pattern, neatly ordering concepts, rules and regulations, but seemingly lacking the zest for religious experience. It is basically traditional in its theology and definition of behavior, family and marriage, but has a noteworthy modernist slant in its advocation of modern science, medicine, education, and progress. Conceptions that smack of folklore and superstition are largely eliminated; beliefs and practices that may appear odd by modern standards are played down; and scientific ideas are seen founded in the authoritative scriptures or at least as not at odds with them. The Mullah's world view reflects also a definitely elitist attitude which considers the populace inherently unable to grasp the truth, and therefore deems it both necessary and justified to make doctrinal changes that would increase the appeal of the religion (and, of course, its ministers).

The LANDLORD's style represents a form of religion of power. Religious concepts, institutions, and authorities are made instruments to exert control, promote interests, and enhance one's status in this world and the next. Symbols of morality are—often tortuously—manipulated in such a way that his position and behavior appear uniquely justified and righteous. Charitable acts, services to the public, and conspicuous performance of rituals serve to visibly demonstrate his moral excellence, display his superior status and power, and evince his devotion to the physical and spiritual well-being of his people. The projected image is that of a landlord who, following the precepts of Islam, uses his power for the benefit of his peasants in such propitious, matchless ways that his domination appears inherently legitimate, and his peasants therefore morally bound to abide by it.

The two TRADERS maintain a type of traditional, popular orthodoxy, incorporating into the strictly orthodox doctrines an abundance of marginally orthodox, folkloric, and magical beliefs and practices—virtually all there are. But between the two there is also a distinct difference in style. The Old Trader's style is one of sincere, quietistic devotionalism in which a sheer inexhaustible knowledge of mythology, dogma, morality, and liturgy is held as absolute truth with deep emotional attachment. The well-nigh perfect fulfillment of moral and ritual obligations appears to be a matter of course. Thus, unlike the peasants with their lingering doubts about teachings and their guilt about moral and ritual shortcomings, the Old Trader faces the sacred with an unmitigated feeling of trust and affinity.

In the Young Trader, by contrast, essentially the same tenets appear like ultra-conservative slogans which, together with fantastic beliefs about science and an air of righteous arrogance, take the form of bigoted zealotry.

The world view of the OLD TEACHER is essentially a form of humanism: doing good to others for the sake of their—and one's own—humanity rather than for the sake of religious injunctions or afterworldly rewards. These humanistic concerns are essentially thisworldly pragmatic: political freedom, decent living conditions, secular enlightenment. Eschatological questions are met with an attitude close to agnosticism. Islam is explicitly relativized as an ethical system which conveys the same humanistic message as other philosophical systems.

The world view of the YOUNG TEACHER represents a haphazard mixture of rationalistic ideas, emphasizing education, unconditional individual responsibility, and psychological explanations, with a firm belief in all fundamental, orthodox doctrines and—somewhat strangely—a variety of folkloric and magical practices.

The style of the CRAFTSMAN is a rather radical form of modernist purism and relativism, in which Islam is supposedly purged from all manipulative, nonsensical, non-essential, and harmful appendages. Basically, he maintains only the belief in God and divine justice, the social morality, and a rather non-committal attitude toward all eschatological issues. Most other doctrines, including such essentials as the absolutist claim of Islam and the Shia imāmology, most ritual injunctions, and most prescriptions are—at least in their customary forms and meanings—repudiated with facetious cynicism and fierce anti-clericalism while folkloric notions and practices are ridiculed.

The REPRESENTATIVE models an Islam of social activism and liberation, put into practice with the zeal and impact reminiscent of an old-testamentarian prophet. Total dedication to the good of others is seen as the only genuine, enduring meaning of life, faith, ritual and morality, making the most trivial of daily chores a sacred act, and the persistent struggle to free peasants from oppression and improve their lot a sacred mission. The system is not derived from modern ideologies but is wholly Islamic in nature, based mainly on the mystic notions of love, detachment, and remembrance combined with an uncompromising, but not vengeful, morality.

The religious style of the PRAYER-WRITER can be called a mysticism of work: withdrawal into the solitude of agricultural work to experience the serenity of the mystic and express his detachment from the affairs of the world. Against this, formal doctrine and ritual as well as folklore and magic appear as outward, non-essential aspects of his religion, though he is vastly knowledgeable in all of this, believes in it sincerely, and uses it conscientiously in service to his fellow people.

The style of the MYSTIC is an intrinsic intertwining of concepts and techniques derived from Sufism with patterns of magical thought and attempts to gain special knowledge, abilities and powers of control—an association of ideas which seems to underlie the process by which in the Middle East and elsewhere mystics become transformed into holy men, saints, and intercessors, and their tombs into places of pilgrimage.

The version of the OLD HUNTER seems to reflect an old religious pattern in which a fearsome, strict, fundamentalist brand of Islam is fused—not without vexing conflicts, though—with the traditions of a local, probably pre-Islamic folklore centering around the dangerous as well as beneficent world of jinn. In his case more than in any other, the high-mountain environment of these people and the traditional, highly valued and emotionally charged game-and-hunting complex are dealt with in terms of an Islamic idiom.

The style of the DEEP BELIEVER keeps a middle ground between intense virtuosity on one side and low-keyed pragmatism on the other. It is a neatly differentiated, well controlled, and highly integrated system that is pervaded by a firm and honest sincerity and, notably, provides also an explicit, positive meaning to peasant work and peasant existence itself.

The FUNDAMENTALIST advocates what he takes to be a strictly Qur'ānic, literal version of Islam as the only true and pure form of the religion, stressing motifs such as the wisdom of Qur'ānic prescriptions, afterworldly punishment, absolutist claims of the Shia as the only right belief, the powers of the Imāms and the Qur'ān, and the decline of morality in modern education and lifestyles. His version turns out to be in many respects just about the opposite of what the modernist Craftsman considers to be the pure Islam. In fact, what either regards as the pure form of Islam constitutes a model of corruptness in the eyes of the other.

The version of the WEALTHY is in terms of both beliefs and practices mainline orthodoxy, but lacks the passion, intricacy or strong personal imprint of others in this category. Characteristically, while the Poor attributes wealth and poverty to the vagaries of good fortune, the Wealthy believes that a person's economic circumstances are predominantly of his own making and reflect his own efforts and morality.

The DOUBTFUL is well-versed in orthodox doctrine, mythology, and ritual, but he holds these beliefs with a certain reserve, and there exists—partly related to an anti-clerical purism—an undercurrent of doubt and skepticism which, when surfacing, may question even the most basic tenets of the religion.

The world view of the CALM is structured mainly by paradigms of universal rather than specifically Islamic character. In terms of these paradigms he formulates an unusually harmonious attitude toward fortune and misfortune, morality, existence, and death. His is not the equanimity of the mystic detached from worldly affairs, but the calmness of one who feels in tune with laws of cosmic order.

The style of the PRAGMATIST is to concentrate on the this-worldly pertinence of religious symbols, conceiving of God as the Good Provider, the afterlife as an intangible issue, worldly defects as man's own fault rather than God's, and of ritual as a means to secure health and welfare.

The style of the MASHHADI is to leave the eschatological question open and undecided while at the same time abiding by the religious laws and performing about all the rituals there are—because as a Muslim he has to, because it is safer to do so, and because, after all, he believes.

What the LOWER PEASANTS formulate can be called a religion of scarcity. They uphold all the fundamental tenets, adhere to the moral code, and see their lives in terms of the religious idiom as much as any other Muslim. However, existential pressure and lack of education all but preclude sophistication in religious expression, be it in the form of ritual practice or conceptual formulation. These aspects exist, as it were, in germinal or potential form. Their actual development is suspended because of external conditions, not because of principal abnegation. Again there are differences in style.

The first Peasant concentrates on two themes characteristic for this level of the peasantry, predestination and hard work. Predestination is his almost stereotypically used concept for explaining general conditions and particular events, yet, within the frame set by predestination, relentless, hard work is indispensable for things to work out.

The second Peasant's style of faithful surrender to God lets him humbly do his hard work and care and share as well as he can. The success of his work, his fate in the afterworld, and such academic questions as to whether his neglect of rituals will be forgiven or his hard work will earn merit—these he puts, as he says, in the hands of God.

The style of the POOR is more a kind of powerless resignation than the thankful contentment enjoined by orthodox code. God ought to give to all, but to call Him unjust or unloving for not doing so is impossible as well as useless. Also, the Poor refuses to accept the afterworldly consolations and promises offered by the religion. On the contrary, the rich, he feels, will also be better off there. It is a system by means of which he faces his condition squarely and realistically, giving way neither to illusionary speculation and escapes nor to fatalism and despair.

NOTES

1. This is one version of the Hafiz verse. The other version, generally considered the original one, finishes: ". . . if I wouldn't *sell* it for one grain of barley," i.e., sell it even cheaper than my father did. The speaker's version, possibly prevalent in his milieu, fits of course his religious views much nicer.

2. The Representative used only personal names when referring to the former chiefs (kadkhudā) of the area. For a number of reasons this cannot be done here. In the following, the term 'landlord' will be used instead of personal names, but with the understanding that it shall only mean 'occupying a position of de facto control over the land'; it shall not have the connotation of 'legitimate landownership,' as this would directly contradict the speaker's conception. Thus, in the present context the term 'landlord' shall be semantically distinct from the term 'landowner' (mālik).

3. I cannot trace the first two lines; the last two lines are Mathnawi, Book II, 1756.

4. The Representative tends to use ma'rifat in the sense of mystical knowledge, deep insight, true understanding, while 'ilm stands more for cerebral, concrete, detailed, factual knowledge of both earthly and transcendental matters.

5. cf. 4.

6. cf. Mathnawi, Book II, 1720 ff. Nicholson edition.

7. Mathnawi, Book III, 3901–4. Translation taken from: Nicholson, 1914: 168.

8. Sa'dī, Gulistān, Introductory. Author's translation.

9. Folklore attributes to the 'Wind of Yemen' a magical force giving life and health.

10. The verses are probably wrongly attributed to Sa'dī.

11. This is a very popular saying; but not from the Qur'ān.

12. A popular saying; but derived from Firdawsī, not religious texts.

GLOSSARY

ākhūnd	a low-ranking cleric; in the village synonymous with Mullah.
Aisha	the favorite wife of Muhammad who, according to Shia tradition, betrayed Ali and his faith.
'ālam-i zarr	lit., Miniature World; said to have existed prior to this world.
Ali	'Ali ibn Abi Talib, cousin and son-in-law of Muhammad; the first Imam.
Amīr al-Mu'minīn	Leader of the Faithful; honorific title of Ali.
'Ashūrā	the tenth day of Muharram, on which, according to tradition, the Imām Husayn and his followers were killed at Karbala. On this day the mourning celebrations commemorating this event reach their climax.
Bībī Hakīmah	a popular shrine in South Iran; according to tradition, a sister of the eighth Imām is buried there.
damband	spell-binding of jaws of wild animals dangerous to livestock.
Dāwud	the psalmist David.
davā	medicine, remedy.

du'a'	invocation, prayer, usually for a favor; also amulets containing a written prayer
dervish	one who renounces worldly goods for the sake of a mystical contemplation of existence and compassion for others. In the vernacular it often has the negative connotation of a fraudulent, itinerant beggar.
fatihah	first sura of the Qur'an; recited for the dead. fatihah khvani: the formal recitation of the prayers for the dead.
Fatima	Muhammad's daughter, the mother of Hasan, Husayn and Zaynab, and the wife of Ali.
fitriyah	alms given to the poor at the end of the month of fasting.
ghufaylah	name of a special prayer for the forgiveness of sins.
gurazband	spell-binding of wild boars.
ghusl	religiously prescribed ablutions, e.g., after sexual intercourse, after parturition.
Hadith	a collection of sayings attributed to the Prophet.
Hafiz	a very popular, famous poet of Shiraz, 1326–1389 A.D.
halal	religiously lawful.
haram	religiously unlawful.
Hasan	elder son of Ali and Fatima.
Hazrat	Excellency; a honorific title.
houri	a beautiful, paradisical virgin.
Husayn	younger son of Ali and Fatima. Husayniyah: place of worship and social gathering, dedicated to Husayn.
'id qurban	the day of sacrifice during the Hajj on which an animal is sacrificed.

Imām	one of twelve Muslim leaders of the line of Ali, held by Shiites to be the divinely appointed, infallible, sinless successors of Muhammad.
Imāmzādah	the offspring of an Imām; the shrine of an Imām or his offspring.
'Isā	Jesus.
'Izrā'il	the angel of death.
jinn	spirit(s).
kadkhudā	the chief of a tribe; in the village used synonymously with landlord.
kākul	wheat stalks twisted into a bunch; said to occur in a field when wheat is especially heavy and yields an unusually rich crop.
Karbala	a place in central Iraq where the battle between Husayn and the forces of Yazīd, the Umayyad regent, over control of the Islamic empire was fought. Now a major Shiite pilgrimage center.
khan	chief of a tribal confederation.
khāngāh	a meetingplace of members of a Sufi order.
khums	a fifth of a person's income; to be paid as a religious tax to religious authorities.
Lūt	Lot; the city of Sodom.
maktab	a traditional school where literacy was taught by means of mainly religious texts.
man	a measure of weight equivalent to 3–6 kilogram, depending on the area and the substance weighed. In the village, 1 man wheat = 6 kilogram.
ma'rifat	divine knowledge.
mi'rāj	Muhammad's alleged ascension to heaven.
misqāl	a measure of weight equivalent to 4.64 grams.

Mu'āwīyah	opponent of Ali; founder of the Umayyad Dynasty that controlled the caliphate 661–750 A.D.
Muharram	the month of commemoration of the death of Husayn and his followers.
Mujahedin	an Islamic-marxistically inspired political group opposing the present regime of the Islamic Republic.
mujtahid	a religiously very learned man and high Shia authority.
mukāfāt	God's retribution. mukāfāt pas dādan: to make recompense, to undergo punishment, to suffer retribution.
mullah	a person learned in theology and often acting as a religious functionary; in local usage the term denotes any literate person, hence also a teacher.
Mūsā	Moses.
Nahj al-balāghah	collection of sayings and sermons of Ali.
navaruzī	an extraordinary yield in crops or livestock.
Naw-rūz	New Year's Day of the Persian calendar on March 21.
pīshānī nivisht	(or: sar nivisht) destiny; literally, "written on the forehead."
qismat	destiny, decree of God.
Qur'ān	Koran; the sacred book of Islam; believed to contain God's revelations to Muhammad.
Ramadan	the month of fasting.
rawzah	recitations of legends about the Imāms. rawzah khvānī: commemorative prayer rituals, sometimes accompanied by a meal.
rial	the smallest monetary unit in Iran. 10 rial = 1 toman; in 1976, 1$ = 77 rial.

Rumi	Jalāl ud-Dīn Rūmī, an influential Sufi mystic and poet, 1207–1273 A.D.
sadaqah	a special form of alms.
Sa'dī	a very popular, famous poet of Shiraz, 1184–1292 A.D.
salavāt	a formula of blessings on Muhammad and his family.
28 Safar	the day on which the martyrdom of Imām Hasan is commemorated.
Sayyid	a patrilineal descendant of Muhammad through Ali and Fatima.
Sayyid Mahamad	the name of an Imāmzādah buried at a local shrine.
Shāh Ni'matu'llah	the founder of a Sufi order named after him. He is highly regarded in Iran as a saint and miracle-worker.
Shahrbānū	a wife of Husayn.
shāns	good fortune.
sharī'at	the Islamic law.
shaqq al-qamar	the miracle of "splitting the moon" attributed to Muhammad.
Shia	the Shia sect of Islam; also, member(s) of this sect, or Shiite(s). The sect maintains that the Imām Ali, rather than the three first caliphs of the Sunnites was the rightful successor of Muhammad.
shī'ah	lit., the faction or party (of Ali); the Shia sect of Islam.
sīmband	a written prayer to protect wheat fields against pests.
sirāt	according to the Hadith, the narrow, sharp bridge across hell which all souls must cross.
sufrah	festive meal offered for religious purposes.
Sulayman	Suleiman, Solomon.

Tāsū'ā	the ninth day of Muharram.
ta'ziyah	the passion play commemorating the events at Karbala.
toman	the largest monetary unit in Iran. 1 toman = 10 rial. In 1976 1 toman = 0.13 $.
'ulamā'	Muslim theologians; learned men. In the vernacular, the term includes Mullahs, Ākhūnds, and Ayatullahs.
vilāyat-i faqīh	political rule exercised by the supreme jurist in the absence of the Last Imām.
Yazīd	second caliph of the Umayyad Dynasty; opponent of Husayn.
zakāt	religious tax; alms given especially to non-Sayyids.
Zaynab	daughter of Ali, sister of Husayn, and a very popular saint in Iran.
zikr	a meditative formula similar to the Indian mantra, usually comprising God's name, and used mostly by Sufis.

REFERENCES

Akhavi, Shahrough. 1980. *Religion and Politics in Contemporary Iran: Clergy-State Relations in the Pahlavi Period.* Albany: State University of New York Press.

Algar, Hamid. 1969. *Religion and State in Iran, 1785–1906.* Berkeley: University of California Press.

Antoun, Richard T. *Islamic Sermons and the Moslem Preacher in the Modern World.* Manuscript.

Asghar, Ali. 1969. "Beliefs of the Shi'a." Summarized in *A Literary History of Persia*, Vol. IV., edited by Edward G. Browne, pp. 381–403. Cambridge: Cambridge University Press.

Atiya, Nayra. 1982. *Khul Khaal.* Syracuse: Syracuse University Press.

Barth, Fredrik. 1961. *Nomads of South Persia.* Oslo: Oslo University Press.

Berger, Peter L. and Thomas Luckmann. 1966. *The Social Construction of Reality.* New York: Doubleday.

Bourdieu, Pierre. 1977. *Outline of a Theory of Practice.* Cambridge: Cambridge University Press.

Burckhardt, Jacob. 1960. *Die Kultur der Renaissance in Italien.* Stuttgart: Reclam.

Casagrande, Joseph B. (ed.) 1960. *In the Company of Man.* New York: Harper.

Castaneda, Carlos. 1968. *The Teachings of Don Juan: A Yaqui Way of Knowledge.* Berkeley: University of California Press.

Coles, Robert. 1967–1977. *Children of Crisis.* Vol. 1–5. Boston: Little, Brown and Co.

Crapanzano, Vincent. 1980. *Tuhami: Portrait of a Moroccan.* Chicago: University of Chicago Press.

Critchfield, Richard. 1978. *Shahhat: An Egyptian.* Syracuse: Syracuse University Press.

Douglas, Mary. 1973. *Natural Symbols.* New York: Vintage Books.

Dundes, Alan. 1972. "Comment to: 'World Views: Their Nature and Their Function'." *Current Anthropology* 13, no. 1: p. 97.

Eickelman, Dale F. 1985. *Knowledge and Power in Morocco: The Education of a 20th Century Notable.* Princeton: Princeton University Press.

Erikson, Erik H. 1943. *Observations on the Yurok: Childhood and World Image.* Berkeley: University of California Press.

———. 1958. *Young Man Luther.* New York: W. W. Norton.

———. 1980. *Identity and the Life Cycle.* New York: W. W. Norton.

Evans-Pritchard, E. E. 1937. *Witchcraft, Oracles and Magic among the Azande.* Oxford: Clarendon Press.

Fabian, Johannes. 1983. *Time and the Other.* New York: Columbia University Press.

Fallers, Lloyd A., assisted by M. C. Fallers. 1974. "Notes on an Advent Ramadan." *Journal of the American Academy of Religion* 42, no. 1: pp. 35–52.

Fernea, Elizabeth, and B. Q. Bezirgan. 1977. *Middle Eastern Women Speak.* Austin: University of Texas Press.

———. 1978. *Some Women of Marrakesh.* Granada Films.

Fischer, Michael M. J. 1980. *Iran: From Religious Dispute to Revolution.* Cambridge: Harvard University Press.

Friedl, Erika. 1980. "Islam and Tribal Women in a Village in Iran." In *Unspoken Worlds: Women's Religious Lives in Non-Western Cultures,* edited by N. A. Falk and R. M. Gross, pp. 159–173. San Francisco: Harper and Row.

———. 1983. "Die Medizinischen Systeme von Boir Ahmad." In *Ethnologie und Geschichte,* edited by Peter Snoy, pp. 163–179. Wiesbaden: Steiner.

———. *The Women of Deh Koh.* Manuscript.

Friedrich, Paul. 1965. "An Agrarian Fighter." In *Context and Meaning in Cultural Anthropology,* edited by Melford E. Spiro, pp. 117–143. New York: Free Press.

Galbraith, John Kenneth. 1978. *The New Industrial State.* 3rd edition. Boston: Houghton Mifflin.

Gardiner, Robert. 1963. *Dead Birds.* Contemporary Films.

Geertz, Clifford. 1966. "Religion as a Cultural System." In *Anthropological Approaches to the Study of Religion,* A.S.A. Monographs No. 3, edited by M. Banton, pp. 1–46. New York: Praeger.

———. 1968. *Islam Observed.* New Haven: Yale University Press.

———. 1974. " 'From the Native's Point of View': On the Nature of Anthropological Understanding." *Bulletin, American Academy of Arts and Sciences* 28, no. 1: pp. 26–45.

Gerth, H. H. and C. Wright Mills (translators and eds.). 1958. *From Max Weber: Essays in Sociology.* New York: Galaxy Book.

Gould, Stephen J. 1982. "Of Wasps and WASPs." *Natural History* 91, no. 12: pp. 8–14.

Grunebaum, G. E. von. 1955. *Islam.* London: Routledge and Kegan Paul Ltd.

Herzfeld, Michael. 1985. *The Poetics of Manhood.* Princeton: Princeton University Press.

Horton, Robin. 1971. "African Traditional Thought and Western Science." In *Rationality,* edited by Bryan R. Wilson, pp. 36–171. New York: Harper Torchbooks.

Ibrahim, S. E. 1982. "Egypt's Islamic Militants." *Merip Reports* 12, no. 2: pp. 5–14.

Jones, W. T. 1972. "World Views: Their Nature and Their Function." *Current Anthropology* 13, no. 1: pp. 79–91.

Keddie, Nikki R. 1963. "Symbol and Sincerity in Islam." *Studia Islamica* 19; pp. 27–63.

Kracke, Waud H. 1978. *Force and Persuasion: Leadership in an Amazonian Society.* Chicago: University of Chicago Press.

Kuhn, Thomas. 1970. *The Structure of Scientific Revolutions.* Chicago: University of Chicago Press.

Lasch, Christopher. 1978. *The Culture of Narcissism.* New York: W. W. Norton.

LeRoy Ladurie, Emmanuel. 1978. *Montaillou: The Promised Land of Error.* New York: G. Braziller.

Lewis, Oscar. 1965. *Village Life in Northern India.* New York: Vintage Books.

———. 1969. *A Death in the Sanchez Family.* New York: Random House.

Loeffler, Reinhold. 1971. "The Representative Mediator and the New Peasant." *American Anthropologist* 73, no. 2: pp. 1077–1091.

———. 1976. "Recent Economic Changes in Boir Ahmad: Regional Growth without Development." *Iranian Studies* IX, no. 4: pp. 266–287.

———. 1978. "Tribal Order and the State: The Political Organization of Boir Ahmad." In *State and Society in Iran,* edited by Amin Banani, *Iranian Studies* XI, pp. 145–171.

———. 1986. "Economic Changes in a Rural Area Since 1979." In *The Iranian Revolution and the Islamic Republic,* edited by Nikki Keddie and Eric Hooglund, pp. 93–109. Syracuse: Syracuse University Press.

Mann, Oskar. 1910. *Die Mundarten der Lur-Stämme im Südwestlichen Persien.* Berlin: Georg Reimer Verlag.

Mottahadeh, Roy. 1985. *The Mantle of the Prophet: Religion and Politics in Iran.* New York: Simon and Schuster.

Munson, Henry, Jr. 1984. *The House of Si Abd Allah: The Oral History of a Moroccan Family.* New Haven: Yale University Press.

Nasr, Seyyed Hossein. 1969. "Ithna 'Ashari Shi'ism and Iranian Islam." In *Religion in the Middle East,* Vol. 2, edited by A. J. Arberry, pp. 96–118. Cambridge: Cambridge University Press.

Nicholson, R. A. ed. and trans. 1925–1940. *The Mathnawi of Jal'al'udd'in Ru'mi'.* 8 vols. London: Luzac.

———. 1975. *The Mystics of Islam.* New York: Schocken Books.

Obeyesekere, Gananath, 1981. *Medusa's Hair: An Essay on Personal Symbols and Religious Experience.* Chicago: University of Chicago Press.

Ortner, Sherry B. 1984. "Theory in Anthropology since the Sixties." *Comparative Studies in Society and History* 26, no. 1: pp. 126–166.

Pandian, Jacob. 1985. *Anthropology and the Western Tradition: Toward an Authentic Anthropology.* Prospect Heights: Waveland Press.

Peters, Emrys. 1984. "The paucity of ritual among Middle Eastern pastoralists." In *Islam in Tribal Societies,* edited by Akbar S. Ahmed and David M. Hart, pp. 187–219. London: Routledge and Kegan Paul.

Radin, Paul. 1957. *Primitive Man as Philosopher*. New York: Dover Publications.

Rahman, Fazlur. 1966. *Islam*. New York: Holt, Rinehart and Winston.

Riedl, Rupert. 1981. *Biologie der Erkenntnis*. Berlin: Paul Parey.

Rosen, Lawrence. 1984. *Bargaining for Reality: The Construction of Social Relations in a Muslim Community*. Chicago: University of Chicago Press.

Rumi, Jalāl ud-Dīn. *Mathnawi Ma'nawi*. See: Nicholson, trans. 1925–1940.

Sa'dī. 1964. *The Gulistān*. E. Rehatsek, trans. London: Allen and Unwin.

Scott, James C. 1985. *Weapons of the Weak: Everyday Forms of Peasant Resistance*. New Haven: Yale University Press.

Shehabi, Mahmood. 1958. "Shi'a." In *Islam: The Straight Path*, edited by K. W. Morgan, pp. 180–223. New York: Ronald Press.

Shostak, Marjorie. 1981. *Nisa: The Life and Words of a !Kung Woman*. Cambridge: Harvard University Press.

Spiro, Melford E. 1967. *Burmese Supernaturalism*. Englewood Ciffs: Prentice-Hall.

Spooner, Brian. 1973. "The Cultural Ecology of Pastoral Nomads." *Addison-Wesley Module in Anthropology No. 45*. Addison-Wesley Publishing Company.

Stromberg, Peter G. 1986. *Symbols of Community: The Cultural System of a Swedish Church*. Tucson: University of Arizona Press.

Tabātabā'ī, A.S.M.H. 1975. *Shi'ite Islam*. Albany: State University of New York Press.

Taheri, Amir. 1986. *The Spirit of Allah: Khomeini and the Islamic Revolution*. Bethesda: Adler and Adler.

Thaiss, Gustav. 1972. "Religious Symbolism and Social Change: The Drama of Hussain." In *Scholars, Saints and Sufis*, edited by Nikki R. Keddie, pp. 349–366. Berkeley: University of California Press.

Thompson, Edward Palmer. 1966. *The Making of the English Working Class*. New York: Vintage Books.

Turner, Victor. 1967. *The Forest of Symbols*. (Chapter VIII: Themes in the Symbolism of Ndembu Hunting Ritual.) Ithaca: Cornell University Press.

Tylor, Edward Burnett. 1889. *Primitive Culture*. New York: Henry Holt.

Witherspoon, Gary. 1977. *Language and Art in the Navajo Universe*. Ann Arbor: University of Michigan Press.

Zborowski, Mark. 1955. "The Children of the Covenant." In *Studies in Motivation*, edited by David C. McClelland. pp. 352–374. New York: Appleton-Century-Crofts.

INDEX

Printed in the United States
96962LV00004B/31-36/A